Anthony Kirk-Greene is Emeritus Fellow of St Antony's College, Oxford. His publications include *Glimpses of Empire: A Corona Anthology* (I.B.Tauris, 2001); *On Crown Service: A History of HM Colonial and Overseas Civil Services, 1837–1997* (I.B.Tauris, 1999) and *Symbol of Authority: The British District Officer in Africa* (I.B.Tauris, 2005).

ASPECTS
OF EMPIRE

A Second Corona Anthology

ANTHONY KIRK-GREENE

I.B. TAURIS
LONDON · NEW YORK

Published in 2012 by I.B.Tauris & Co Ltd
6 Salem Road, London W2 4BU
175 Fifth Avenue, New York NY 10010
www.ibtauris.com

Distributed in the United States and Canada Exclusively by Palgrave Macmillan
175 Fifth Avenue, New York NY 10010

ISBN: 978 1 84885 514 4

A full CIP record for this book is available from the British Library
A full CIP record is available from the Library of Congress

Library of Congress Catalog Card Number: available

Printed and bound by CPI Group (UK) Ltd, Croydon, CRO 4YY

MIX
Paper from
responsible sources
FSC
www.fsc.org   FSC® C013604

CONTENTS

Introduction by Anthony Kirk-Greene   VII

I. The Colonial Office   1

II. Colonial Policy in the Decolonizing Decade   33

    a) Statements and Initiatives   34

    b) Colonial Affairs in Parliament   122

    c) From the Secretary of State for the Colonies   156

III. The Colonial Service and the Transfer of Power   183

    a) H.M.O.C.S. and Localization   184

    b) Retirement and Re-Employment   228

IV. The Colonial Service: *ave atque vale*   271

Index of Contributors   291

INTRODUCTION

by ANTHONY KIRK-GREENE

T his is the second volume of the anthology drawn from *Corona*, the official journal of the Colonial Service/Her Majesty's Overseas Civil Service published monthly from February 1949 to December 1962. The first, *Glimpses of Empire*, concentrated on the life of colonial officials, both professional and administrative, at work and, *en passant*, at leisure: in a word, on the Colonial Service. *Aspects of Empire* on the other hand has been premised as the necessary complementary volume, focusing on colonial policy, Parliament and its colonial debates, and on the metropolitan modalities of decolonization as they affected the transformation and the eventual termination of the Colonial Service as a career: in brief, on the Colonial Office. If the primary appeal of *Glimpses* was aimed at former members of H.M. Colonial Service, with a sprinkling of British social historians among its academic readers, *Aspects* will likely count a large number of imperial history researchers among its readership, as well as the positive insider following of 'those who were there'.

This second volume calls for no detailed description of the context and chronology of *Corona*, since such a historical account of its origin, progress and closure formed the essence of the substantial Introduction to the first volume. Of additional relevance to the *Corona* story are the memoirs of *Corona*'s founding editor, K.G. Bradley, as set out in chapter 13 of his autobiography, *Once A District Officer* (1966) and in his article 'Midwife to *Corona*' (VIII, 406–409). Suffice it here to say that the *Corona* journal came into being as one of the items in the package deal of Colonial Office reforms (along with the turning point Despatch on Local Government, the *Journal of African Administration*, the Colonial Office Summer Schools at Cambridge University, and the African Studies Branch in the Colonial Office, put together by the Secretary of State for the Colonies, Arthur Creech Jones, in 1947). Its aim was, as Creech Jones outlined in a pre-publication address to members of the Colonial Service, 'to keep members of the Service informed about the recent pronouncements and developments in colonial policy and practice'. As he saw the problem of the Colonial Service in its complex and internationally scrutinized post-war setting, it could no longer afford to 'perform independently, each of us working in comparative isolation in our own office, our own village, our own district, or even our own Colony or Protectorate'. The answer lay in a forum for the exchange of information and a pooling of ideas; in short, a Colonial Service journal, 'whereby such knowledge, gained from day to day by officers at work in field, may be put into a common pool from which all their colleagues may draw with advantage' (I,1,4). In place, therefore, of another meticulous *Corona* historical narrative introduction, the opportunity is taken here to comment on the categories and nature of the text selected, out of a corpus of over 1,500 articles, for inclusion. It thus serves, if you like, as a guide to and elucidation of the contents.

One word of explanation is in order to underline the fundamental difference between the aims of *Glimpses* and *Aspects*. While the first volume was dedicated to the nature of the work of members of the Colonial Service (later the Overseas Civil Service), covering the men and women recruited to work overseas in the Service's different professional departments, the present volume focuses on the Colonial Office and on Whitehall policy rather than on the Colonial Service in individual colonial territories. In other words, here the subject matter is those in London who drew up the colonial policies and schemes, which those in the field were expected to implement. In contrast to Foreign Office practice, the Colonial Office was staffed by members of the Home Civil Service, with just a handful of Colonial Service officers attached on temporary secondment (a practice internally known as 'beachcombing'). In a way, then, the publication order of *Glimpses* and *Aspects* reflects the reverse order of my two Colonial Service studies also published by I.B.Tauris. While *On Crown Service* (1999) is a history of the structure and development of Colonial/Overseas Civil Service between 1837 and 1997, it is the second volume, *Symbol of Authority* (2006), which analyses the character and nature of the work of the colonial administrator in the field.

Part I consists of articles on the Colonial Office, its organisation and work. Creech Jones had been quite adamant that in launching a Colonial Service journal it was at the same time to be an instrument for keeping the Colonial Office in touch with what the Colonial Officer was thinking; 'We here [in the C.O.], I may say, do *not* intend to keep out of the arena' (*ibid*). To the outside observer, whether he or she be foreign or even British, it has often been a matter of puzzled surprise that Britain's Colonial Office and Colonial Service were two distinct services, recruited and paid quite separately and – unlike the Foreign Office and Diplomatic Service – innocent of any regular cross-posting or interchange of personnel. Furthermore, not only did a major component of the British Empire, India, come under yet another and quite separate Whitehall Department, the India Office, but after the second World War the Dominions became the responsibility of a fourth overseas department, the Dominions (later the Commonwealth Relations) Office. In partial if minimal mitigation, as it were, of the Colonial Office/Service divide, the Warren Fisher reforms of 1930 introduced a scheme of limited exchange. Junior Principals in the Colonial Office might be seconded for a year to a colonial government to work as an understudy Assistant District Officer, while mid-seniority District Officers were from time to time seconded to the Colonial Office to learn how things worked at the London end. This latter practice came to be known as 'beachcombing'. In the decolonizing decade, a more senior Colonial Office official was now and again seconded to a territorial government, to advise on constitutional or ministerial matters or perhaps to help in the establishment of the new Cabinet Office or local Diplomatic

Service. Enabled by the convenience of air travel, from time to time in the 1950s a top official from the Colonial Office flew out to brief himself or maybe support the governor in moments of constitutional impasse. The Secretary of State, too, became measurably more itinerant than any of his pre-war predecessors could ever have been, while colonial governors could now be recalled for consultations in a matter of hours rather than weeks. The Colonial Office professional advisers, on the other hand, had long been expected to visit the colonies as part of their role, and were well acquainted with the Colonial Service scene.

Yet quite deliberately, and despite several internal enquiries and reports over the years on the issue of amalgamation, the Colonial Office and the Colonial Service remained separate entities right up to the closure of the former in 1966. True, there were instances of a senior Colonial Office official being offered a colonial governorship, the plum job which the Colonial Service defensively felt lay in its gift and should go to its own. Consequently, not all such 'Whitehall-wallah' appointments were greeted *in situ* with approval at the time or their incumbency looked back on with enthusiasm. In the worst-case scenario, the relationship between the Colonial Office and say one of its Colonial Service governors could degenerate into the same sort of mutual antipathy and disdain which has conventionally characterized relations between the General Staff and front-line commanders. Many a governor would have been appalled had he read some of the minutes written by relatively junior officials on his dispatches as they circulated in the Colonial Office. Within the history of the Colonial Service, including the post-war period, it is possible to identify a handful of colonial governors who were virtually sacked by the Colonial Office. Overall, then, while in personnel terms it was the Colonial Office which was responsible for the beginning and end of an officer's career in the Colonial Service (his recruitment, training, appointment and retirement), it was essentially the Colonial Service – staffed territorial governments which posted, paid, promoted (up to superscale ranks) and paid the pension of their officers.

By the late 1950s, the staff structure of the Colonial Office consisted of a Permanent Under Secretary, two Deputy Under Secretaries, nine Assistant Under Secretaries, 31 Assistant Secretaries and 70 Principals. To manage its Colonial Service responsibilities, after 1930 the Colonial Office set up a Colonial Service Division. By the mid-1950s, the high noon of the Colonial Office's involvement in the transformation of the Colonial Service as an integral part of the transfer of power, the Division's schedule of portfolios looked like this, headed by no less than a Deputy Under Secretary:

Department A: Recruiting and Training.

Department B: Conditions of service, discipline, pensions, honours, ceremonial.

Departments C, D and E: Appointments, transfers, promotions for the Administrative and all the professional branches.

A final point on the separate identities of the Colonial Service and the Colonial Office. While every Colonial Service officer would be aware of who his 'own' governor was and likely the names of their immediate

predecessors, the succession of top Whitehall mandarins in the Colonial
Office was far less readily known among Colonial Service officers in the field.
For the record, the post of Permanent Under-Secretary (PUS) at the Colonial
Office and that of his deputies were held during the period 1945–1966, by
the following officials:

Year	PUS	Deputy PUS (joint)
1947	Sir Thomas Lloyd	Sir Charles Jeffries and Sir Hilton Poynton
1956	Sir John Macpherson	Sir Hilton Poynton and Sir John Martin
1959–66	Sir Hilton Poynton	Sir John Martin and Sir William Gorrell Barnes

In such a momentous imperial era as that of post-war reconstruction and
then decolonization, both the Colonial Office and the Colonial Service were
fortunate to have had such positive and experienced continuity in their final
periods: just three permanent under secretaries and four joint deputies in
twenty years.

After this introduction to the role of the Colonial Office, Parts II and III
present the central themes of this second *Corona* anthology, the dissemination of information on colonial policy among its readers, overwhelmingly men and women working in the Colonial Service, and the
impact on them of plans for decolonization.

In retrospect, analysts of the Colonial Service will regret how scant was
discussion of colonial policy by those readers. Despite *Corona*'s disclaimer,
repeated in every issue, that 'the Secretary of State does not necessarily
endorse any opinions expressed in this journal' nor did it express the views
of territorial governments, neither the editor nor the contributors seemed
inclined to submit articles of a critical vein. Maybe the requirement that
every manuscript from a colonial civil servant had to be accompanied by an
assurance that it had been approved by his own government 'in accordance
with the regulations [General Orders]' was too much of a constraint. At any
rate, the feedback was minimal in the underused Correspondence pages. In
general the editor took the line that to query or criticize government policy
was not part of his brief, despite some outspoken comments on what he saw
as the inadequacy of the second H.M.O.C.S. White Paper of 1956 to arrest
the decline in Colonial Service morale. Indeed, when HMG introduced its
Special List 'A' (and later 'B') to handle the exodus of Colonial Service staff
by holding out hopes of some measure of continued government service,
Corona came under fire for not serving as a forum for encouraging its readers
to air their views. (The debate and the editor's defence of his ban is
rehearsed at length in the introduction to the first volume of this anthology,
p.xvii ff). But the editor remained firm in his rejection of the charge that
Corona eschewed political comment. *Corona*, he declared, 'must avoid any
hint of suspicion of partiality: and politics are the stuff of partiality' (XIII,
404). His cautious concern was made manifest in his declaration that the
journal was emphatically 'NOT a show window for chips on individual
shoulders or for personal grouses' (VII, 403). What all this means is that if

one is looking for 'the Colonial Service voice' during the rapidly changing 1950s, it was not often to be heard in the pages of *Corona* Instead, it is to the minutes of the territorial Senior Civil Servants' Associations that the historian should turn.

Under the rubric of Colonial Policy, the articles in Part II have been grouped under three heads. Section (a) presents a succession of C.O. statements of policy. Most of these are of an economic or political nature such as the Colonial Development and Welfare (C.D.W.) schemes; the UN Visiting Missions to Trust Territories like Tanganyika, Togoland and the British Cameroons; the emergencies in Malaya and in Kenya, including the resettlement of Mau Mau detainees; constitutional issues like those of the pacemaker Gold Coast and the complex Malta; the Enugu shooting and the Seretse Khama affairs; and the controversial (though that aspect was not emphasized) creation of the Central African Federation. There are also exposés of socio-developmental matters, for instance the colonial cinema and broadcasting (including the locally famous 'saucepan radios'), relations between governments and mission societies, and the purposes and problems of colonial economic development and co-ordination.

Section (b) switches the focus from Whitehall to Westminster. The reporting in *Corona* of the annual colonial debate in Parliament was accorded high priority by the editor, who devoted a regular column to 'Parliament' (soon rephrased more catchingly as 'Beneath Big Ben'). This also took in other debates on matters of primary concern to members of the Colonial Service, not only on such emergencies as Malaya and Mau Mau but notably the legislative debates over the creation of H.M.O.C.S. and later the Overseas Service Bill. Finally, Section (c) reproduces some of the messages, traditionally sent or broadcast by the Secretary of State at New Year, to the colonial peoples and to his Colonial Service.

Probably the most far-reaching of the CO's decisions on the Colonial Service, apart from its replacement from 1930 of the 40 or so territorial services by a single, unified, inter-transferable Colonial Service in each of its twenty Departments (Administration, Education, Forestry, Medical, Police, etc.), came in 1954. This change abolished the Colonial Service and established instead Her Majesty's Overseas Civil Service (after an abortive call for a new Commonwealth Service), replacing a primarily permanent and pensionable service with one predominantly staffed by contract appointments. The dismantling of the Colonial Service and transfer of power in the mid-1950s were now to replace the post-1945 mantra of 'development' as the central thrust of colonial policy. To an extent, Part III carries undertones and aftermaths of Part II (b), for many of the arguments which were so decisively to condition the morale and shape the mind of the Colonial Service during the transfer of power were first vigorously debated in Parliament and widely rehearsed in the UK press. Of particular significance were the milestones of the disbandment of the Colonial Service in favour of a new H.M.O.C.S. and the schemes proposed for compensating serving officers for loss of career, set out in a series of White Papers between 1954 and 1962. Part III thus focuses on the effect of decolonization on the Colonial Service at three major levels: the impact of the establishment of

H.M.O.C.S.; the linked localization of the territorial civil services; and, the other side of that particular coin, HMG's plans (and their acceptance or modification by the territorial governments as the final stage of self-government approached) to facilitate the early retirement of its overseas civil servants through the creation of Special Lists and provision for lump sum compensation to those whose careers had been prematurely terminated. These schemes were based on a sliding scale of age and length of service, sometimes of Byzantine complication to the non-actuarial mind. The whole process culminated, a few years before the end of *Corona*, in HMG's decision to set up an Overseas Service Resettlement Bureau (OSRB) and hence the whole latterday field – as yet insufficiently explored in the literature – of 'second careers'. Together these multiple and interlocking events were profoundly to exercise the 'Colonial Service mind' as officers forced themselves to face up to the crucial personal question: to stay on, to go now, or to go when.

By way of finale, Part IV is – like the transfer of power itself – short and to the point. Much of it is derived from the very last issue of *Corona* (December 1962), in which the editor purposely sought from Colonial Office and Colonial Service luminaries articles which together would combine looking forward with looking back. To these heavyweight pieces I have added three quite personal reflections on the ending of a career from 'ordinary' readers and on what 'going home' meant for them. As for the contribution of Alan Lennox-Boyd, former Secretary of State and the post-war Colonial Service's most popular Minister, he left *Corona's* readers in no doubt as to what it meant: 'The end of *Corona* marks the end of an era, but the men and women of that era whose way of life is set down in their journal can rightly feel that they belonged to the best Service in the world'.

OXFORD
2012

I. THE COLONIAL OFFICE

While the recruitment, work, conditions of service and career of Colonial Office officials were quite separate from those operating for the Colonial Service, the link was nevertheless so immediate and so intimate that the relationship was inevitably a close if not necessarily an integrated one. Part I looks at some of the articles on the Colonial Office in the Colonial Service's journal, subtly encouraged by an editor who was wisely aware of the need to break down the conventional 'overseas' barrier of 'home' suspicion and promote the imperative for the Service to know more about the Office as well as vice-versa.

On occasion there was a real need for the average Colonial Service officer to realize that the Colonial Office had a human face (and heart) after all, and to appreciate the extent of the Office's genuine knowledge about and interest in the Service and its work. At the same time, *Corona* never failed to underline its total independence (in anything other than the hospitality of office accommodation in Great Smith Street) from the C.O. and to emphasize that in no way did its contents or opinions reflect the official policy of either the Secretary of State for the Colonies or of any territorial government.

In 1961, just as *Corona* was coming to an end, the UK government created out of parts of the Colonial Office a Department of Technical Co-operation (D.T.C.), to direct a more coherent approach to the technical support of the newly independent countries. This became the Ministry of Overseas Development in 1964, later restructured into the Overseas Development Administration (O.D.A.). The Colonial Office was closed down in 1966, 112 years after its establishment, with its own Secretary of State, following its separation from the War Office in 1854. From 1966 responsibility for the new independent territories became that of the Foreign and Commonwealth Office (F.C.O.).

The Colonial Office

by A. R. THOMAS, C.M.G.

L et me begin with a few facts and definitions. The Colonial Office is the Department of His Majesty's Government in the United Kingdom which deals with the affairs of the non-self-governing countries of the British Commonwealth. It does not deal with the self-governing Colony of Southern Rhodesia, which comes under the Commonwealth Relations Office. Nor does it deal with the High Commission territories of Basutoland, Swaziland and Bechuanaland, which also come under the Commonwealth Relations Office. It does not deal with the Anglo-Egyptian Sudan or certain small territories in the Persian Gulf, which also come under the Foreign Office. And finally, of course, it has no responsibility for relations with the great self-governing countries of the Commonwealth, such as Australia and India, which are the concern of the Commonwealth Relations Office, or the dependencies of those countries.

What is left, however, for the Colonial Office to deal with is a formidable responsibility, comprising an area of some two million square miles, populated by seventy million peoples and administered by thirty-five separate Governments. The task is rendered more complex by the great variations of climate, religions, languages, races, colour, customs and standards of education and development. These variations make it necessary to treat each territory as an individual entity and not merely as a unit in a general scheme.

I will not attempt to distinguish between the status of the various territories. My subject is the Colonial Office, and it is sufficient for this purpose to note that whether a territory is a Colony or a Protectorate, a Protected state, or a Trust territory, it has available to it precisely the same measure of assistance and advice from the Colonial Office. Of course, His Majesty's Government has special responsibilities *vis-à-vis* the United Nations in respect of its Trust Territories; but that does not mean that they receive any greater assistance or better treatment than the other territories. On the contrary, we aim at governing all out territories in accordance with the principles which we are expected to apply to the Trust territories. Also, for the sake of simplicity I propose to use the word 'Colony' somewhat loosely to describe all the territories – no matter their precise constitutional status – which come under the Colonial Office.

The Head of the Colonial Office is the Secretary of State for the Colonies. In fact, without him, the Colonial Office has no existence. The Colonial Office is in origin the Secretariat of the Secretary of State and all its actions are performed in his name and he takes responsibility for them. The Secretary of State is the Minister responsible to Parliament – and through

Parliament to the electorate of the United Kingdom – for the general administration of the Colonies. As a member of the Cabinet he has the duty and the opportunity of voicing Colonial interests on all matters which may affect them. He has to assist him on the political side a Minister of State and a Parliamentary Under-Secretary of State, whose appointments – like that of the Secretary of State – are subject to changes of Government at home; though it is fair to say that there is a wide measure of agreement between the principal political parties of the United Kingdom on the subject of Colonial policy.

On the official side the Secretary of State has to assist him the permanent staff of the Colonial Office. These are career civil servants and their position is unaffected by changes of Government. The permanent staff of the Colonial Office numbers about 1,300 in all. This includes all grades – administrative, executive, clerical, typists and messengers. The number of officers who are concerned with matters of policy – broadly speaking, the administrative grade and the professional advisers – is of course much smaller, about 200 in all. All these officers belong to the Home Civil Service, which is separate and distinct from the Colonial Service, except that a number of administrative and professional posts are filled by Colonial Service officers either on secondment or after their retirement from the Colonial Service.

The permanent head of the Colonial Office is the Permanent Under-Secretary of State, who is responsible for the staffing and organisation of the office and is the principal link on policy matters between the permanent staff and the Ministers. There are also two Deputy Under-Secretaries of State, who may deal direct with Ministers on certain groups of subjects, at the same time keeping the Permanent Under-Secretary informed. Next in seniority come the Assistant Under-Secretaries of State, of whom there are eight, and who are generally responsible for co-ordinating the work of various groups of departments. And below these senior officials comes the main departmental organi\sation of the office.

Originally the Colonial Office was organised on a territorial basis; that is to say, there were separate Geographical Departments which dealt with all matters affecting a particular group of Colonies. Thus you had a West African Department which dealt with everything arising in the Colonial Office to do with the four West African territories. Similarly, there was an East African Department, a West Indian Department, a Mediterranean Department, a Far Eastern Department and so on. Sometime in the late 1920's and the early 1930's it became apparent that this was not by itself a completely satisfactory system. Certain subjects – I instance tariff policy, the conditions of service among Colonial Service officers, and the application to the Colonies of international conventions – could obviously best be dealt with on a centralised basis. Hence a number of new Departments were created whose function it was to deal with certain groups of subjects on a Colonial Empire-wide basis. We now have separate 'subject' departments dealing with defence, Colonial Service staffing matters, economic policy, social services, communications, international relations and research – so that in fact they now easily outnumber the geographical departments. We still retain the original geographical departments, however, and very important they are – dealing as they do with constitutional, political and other matters and maintaining close contact with the subject departments in order to ensure that general decisions of policy are not applied without taking fully into account the individual variations and the political background of the different territories.

Thus the Colonial Office is organised on a dual basis. In one official document, owing to a printer's error, the word dual was spelt 'duel.' But in truth there is a very close and friendly liaison between the geographical and the subject departments, and indeed if this were not the case, the wheels of the Colonial Office would quickly draw attention to it by their creaking!

There is yet a third important element in our organisation, namely the Advisory Staff. The Secretary of State has to advise him on professional matters a team of Advisers who are appointed because of their special qualifications and expert knowledge and experience in various groups of subjects. For instance, there is a Legal Adviser, a Medical Adviser, an Agricultural Adviser, an Educational Adviser and other Advisers on Labour, Social Welfare, Forestry, Fisheries, Co-operation and so on. In some cases these Advisers have their own small separate staffs and there are also Advisory Committees which enable the Secretary of State and the Colonial Office to draw on a wide range of expert advice outside the Colonial Office. The advisers (apart from the Legal Adviser) have no executive functions, but their advice is always available to Ministers and to the Office and they are in regular touch through visits and reports with the professional departments in the Colonies.

I have dealt in some detail with the organisation of the Colonial Office because it seems to me to be a necessary background against which to consider the present-day functions of the Colonial Office. I stress the word 'present-day,' because its functions are very different from what they were twenty years ago, and will probably have changed again quite considerably in another ten years from now. Perhaps I have put the cart before the horse. Perhaps I should have discussed the functions of the Colonial Office before describing its organisation, since it is the organisation which must adapt itself to changing functions, and not the functions which must be governed by the organisation. Anything in the nature of a rigid organisation would indeed be fatal to the pursuit of a dynamic Colonial policy and I therefore emphasise that the Colonial Office must be continually prepared to adapt its organisation and staffing arrangements to meet the changing times.

As a broad generalisation, it may be said that the Colonial Office has three general functions to perform. The first is to act as the mouthpiece of His Majesty's Government in conveying to Colonial Governments the broad policies and the particular decisions and wishes of His Majesty's Government. The second is to act as the mouthpiece of Colonial Governments by seeing that the interests of those Governments and the Colonial peoples are fully safeguarded and promoted in matters arising here in this country or elsewhere outside their territories. The third is the provision of expert services and advice of all kinds of which our organisation is capable, including the provision of moneys for development purposes and also – very important – the provision of staff.

Let us take first what I have described as the function of conveying to Colonial Governments the decisions and wishes of His Majesty's Government in broad matters of policy. Throughout this note I have been at pains to avoid giving any impression that the Colonial Office administers the Colonies. There has never been a time when that was the case. Each territory possesses – and has always possessed – its own separate administration, and even in the days when the simplest form of direct rule was practised, there was a very healthy prejudice in favour of relying on the man on the spot. Nevertheless, when the administration of a territory consisted only of the Governor and his official advisers, and there was no obligation to accept – or even to seek – the advice of local leaders, it was always possible for decisions to be taken in London and to be conveyed to Governors in the form of instructions. Today the picture has changed. In many territories there is now a majority of unofficials in the Legislative Council and in most places there is some form of electoral system; with the result that in accordance with the declared policy of His Majesty's Government control is steadily passing to the representatives of the local peoples. This imposes very distinct limitations on the control which can be exercised by the Home Government. This fact is not always fully appreciated by those who criticise us in international discussions. You can't have your cake and eat it. Either you have to accept the risk that in moving towards self-government Colonies may deviate from the approved pattern and may decide, for example, not to accede to an international convention; or else you have to retain the power to require them to go the way you want them to go, by maintaining what is sometimes described as an out-of-date colonialism. We have definitely chosen the former path. That, however, is by the way. What I wish to emphasise is that the range of matters on which the Home Government would deem itself justified in laying down the law is now narrowly limited. There are, however, many matters on which the Home Government has views; and if – as may happen – these run counter to the views of a Colonial Government, it is up to the Colonial Office to make use of its powers of reasoning and persuasion. Thus the task of the Colonial Office has in many ways become a much more difficult and delicate one than in the old days when local reactions were not so carefully studied as they are today.

The second general function of the Colonial Office is to see that the interests and views of Colonial Governments and the peoples which they represent are fully safeguarded when matters affecting those interests come up for consideration either by the Government at home or in international discussions. This again is a task which calls for qualities of discretion and diplomacy – and at times of forcefulness. The Secretary of State for the Colonies and his Department have – by virtue of their special knowledge of the Colonies and their constant contacts with Colonial Governments – the right and the responsibility of being the particular advocates of Colonial interests in the Cabinet or elsewhere. The great self-governing countries of the British Commonwealth have their own Ambassadors and High Commissioners to represent their interests. The non-self-governing territories do not have this direct from of representation. This makes it all the more incumbent on the Colonial Office to see that their interests do not go by default. If, example, the Service Departments are planning defence measures which affect a Colony or group of Colonies, it is up to the Colonial Office to ensure that the Governors are fully consulted at an early stage in order that they may have an opportunity to represent the repercussions which such measures may have on local civilian interests. Or again, if a commodity is in short supply – a situation which is nowadays unfortunately all too frequent – it is the job of the Colonial Office to see that the vital needs of the Colonies are met, or at any rate taken fully into account, and that there shall be fair shares for all. Or again, in the international field, it is the duty of the Colonial Office representative on the United Kingdom delegation to ensure that the interests of the Colonies are safeguarded and that incorrect statements and unfounded criticisms are corrected and rebutted. This work of representation calls for constant vigilance and for the closest possible contact between the staff of the Colonial Office and Colonial Governments in the field. Of course there are times when it may not be possible to support the views of Colonial Governments for certain reasons which may not have been apparent to them. It is very important that the Colonial Office should exercise its discretion wisely, because if support were automatically given to Colonial requests in bad cases as well as in good, the currency of the Colonial Office would rapidly depreciate and it would not enjoy the reputation which I think it has gained for itself of making other Government Departments at home and other outside organisations take serious heed of its representations on behalf of Colonial interests.

The third general function of the Colonial Office is the provision of services of various kinds to Colonial Governments. I have already mentioned the work of our specialist advisers and Advisory Committees, and I would only add that we are generally able to respond to the request of a Colonial Government for an expert or a team of experts to go out to a territory and advise the local Government on some matter affecting its health and educational problems, its agriculture or some other aspect of its development programme on which it has not got the necessary expert professional assistance available locally.

The Colonial Office is also responsible for the allocation to Colonial Governments of the money voted by Parliament under the C.D. and W. Acts for development and research in Colonial territories. It is also responsible in consultation with the Treasury for deciding what proportion of the moneys available shall be devoted to centrally administered schemes such as scientific research in which it would be wasteful for activity to be duplicated in the different territories.

Finally, it is one of the most important duties of the Colonial Office to see that the staffing needs of Colonial Governments are properly met both in numbers and in quality. Although an increasing number of administrative and professional posts are now being filled by local recruitment, a large proportion of the staff is, and for some considerable time to come must be, recruited in the United Kingdom with some assistance from other Commonwealth countries. The Colonial Office has to deal both with the selection of candidates, and also with the filling of higher vacancies in the Colonial Service by the promotion or the transfer of serving officers. The Colonial Office has also to see that the necessary degree of co-ordination is maintained between the levels of salaries and conditions of service offered by the various Colonial Governments.

There are other important activities in which the Colonial Office engages, but I am afraid that space does not permit me to do more than to make very brief mention of two of them. In the field of Information, the Colonial Office is responsible for the dissemination in this country and in other countries of accurate information about current events and policy. It also transmits to the Colonies information about British institutions and the democratic way of life. In these days of Cold War this work has taken on an added importance, as a means of strengthening the faith of Colonial peoples in Western ideals and in countering hostile propaganda from certain sources.

The second particular activity which I should like to mention is that of the care of Colonial students who come to this country for their higher education. We have a special department dealing with this. With the ever-rising standards of education in the Colonies more and more of these students are coming over here and we do our best to place them in Universities suitable to their particular studies and to ensure that their stay over here is made generally pleasant and comfortable.

That ends my list of the activities of the Colonial Office, though there are many more that could be added. I should just like in conclusion to say a word about a scheme which we have for the two-way exchange of Colonial Office and Colonial Service officers. No one is more conscious than we who work in the Colonial Office of the difficulties and dangers of trying to deal intelligently with matters which are happening thousands of miles away in widely-scattered parts of the Commonwealth. We therefore try to educate ourselves! We do this in two ways. First, it is the policy to send as many of our administrative officers as possible to the Colonies for a period of two years in the early stages of their careers, in order that they may learn to understand how the thing looks from the other end and in particular to gain practical experience of Colonial administration in a District. Secondly, we have a reverse scheme in operation under which Colonial Governments may recommend certain of their officers to serve in the Colonial Office for a two-year period, in order to gain experience for themselves and their Governments of the workings of the Colonial Office and Whitehall. There is considerable competition for these vacancies, but at any one time we have something of the order of twenty Colonial Service officers performing responsible adminis-trative work in the Colonial Office. Also, many of our professional advisers are men who have had long periods of service overseas before receiving their appointments in the Colonial Office. There is also a great deal of personal contract between members of the Colonial Office and officers in the field by visits by members of the Colonial Office to the territories with which they deal, and also by discussions with senior Colonial Service officials – and unofficials – visiting this country. In these various ways we do our best to bridge the gap between Whitehall and the wide open spaces.

The Colonial Month

Delightful weather welcomed their Majesties to Church House for the opening of the Colonial Month on the 21st June and, indeed, it has continued (though with rather excessive heat at times) until the time of writing. On that first morning Great Smith Street was gay with flags, with Oriental and African dress and with the green and red uniforms and bright lances of the Gold Coast Mounted Police on parade outside the entrance to the Colonial Office.

On the platform with their Majesties, who were accompanied by the Earl of Athlone and Princess Alice, were Mr. and Mrs. Attlee, the Secretary of State, Lord Listowel and Mr. Rees Williams. The Gold Coast police and Scouts and Guides from the colonies came in and lined the walls and there was a very distinguished gathering in the body of the Hall.

We are printing the King's speech in full elsewhere in this issue. The only other speaker was Mr. Kenneth Blackburne, who, before the King arrived, told us all, very charmingly, about the Month and what we ought to see and how to get there. After the King's speech the Secretary of State made thirty-two presentations to His Majesty. Those so honoured were nearly all visitors from the colonies, almost every one of which was represented. The whole ceremony, which was very simple and not very long, was broadcast with a commentary by Richard Dimbleby.

Daisies may be nearly over in the fields but there has been a remarkable crop of them in the streets of London since the 21st June. The Daisy has been chosen as the emblem for the Colonial Month and it appears on posters everywhere, with the crest of a different colony on each of its petals. Everywhere, too, appear the flags of the colonies; crested Red Ensigns on flag-poles above the new bank of flowers in Trafalgar Square; Blue Ensigns, crested too, cascading down the gutted walls of the old Westminster Hospital, which is to be the site of the new Colonial Office, while blue streamers, with 'Colonial Month' on them in big white letters, have appeared all over Town, along balconies and above shop windows. In the windows themselves throughout the West End and in other shopping centres, the colonies and their products are a constantly recurring motif. Over a hundred firms, and shops large and small, have co-operated in these displays. They range from a complete model of a cocoa tree, with photographs of the harvesting and samples of the product, in a big window in Oxford Street, to the hopeful, if rather misguided, marshalling of little Canadian and Australian flags round some bottles of Cyprus sherry in a corner grocery. It is, in fact, almost impossible to walk for more than a hundred yards down any main shopping street in Central London without seeing evidence of the colonies, and that was one of the objects of those who organised the Month.

This kind of publicity has, of course, only a limited object: to rouse the interest of the great London public and so to encourage it to go in search of information. Over 100,000 of them went, in the first two weeks to see the exhibition organised by the Central Office of Information in Oxford Street, just opposite the Marble Arch Pavilion Cinema. This exhibition is the focal point of the Month and is aptly called 'Focus on Colonial Progress.' The two troopers of the Gold Coast mounted police, who stand guard outside, draw endless crowds and are performing a most gallant and valuable service.

The exhibition is remarkably good, in spite of its very cramped quarters. There is no need for us to describe it here, as you will have already seen pictures of it and read about it in the Press. The exhibits were carefully arranged – atmosphere, geography, peoples, art, history, policy, problems and achievement, in that order. We particularly liked the 'equatorial forest' at the entrance. It was well and accurately done – including the 'Ashanti blood' and the humid heat. (During the last week in June there were longer queues than ever outside because people said that the air-conditioned 'forest' was the coolest place in Oxford Street); we liked, too, the 'talking room,' the glass case containing live locusts, and the maps and prints in the historical section. The thirty lifesize wax-work figures of colonial types were accurate as to costume and background, but some of them were rather ugly; the Masai warrior, for instance, had no grace. There is, perhaps, still too great a tendency to over-emphasise the crude and the barbaric. Some people made the same criticism of the otherwise excellent B.B.C. programme 'Colonial Round Up,' the script of which was so beautifully spoken by John Gielgud. Their Majesties went to see the Exhibition on the 11th July.

The B.B.C. has been co-operating splendidly during the Month. In the home services they have put on nearly twenty programmes concerned with the colonies as well as many in the European and other foreign services.

The Press gave the Month a good send-off and in several newspapers there has throughout the period been a stronger colonial motif than usual. Two at least of the popular Dailies are sending special correspondents round the colonies by air to cable home despatches as they go. The *Overseas Daily Mail* brought out an eight-page supplement on Malaya and the *Daily Express*, in conjunction with Cable and Wireless, has promoted a scheme by which the public have been able to cable questions and receive answers from six colonial stations. Throughout the Month there have been special film shows and lectures organised by the Central Office of Information and others at many different centres in London.

In addition to 'Focus on the Colonies' there have been no less than nineteen special exhibitions or displays put on by Museums and Societies of all kinds, ranging from the West India Committee to the Victoria and Albert Museum, and including the Boy Scouts Association and Missionary Societies. We have not had time to go and see them all, but pride of place should probably be given to the exhibition of the 'Traditional Art of the British Colonies' at the Royal Anthropological Institute. As Mr. William Fagg said of it in a letter to *The Times*: 'African genius especially is seen at its finest and in astonishing variety, from the Ife sculptures which outdo Praxiteles in naturalism to the awe-inspiring cubism of the Niger delta tribes.'

And last, but not least, a special service was held at Westminster Abbey on the evening of Sunday, the 26th June. The Reverend R. W. Stopford, formerly Principal of Achimota, preached and there was a big attendance of people from the colonies.

The Colonies on Tour

The 'Colonial Month,' held in London last year was so successful that arrangements have been made for holding similar 'Colonial Weeks' in eight provincial cities during the coming months, the centre-piece on each occasion being a smaller touring edition of the original Oxford Street exhibition, 'Focus on Colonial Progress.' In fact the tour has already started; it began at Southampton, from the 6th to the 20th May, and it arrived in Bristol for a stay of nearly three weeks on the 5th June. We hope to be able to give our readers a personal impression of the Bristol 'Weeks' in our next issue, but meanwhile we are concerned with Southampton.

The Secretary of State went down there to open the affair and his inaugural speech was made at a civic luncheon given at the Polygon Hotel. He began by reminding the citizens of Southampton that 'on the 15th day of August, 1620, it was from the nearby West Quay that the little company of Pilgrim Fathers embarked on the *Mayflower* to found the New England States of America,' and that 'it was on the 13th day of October, 1948, that the ship *John Biscoe* of the Falkland Islands Dependencies Survey set out from Southampton.'

Having thus happily reminded his audience of the earliest and the latest of the many links of their Imperial connection, he said, 'We need today more than the links of trade which shipping has created. We in the Commonwealth need more than ever before to be able to strengthen our association one with another; for no one can doubt that a powerful and united Commonwealth can contribute possibly more than anything else to world peace.' 'If,' he added, 'we are to strengthen our association, we must get to know one another better,' and he emphasised the urgent need for combatting the 'appalling ignorance' in this country about its Colonial Empire and emphasised that an enlightened colonial policy must be based on a well-informed public opinion.

The exhibition was held in Blighmont Drill Hall and attracted a great deal of attention. More than 28,450 people visited it during the next two weeks. Those who saw it last year will, incidentally, be interested to know that, for touring purposes, a replica of a Zanzibar gateway has now been substituted for the rather immobile West African forest.

On Sunday, the 7th, a large congregation went to Christ Church, Freemantle, for a special civic service at which Archdeacon S. M. Collier of Penang preached, and the second lesson was read by Mr. J. K. Fiergbor, a student from the Gold Coast. There are about sixty colonial students at Southampton University and other local institutions and some of them were introduced to the Secretary of State when he opened the Exhibition. The Mayor also entertained many of them to tea on the following Friday.

In addition to the Exhibition twenty-eight lectures were given to various groups in Southampton, and at Ringwood, Ryde and other places; some of the shops put on special displays and, as in London last year, Cable and Wireless organised a special and much appreciated service of free messages of greetings to friends in the colonies. A special message was sent by the Mayor during the civic luncheon, to the Mayor of Nairobi, 'the principal city of East Africa, and recently honoured by Royal Charter,' and the reply came within half an hour.

The tour, then, went off to a fair start. By the time the exhibition has been to Bristol, Cardiff, Liverpool, Glasgow, Newcastle, Birmingham and Bradford and all those places have carried out their ambitious supporting programmes, another 'Gallup poll' will perhaps show that rather more than twenty-eight per cent of the victims may be able to name one colony, and rather less than seventy per cent be unable to explain the difference between a colony and a Dominion.

Colonial Weeks

A VISIT TO BRISTOL

As my new cream and crimson train slid westward across the rumpled green and gold quilt of the summer fields, I reminded myself very carefully that I must not expect to find Bristol *en fête coloniale*. There is nothing of the Festival about these 'Colonial Weeks'; their purpose is not to organise pride and sentiment but simply to increase knowledge; not to tell people only of our achievements but also of our problems and difficulties and how they can help. Very rightly the spearhead is aimed at young people and children, and I found hundreds of them going through the exhibition, with teachers and with a lecturer for each party. I saw one teacher scribbling hard. She had a gleam in her eye and I knew that her notes would appear next morning as examination questions. If any of the ladies who had been trying to send free greetings under the Cable-Wireless scheme to nephews in Australia were the parents of these children they were likely, I thought, to have a pretty sharp experience of adult education. On Sunday afternoon, which was fine and hot and not at all the sort of day for visiting museums, I found the people coming in at the rate of three hundred an hour. Most of them were family parties, with father holding forth, and almost all the others were young men and girls. The target was being hit. The exhibition was set up in the City Museum and it was well arranged in much lighter and more spacious conditions than in Oxford Street. Every hour, too, there was a film show. Indeed, the use being made of the cinema at Bristol was very encouraging. In addition to those films shown at the exhibition, others were being taken out by van to Durdham Down, to the Suspension Bridge and to all the parks and other places where people sit about and play in this lovely summer weather. And with the van went other lecturers. The young came running and their elders lingered, and a few more seeds were scattered. Most striking of all, I thought, were the film-shows being given in the Chapter-house of the Cathedral, which is the most perfect piece of interior Norman in the whole of England. One of the films was *Daybreak in Udi* and I wondered whether the ghostly Brothers were any more amazed than the wide-eyed audience. In Bristol a particularly big part in the campaign was being played by the Church, partly because of the keen interest of the Dean, who is Kenneth Blackburne's father. He and Canon Peacey had organised in the nave of the Cathedral an excellent exhibition of photographs, posters, literature and some very interesting relics, illustrating the history, the work and the purpose of missionary endeavour in all parts of the Empire. Every Missionary Society in Britain, except the Roman Catholics, had contributed. My only regret was that, in spite of everything, this exhibition could not do justice to the importance of the Mission's work at the present time. Kenneth Blackburne opened the exhibition himself and, I am sure, though I was not there, that he took the opportunity of saying so.

The 11th June was 'Colonial Sunday' and I went to the morning service in the Cathedral. The Lord Mayor came in his state carriage with its prancing bays and his coachman and footman in blue and scarlet. The singing was beautiful, both the Lessons were read, very well, by colonial students, and the Dean's address was forthright and timely.

As I made my way to the Temple Meads station through the bomb-torn heart of the City and past the cloud of blue colonial flags floating over the still water of the dock by Neptune's statue, I realised that at Bristol it was not only the ignorant who could profit from these Colonial Weeks.

Calling at the Colonial Office

by RAYMOND NORRIS, M.B.E.

Since I first knew the Colonial Office – more than twenty years ago – there have, of course, been tremendous changes, particularly in the expansion of its activities and the emphasis on economic affairs, but none more striking than the vastly improved arrangements now made at Church House and Sanctuary Buildings for the reception of visitors.

The memory is still vivid of my first arrival to assume duty in the old Colonial Office, not a little overawed at the prospect of working in an office with so distinguished an address as Downing Street. The glamour became tarnished, however, in the over-crowded, grimy building which the Colonial Office shared with the Dominions Office (as the latter was called in those days). Many readers of *Corona* will remember the Downing Street office, with its poky little entrance hall, small, dimly-lit, sparsely-furnished with two or three straight-backed chairs, at the foot of a narrow flight of stairs which seemed to lead up into a blank wall, with another flight leading down to what, from its gloomy lighting, could only be the cellars. Callers who passed the doorman usually ventured down the stairs to the lift, which wheezed its way upwards with frequent breakdowns necessitating calls for help to the Admiralty (I never quite knew why) to release the unfortunates who were often stuck between floors. Narrow corridors stacked with cupboards of old files and tiny waiting rooms – or even a hard chair in a corridor were the next stage before a visitor could reach the officer he or she wanted to see. Not a very encouraging start to an interview, particularly if one had called on the off-chance without an appointment. No one was more aware of this than the Colonial Office authorities themselves and many were the embarrassed officers who had to see callers in such crowded surroundings. Lack of space, however, was such that it was difficult enough to find room for officers to work in and what little space was originally available for waiting rooms had reluctantly to be taken for offices.

Then – starting during the war – came an even more difficult period for callers and Colonial Office officials alike, when the Downing Street office burst its seams and room had to be found elsewhere. The Downing Street office, with its 'out-stations' at Richmond Terrace and Queen Anne's Gate, extended to Dover House, Palace Chambers, Victoria Street, and even as far afield as Park Street. Finding a member of the Colonial Office staff was difficult in the extreme – even, I imagine, for officers of the Department, let alone visitors. Many were the complaints that one called to see Mr. X at Downing Street, to learn that he was in Park Street; on deciding to return at a later date, it transpired that he had been moved to Palace Chambers – and so on. No wonder that the Colonial Service regarded members of the Colonial Office staff as being elusive in the extreme!

Remembering all this, it was with interest that I called at Church House for the first time early this year. The change is truly remarkable. The large, pleasant entrance hall is well-lighted and decorated and has badges of some of the colonies on the walls. The Enquiries Room might well be the waiting room in a club or large corporation; comfortably furnished with armchairs and tables and with up-to-date magazines and pamphlets on Colonial Affairs. The Reception Desk is staffed with pleasant, efficient officers, who obviously have the good name of the Department at heart and really want to help callers. So much for the new atmosphere. The service?

If you have an appointment, a rapid telephone call confirms that the officer is expecting you (or his whereabouts determined if possible) and you are then placed in the care of a messenger who takes you to your destination. This latter is a necessary precaution for callers who are not familiar with the six floors and dozens of corridors of Church House. I rashly tried to find my way around on a second visit unaided but had to call for help. If you have not made an appointment, the Reception Desk will help you to decide whom it is you want to see and will then find out if he or she is available before sending you on your journey, or will try to make an appointment for you later on. If, for example, you have gone to Church House instead of to Sanctuary Buildings, just across the way, a telephone enquiry will ascertain for you whether it would be a lost journey or not to cross the road.

The caller who does not want to see anyone in particular but who is in search of information about the colonies – the population of Nigeria, the cost of housing in the Bahamas, the climate of Jamaica, and the thousands of other miscellaneous enquiries which reach the Colonial Office every year – is also well looked after in the Enquiries Room. Reports, pamphlets and other information are available to be perused in leisure and comfort. Should an interview subsequently be desired, the caller is then put on the right path.

The office in Sanctuary Buildings has not the same impressive appearance but the service is the same in the Enquiries Room. The room there has an interesting addition in the shape of a board giving details of theatres and shows in London, so one can while away the time waiting for an interview in picking out a show to see later on in one's leave. So far as I know, the Reception staff will not book seats but I am sure that they will be only too happy to put a stranger on to a ticket agency – a service which my friends in the Establishment Division would not, I am certain, wish to see taken advantage of in too many cases!

During my ten years or so in the West Indies I have on several occasions been asked by officials and unofficials whether the invitations to call at the Colonial Office are genuine and sincere. Such invitations are genuine, for the Colonial Office realises as well as anyone how valuable such contacts are to both sides, and I think that the doubts have arisen from the difficulties in the 'bad old days' of getting to the right man without disheartening and time-consuming searches, often in different parts of London. All honour to the officers of the Colonial Office who, realising the importance of first impressions, were responsible for the present arrangements for the reception and comfort of callers at Church House and Sanctuary Buildings today. The title of the Reception Department is significant and is indicative of the service given there. What the new Colonial Office will be like when it is built I know not, but of one thing I am certain – the caller's welcome will not be a warmer one than it is now, nor will he be made to feel more at home.

The sceptic will say that I've been dreaming or am drawing a long bow. Well, call at the Colonial Office during your next leave and try it out. If your reception in the Enquiries Room is not a pleasant one and if everything possible is not done for you, then ask one of the Reception Officers at Sanctuary Buildings to pick out the best show on the theatre board and come with me to it at my expense during my next leave.

Beachcombing

by J. DARRELL BATES

Administrative officers in the Colonial Service seconded to the Colonial Office are commonly known as Beachcombers. Why this is so I don't know. Beachcombing conjures up visions of retired civil servants sitting outside gimcrack bungalows on a Tropic Shore in well-worn tennis shoes, waiting for last month's Blackwoods. It describes a picturesque way of doing nothing in particular abroad on a small income. It is idleness in exile. None of this, however, really seems to explain why we Beachcombers are called Beachcombers. So, having no dictionary at hand, I asked my wife what she understood by the word. 'Cheerful old men picking up anything they can find as they wander in strange places, and spending the proceeds on gin,' was the answer. Asked if this really applies to D.C.s on loan to the Colonial Office, she said: 'It doesn't. They are not old.' Perhaps we had better leave it at that.

First of all, how does one become a Beachcomber? The only answer I can think of is Malvolio's. 'Some are born Beachcombers. Some achieve beachcombing, and some have beachcombing thrust upon them.' There doesn't seem to be any one answer. Some are no doubt carefully chosen on merit for this honour – but most of us, I think, get to the Colonial Office more by accident than by design. One thing's clear, though: you don't become a Beachcomber by going to the Colonial Office and asking to be taken on. If you do you will properly be told that the decision lies in your colony. Beachcombers are drawn from all parts of the Colonial Empire. They come generally when they are about thirty, and stay for two or three years. At present there are about twenty of them in the Office.

The first six months are usually depressing. There is United Kingdom income tax to pay and the 8.15 to catch every morning. One has to wear a tie, and pay for firewood. In the office one must get to understand strange formalities of method and phraseology, as bewildering, and sometimes as archaic as the sacrosanct peculiarities of school or university. Not only the procedure but the people are, for the most part, new to one, and one has to cope, perhaps for the first time, with horrors like the disconcerting aliveness of a stenographer and the disconcerting deadness of a dictaphone. If in the first six months you have discovered how to get your drafts typed and your telegrams despatched; if you can extract both the right file and a morning cup of tea from the registry staff, and know half the office staff by sight, by location and by illegibility of signature, you won't have done too badly.

The Colonial Office is divided into Geographical Departments, which are concerned with groups of territories, and Subject Departments which deal as experts with particular things like supplies, finance and communications.

19

Beachcombers are, of course, distributed to Departments as vacancies exist: but often there is a choice of vacancies at the outset, and opportunities of transferring from one Department to another while one is at the Colonial Office. This being so, it is helpful to know beforehand enough about the organisation of the office, to know which Department to choose, or to set as one's goal. My own view is that every Beachcomber should at some stage go to a Geographical Department – where he can, I think, best see the Colonial Office end of his own work as an Administrative Officer, and study, so to speak, the reverse of his own particular medal.

This leads me on to make two other points. Generally speaking the best way in which an Administrative Officer can hope to make any contribution of his own to the Colonial Office is to bring to bear on his work and on the permanent staff of the office the realities of his own experience and responsibilities in the field as a District Officer. It is less often that experience in a Colonial Secretariat is of the same value to the Colonial Office, whose own staff are so obviously much more competent and experienced in this type of work. For this reason I feel that, as a general rule, Administrative Officers should be sent as Beachcombers when, and only when they have actually been in charge of a District. Secondly, it is clearly desirable that territories should be encouraged to send to the Colonial Office the people they think best able both to benefit from this experience themselves, and to make some contribution of their own to the Colonial Office. It is unreasonable to expect them to do so, however, if, as sometimes happens, the Beachcomber gets posted to another job or another colony when he has finished at the Colonial Office. Colonies may well feel that a man sent to the Colonial Office is a man lost, and consequently tend to send the people they are quite prepared to lose rather than those they want to keep.

I personally enjoyed my time at the Colonial Office immensely, and came away with great respect and admiration for the work of the office and for the people in it. This I think is the impression made on most Beachcombers. There is, however, a danger in excessive admiration of this kind. Administrative Officers should come to the Colonial Office not only keen to learn, but keen also to inject – if they can – something of what they regard as the hard realities and practical difficulties of colonial administration. Too often this zeal is quickly exhausted and the Beachcomber assimilated by the office until, after a time, he is almost indistinguishable from the genuine article. Instead of converting his chosen flock the missionary from the bush is converted by the heathen of the city. I think myself that Beachcombers should continuously resist this tendency and try to retain their distinctive status as long as they can. To succeed in this it should not be necessary to exude all the time the obvious aroma of the bush or the rugged atmosphere of I've-quelled-a-riot and remember-the-lion-I-shot-in '37, but better this than the furled umbrella and the black hat.

A word about the functions of the Colonial Office as they appeared to an outsider. They seem to fall roughly into two parts, which can be summarized as positive and negative functions. The positive functions of advice, of direction and of co-ordination are, I think, well enough understood and appreciated in the Service. But it was oddly enough the negative functions which seemed to me to be the more important of the two. I would define them firstly, as ensuring that nothing is done in the Colonial Empire which cannot, if necessary, be justified in an Answer to a Parliamentary Question; and secondly, as seeing that nothing is done which is contrary to the general policy of His Majesty's Government. The constitutional importance of collective Cabinet responsibility dictates the necessity for the latter, and the absence of reasoned and detached criticism in many colonies emphasises the need for the first. These two functions alone, to my mind, entirely justify the existence of the Colonial Office, and explain a large part of the otherwise inexplicable attitudes sometimes taken by the Colonial Office to what goes on or is proposed in the colonies. If every member of the Colonial Service had these negative functions of the Colonial Office clearly in mind, a host of misunderstandings, of irritations and of correspondence would, I am sure, disappear.

It is not, I think, generally known that not only are there Administrative Officers serving as Beachcombers in the Colonial Office, but that there are also members of the permanent Colonial Office staff serving in District Offices and Secretariats. As far as I know no corresponding term of abuse has yet been invented for them. Since 1939 this excellent practice has, owing no doubt to shortages of staff, tended to fall into abeyance, but it is, I believe, now being revived. Certainly there are many of the Colonial Office staff who are desperately keen to serve for two or three years in a colony.

When we were in the field we all get irritated with our Headquarters; and when we are at H.Q. we all get equally irritated with the field staffs. To serve at both ends is perhaps the only cure for this irritation, which is so often unreasonable on both sides and never does anybody any good at all.

A Beachcomber in the Colonial Office

by GERALD SAYERS

They called us 'beachcombers' – those of us seconded from the Colonial Service to work for a time in the Colonial Office. I was not the first of them; but certainly one of the first when, in 1924, I was lent to work in Whitehall for six months. In the end the period stretched to a year and a half.

I went in as the lowest form of animal life, an Assistant Principal, so it was with due humility that I presented myself at the Downing Street entrance of a Colonial Office which then dealt also with the self-governing nations of the Commonwealth.

My spiritual home was to be the Pacific Department which then included the Dominions of Australia and New Zealand and, at the other end of the scale, Tonga and the New Hebrides.

Climbing the vast circular stone staircase in the wake of a messenger I kicked my heels in the corridor until the Departmental Head, whom I will call Mr. Majani, was ready to see me.

In those days there was, believe it or not, no waiting room in the Office. Visitors shivered in draughty passages until the 'high-ups' were ready for them. Indeed, I recall once seeing a slim figure huddled up on a bench in the corridor awaiting an interview – no less a person than the famous Admiral Jellicoe, then Governor-General of New Zealand. The Office was, indeed, aloof and inhospitable in the inter-war years, and in the time I was lent to it I do not recall meeting a single soul from the territories I was dealing with.

My boss, Mr. Majani, was a relic of the Victorian era. About to retire, he had spent over forty years in the Office. With his white hair and walrus moustache, he looked like some benign ecclesiastic, so that it was no wonder that a short-sighted Secretary of State had once mistaken him for the Bishop of Melanesia. He had no hobbies, no friends. Downing Street was his home, his wife, his life: and he retreated to his burrow in Brondesbury or Belsize Park only to eat and sleep.

From him I went to THE ROOM, a vast apartment overlooking the Cenotaph which housed half a dozen of us, a cheerful lot of juniors about my own age. THE ROOM was commonly known as the 'bear garden', partly because there was always one or more of us talking or arguing and partly because, to overcome the tedium of dealing with dull despatches, we would indulge in a mild rag.

My Principal, away on leave when I arrived, came back in due course. He was a promoted clerk and he had an inferiority complex; but to emphasize his superiority over me left no draft of mine unaltered. But it was the same for all. My predecessor, a 'Double First' and an historian of some note, had had every draft of his cut to ribbons. So one day I laid a trap for our 'Mr. Smith'. A routine despatch went yearly to Fiji. Digging up a precedent I found one which had been drafted by him and I copied it word for word. Back it came, slashed out of recognition. I confronted Mr. Smith with the fact but, blushing furiously, he had the last word. 'It's just as well,' he said, 'to have a bit of a change now and again.'

The Head of the Office, the Permanent Under-Secretary, was brilliant and lethargic. I remember him chiefly for a collection he had made of newspaper posters with double meanings. There was, for example, the one issued during the war when the Ministry of Food, as an economy, had banned the making of fancy pastry. An evening paper's poster announced the news under the caption of 'No More Tarts'.

The Office kept odd hours. No one came in before half-past ten, and there was one senior Under-Secretary who was never at his desk much before mid-day. But if they came late they worked late too and they would look askance at me if I put my pen aside at 6 o'clock. Peculiarity over hours was not confined to the Colonial Office, for once when I rang a colleague in the Foreign Office at 11 o'clock one Saturday morning I was told 'Mr. X hasn't come yet.' And when I tried again at half past eleven the reply was 'Sorry, just gone.'

After I had been there a year the Government decided to separate the self-governing Dominions from the Colonies and so in July, 1925, the Dominions Office came into being. The staff remained much as it had been and for a year there was one Secretary of State for both Dominions and Colonies. Outwardly all that happened was that another nameplate went up on the door – so that one saw 'Dominions Office' on one side and 'Colonial Office' on the other. But the change meant that I was seconded to the former and lost my Pacific Colonies. I found myself attached to the foreign relations side where one was little more than a post office.

One of my last jobs was to read through the secret papers for a five year period and to advise which could be made public in fifty years time. That's the sort of job one enters on lightheartedly, for who can tell what will be of consequence and what will be trivial two generations ahead? And if one has erred, one will be in one's grave.

A less lighthearted task was when I had to compose a telegram of condolence from the British Government to the prospective widow of a man who was not yet dead. It happened that a Dominion Premier was ill with an incurable disease and had only a few weeks to live – a fact not known even to his wife or relatives. So the message was drafted in advance and lay in a locked box next to my out tray, waiting and waiting. It was as if the shadow of death hovered over my desk. In time the end came.

Just before I left to return to Africa, the Office had a new recruit, Cecil Syers, who later rose to high office as High Commissioner in Ceylon. It was as well that I left when I did, for with our similarity in names we began to get mixed up. To the office messengers and telephone operators there was no difference between Sayers and Syers and we often got each others' *billet doux*. The worst mix-up happened a few years later when I returned for a further spell of duty at a time when Cecil Syers was Private Secretary to the Secretary of State. About lunch-time one day my telephone rang and a voice asked for a name which might have been mine or his. 'Who do you want,' I said, 'Sayers or Syers ?' There was a snort of rage from the other end of the telephone. 'I don't know what he calls hisself but I want my b - - - y private secretary.' It was Jimmy Thomas, the then Secretary of State, to whom all aitches were superfluous and 'a's' and 'i's' were much the same.

The New Department

by PHILIP ROGERS, C.M.G.

I have been asked by the Editor to produce for the readers of *Corona* a short account of the new Department of Technical Co-operation which was set up on the 24th July. I am glad to do this because, as the head of the Division of the Colonial Office which is particularly responsible for the lives and careers of members of Her Majesty's Overseas Civil Service I have a very real, lively and constant interest in all who serve overseas.

The creation of the new Department was foreshadowed by the Colonial Secretary in a speech on the 19th December, 1960, and the decision of Her Majesty's Government to set it up was formally announced to Parliament by the Prime Minister on the 21st March this year. The necessary Bill received its Second Reading in the House of Commons on the 25th April and the Bill was given the Royal Assent on the 22nd June.

A word or two about the Act setting up the new Department seem called for. It is short and simple, merely providing that there shall be a Ministry entitled the Department of Technical Co-operation, which shall be under a Minister of the Crown called the Secretary for Technical Co-operation who 'may appoint such officers and servants as he may with the consent of the Treasury determine.' And the Department was established 'for the purpose of co-ordinating and promoting and carrying out arrangements for furnishing countries outside the United Kingdom with technical assistance, including in particular assistance in the fields of economic development, administration and social services.'

I have purposely quoted that part of the Act which deals with the appointment of 'officers and servants' because it may occur to some of you – particularly those of you who are having to face all the problems of finding new jobs after premature retirement – that there may be openings in the new Department. There may be – but I am sorry to record that within the Department itself there will be only a very few, and only temporary jobs at that, probably at levels which would not appeal to officers used to the varied responsibilities of running their own districts, or to responsible departmental officers. This is the only frank and honest answer that I can give, but I would like to explain why this is so.

This new Department is going to be a Department of the Home Civil Service. But though the Department is new, the work it does is not. As members of the Overseas Service know – better than most people – this country is responsible already for an impressive amount of technical assistance to the under-developed territories overseas. At the moment, this work is done mainly under the aegis of the three great Overseas Departments – the Foreign Office, the Commonwealth Relations Office and the Colonial Office – according to the part of the world in which the assistance is given. But the fact that three departments are mainly involved leads to a certain amount of duplication of effort, which ought to be removed in the interests of efficiency. For example, the Foreign Office may be recruiting an engineer for the Middle East whom the Colonial Office is attempting to recruit for East Africa. Therefore it is planned to bring together in one Department the existing work which is at present done in several – and of course the staff which is already doing that work will move over to the new Department, integrate with each other, and continue to do their work – it is hoped with greater efficiency, and with all the benefits that come from pooled experience and shared expertise. The effect of all this will be, as I said above, that there will be very few new jobs to be filled from outside the existing cadres of the Home Civil Service at present doing the work. Indeed, it may not be realised how few senior posts there will be in the Department altogether. The administrative posts, from the Director-General down to the most junior, will only number 52, and the advisory posts 27. It will be of interest to readers of *Corona* to know that of these the great majority of the advisory posts, and 20 of the administrative posts, are already held by former members of the Overseas Service (including one from the Sudan). But I can repeat what has already been announced to Parliament – that where new jobs are created, the claims to them of suitably qualified ex-members of the Overseas Service will be fully taken into account. Moreover – and this is the most important aspect – we all hope and believe that the new Department will increase the opportunities of members of the Overseas Service in other fields of work overseas. And it may be of interest to readers that the Overseas Services Resettlement Bureau will be taken under the wing of the new Department.

I come now to the functions of the new Department. As I have attempted to show above, its general purpose is the co-ordination of technical assistance work which it is to take over from the three existing Overseas Departments. But the new Department will, of course, work within the broad lines of overseas policy as determined by the Foreign Secretary, the Commonwealth Secretary and the Colonial Secretary. In defining the scope of this work, technical assistance is given a wide interpretation to include the provision of experts in engineering, agriculture, administration (to name only three types of assistance). It will also provide certain facilities for education and training in the United Kingdom and elsewhere, equipment for schools and colleges and teaching hospitals and so on.

Another part of the responsibilities of the new Department will be concerned with the technical assistance provided with the help of the United Kingdom through the United Nations, in particular the United Nations Expanded Programme of Technical Assistance and Special Fund. It will deal with technical assistance under the Colombo Plan and the newly formed Special Commonwealth African Assistance Plan. It will be responsible on behalf of the United Kingdom for technical assistance matters discussed in the Development Assistance Group, and for any such discussions held in the new Organisation for Economic Co-operation and

Development. It will also provide technical assistance to a number of Middle East countries under the Central Treaty Organisation arrangements and through the Middle East Development Division. Indeed, the increased importance of international co-ordination is one of the strongest reasons which have led to the creation of the new Department.

The Headquarters of the new Department are in Carlton House Terrace. The Secretary (Minister of State) is Mr. Dennis Vosper and the permanent Head (Director-General) is Sir Andrew Cohen who, as a one-time Governor of Uganda, has close links with the Overseas Service. It is particularly happy that this is so, because one of the largest and most important duties of the new Department will be to administer the scheme set out in the White Paper presented to Parliament last October for the continued employment of overseas officers. Although members of H.M.O.C.S. may find themselves serving in independent territories they will continue none the less to be members of that Service and, as is generally accepted, one of the most valuable forms of technical assistance known is the provision of experienced administrators – 'professors' of the arts of government and administration. And the scheme is designed to assist those Governments who wish to take advantage of it to retain the services of overseas officials until local public services can be firmly established with well-trained and experienced officers. The estimated cost of the scheme is likely to be some £12,500,000 a year, excluding compensation payments – over one-third of the provisional budget of the new Department.

I should like to make two points arising from this last paragraph. The first is that, as has already been announced in Parliament, the new Department will not be responsible for the transfer, promotion and discipline of the Overseas Service in dependent territories – that responsibility will remain with the Secretary of State for the Colonies. And the second is that members of the Service should know that their personal affairs will continue to be dealt with by the same people whom they have got to know over the years, who will be continuing to apply the policy of the Secretary of State for the Colonies, including of course all the agreements designed to protect the interests of the Service. And, if I may say so, it is a great satisfaction to me personally and, I am sure, to the other members of my Division, that we shall continue to be associated with members of a Service whose work we all admire so much.

One last point. It is the hope of all concerned that the new Department will be able to assist in continuing all over the world the sort of work which H.M.O.C.S. has done so long, without the stigma which has come to be attached to 'Colonialism'. Members of H.M.O.C.S. will recognise that people recruited by the new Department will be coming out to do the same sort of things that the Service has done and is doing – and will no doubt be able to give them a hand accordingly.

Other Times, Other Needs

SIR ANDREW COHEN, K.C.M.G., K.C.V.O., O.B.E.

R eaders of *Corona* will remember that the origins of the new
Department of Technical Co-operation were described in the
September, 1961, issue. We have been in existence, as a separate
Department of Government, for a year and a bit; and it has been suggested
to me that some kind of personal progress report on what we are doing may
be of interest. Those *Corona* readers who are also avid consumers of White
Papers and Blue Books will already have taken in our two Command papers
and will know a good deal of our plans and policies; the present article is
necessarily a much briefer summary, but it may perhaps be particularly
appropriate at this time. The news that the journal of the Overseas Service is
about to cease publication will have caused much regret, for it marks the
end of an epoch for members of the Overseas Service and the former
Colonial Service. I welcome the chance to show how we are trying, under
changed conditions, to help those countries in which the Services have
worked so hard and so successfully.

One year is a short time in the life of a Government Department, and
we have naturally needed some time to get our bearings, to settle the broad
lines of our policies and our priorities, and to adjust our staff and our
organisation so that these policies can be carried through effectively. We
were called into existence to meet changing conditions in our relations with
the new countries overseas, and we have to adapt and adjust our aims and
methods to meet the different requirements of these new countries to which
we hope to give technical aid. The requirements are different – let there be
no mistake about that – and in general they are the requirements decided
upon by the recipient countries themselves. We have no wish, even if we
were able, to impose upon them forms of assistance different from what they
want or are willing to have. By consultation with the new Governments and
in agreement with them we have to work out the fields in which British
technical assistance can best be provided and most profitably used.

This shift of emphasis is nowhere more clearly seen than in the work of
our Recruitment Division. No longer is a substantial part of overseas
recruitment made up of straightforward administrators, policemen, customs
officers and the like – those who formerly were selected for career
appointments in the actual cadres of the overseas Governments and who
carried out the Secretary of State's responsibility for ensuring good
government, law and order, and the protection of the local revenues. Some
appointments of this kind are still made, because there are still a few
territories where independence is still some way off, but they are few in
number. It is natural and right that the newly independent countries should

28

wish to man their own cadre services as soon as they are able to do so – indeed, one of our principal aims is to help them to achieve this by the training we can help provide, here or in their home countries, for their public services. The major part of our recruitment now is of men and women with professional and technical skills – teachers for secondary schools, colleges and universities; doctors and nurses, engineers of every kind; agricultural experts and advisers; economic planners; industrial managers. They are, in the main, people who have established themselves in their own professions at home, but who respond to the challenge and opportunity of applying their skills for a few years in the service of the new countries, and who see in this a chance both to give something of value to the peoples of these new nations and to extend and enrich their own experience.

But we are also most anxious to secure the services of young people, as we have indeed done in the recent recruitment of teachers for East Africa under the so-called Makerere Scheme – a joint Anglo-American venture. And we are planning with the Voluntary Societies to get many young graduates sent abroad next year – to match Voluntary Service Overseas' excellent School-leavers Scheme.

Recruitment is the mirror of policy; the means to the end. The change in the pattern of recruitment reflects the change of circumstances and the consequent re-alignment of policies. We had to consider very carefully, when we were brought into being, what fields were most appropriate for British technical assistance; what would be welcome, what we could supply. Our first conclusions were set out in the first White Paper on the Department's work (Cmnd. 1698), and since not all the readers of this journal will have seen that document. I cannot do better than to quote the summary in the introduction to it. The relevant paragraph reads:

The Department is giving special attention to twelve main heads of activity in which Britain is well placed to provide technical assistance. These do not cover everything we are doing or hope to do. Other types of assistance will be asked for and where possible provided; for it is the overseas countries themselves who must say what help they most need. But the twelve heads show broadly what kinds of technical assistance the nation's efforts should be most closely geared to supply. The twelve main heads are:

(i)   Training of public servants;
(ii)   The supply of university and secondary school teachers and staff for teacher training colleges;
(iii) Technical education and training;
(iv)   Staff and training for economic and financial planning;
(v)   Geodetic and topographical surveys, geological surveys and help developing mineral resources;
(vi)   The supply of staff, advice and training to develop agricultural and other natural resources;

(vii)   Advice, staff and training for industrial development;
(viii) Engineering surveys and assistance in telecommunications;
(ix)   The development of scientific research;
(x)   The supply of qualified medical and nursing staff and medical and
        nursing training;
(xi)   Individual service overseas through voluntary societies;
(xii)   Management training.

These twelve main heads are in no order of particular priority, nor do they cover everything we can hope to do. But it is clear enough that two constant threads run through the pattern – training and the provision of staff. It is clear, too, that many of these objectives cannot be attained simply by direct Government action alone. The Government's direct activity is itself divided into many separate but related channels; there is direct Government-to-Government negotiation, direct sponsorship and subsidy of particular projects and particular posts and the finding of people to man them, and co-ordinated action with the United Nations and specialised agencies and their various regional programmes. But there is also the need to promote help and co-ordinate the efforts of institutions, individuals and firms outside the Government. All these – universities, technical colleges, schools, voluntary societies, industrial firms, learned and professional bodies and local authorities – all play their part in the sum of British technical assistance. Our job is to co-ordinate, to promote, and to carry out; to make sure that those who can give much needed assistance overseas are enabled to do so.

For this purpose, we have to build up a store of expertise, experience, and personal contacts. We have to know the new alphabet of the United Nations and its subsidiary bodies and the ever-growing alphabet of technical education. Inevitably this leads to committees, and we have established several. We have been very fortunate in securing the services of many distinguished and busy men to serve on these. One is considering the provision of training in public administration; another, the whole range of technical and commercial training and training in industry; a third, the provision of personnel, advice and training in the natural resources field; a fourth, technical aid in geology and mining. We have taken part in a Working Party set up by the medical profession to advise on assistance in the field of medicine and health; and, most recently, in a new body set up by the Voluntary Societies to help co-ordinate the effort made by the many organisations working in the field of voluntary overseas service. And in addition to these committees, and our own powerful advisory team, we are represented on many other specialist bodies concerned with the many fields in which we have to work, and we work in co-operation with them.

There is of course another side to the picture. All the developments which have led to the creation of the Department of Technical Co-operation and given stimulus to the activities with which we are concerned, have led also to displacement and redundancy of many members of Her Majesty's Overseas Service. Nobody with a feeling of responsibility or any recognition of what has been done in the past by these men and women, can regard this result without profound regret and a sense of waste. Through the Overseas Service Aid Schemes and other measures associated with it, we are doing what we can to cushion the blow and eliminate hardship and suffering for individuals, and through the Resettlement Bureau we try to help those who have retired to find satisfying second careers. Resettlement is a great and growing problem; the Bureau have achieved a notable degree of success in their work, even although much still remains to do.

II. COLONIAL POLICY IN THE DECOLONIZING DECADE

a) STATEMENTS AND INITIATIVES

One of the declared purposes of *Corona* was to help members of the Colonial Service, faced with a growingly intolerant and even hostile public opinion abroad (especially in the USA and at the UN) towards colonial rule, to become aware of international issues and statements on colonial policy, in particular in territories other than their own. The time had come to end what the C.O. felt to be an earlier mood of Colonial Service parochialism and to encourage officers to understand what was going on elsewhere. Reading *Hansard*, White Papers or Blue Books was rarely an easy option for the colonial civil servant overseas, but a résumé carried by *Corona* could prove an invaluable conduit for keeping members of the Colonial Service up-to-date with policy issues and constitutional conferences. As an extension of this current information role, from time to time the editor commissioned or reproduced special articles on some wider aspect of colonial policy or its field application, for instance Trust Territories, local government, colonial development, the colonial cinema and broadcasting, etc. Special attention was paid to reports on constitutional change in different parts of the Colonial Empire, and Colonial Service readers were helped to keep abreast with what was going on, politically and economically, in other colonial territories by the editor's careful compilation of a 'Monthly Chronicle'.

The catalyst that converted the watchword of colonial policy from 'trusteeship' and 'partnership' to post-war 'development' was the passing of the major Colonial Development and Welfare (CDW) Acts in 1940 and 1945. Three years later saw the establishment of the Colonial Development Corporation (CDC), with a private sector remit to foster economic development in the colonies. By the mid-1950s, the key concepts of colonial policy began to revolve round the imperative of the transfer of power.

Stocktaking

The White Paper issued shortly before the Colonial Development and Welfare Bill was debated in Parliament, gives a background to the present legislation by tracing the history of the Acts since 1929. At a time when the development of under-developed countries is recognised as part of international policy, a backward glance at the beginnings of this type of aid from Great Britain to the eighty million people of her own dependent territories will be of interest, but it is right to set the Colonial Development and Welfare Acts in their proper setting. As Mr. Lennox-Boyd said in a foreword to the White Paper, there are four points to consider: firstly, Britain offers security at her own cost by being ready at all times to the extent of her military capacity to defend the Colonial territories against external aggression or internal subversion; secondly, Britain gives grant aid to Colonial administrations whose revenues are insufficient for essential undertakings; thirdly, Britain is the main source of public loans and private capital in the Colonies; and fourthly, Britain provides much of the technical knowledge, skill and training necessary to frame and carry out development projects.

It is against this background that the growth of Colonial Development and Welfare provision should be considered. The White Paper makes it plain that growth has not been confined to sums available but has been extended to the types of development eligible ... the Acts lay down that the Secretary of State may, with the concurrence of the Treasury, make schemes 'for any purpose likely to promote the development of the resources of any Colony or the welfare of its people.'

The first step to provide regular funds for the development of the Colonial territories over a period of years was taken with the Colonial Development Act, 1929. This set up a Fund of £1 million a year with the dual purpose of relieving the economic depression in the United Kingdom and stimulating agricultural and industrial activity in the Colonial territories. Expenditure during the eleven years up to 1940 totalled £8·8 million. But though the Act made a valuable start, it had drawbacks. The funds were inadequate. The emphasis was on capital works of an economic nature and there was difficulty in making grants for recurrent charges; and important fields of social development, notably education, were excluded from its terms.

A new Act was therefore passed in 1940. In introducing it to Parliament at the height of the German victories in France, the Secretary of State said, 'It is characteristic that, whilst every ounce of our energy is being thrown into the battle, this House nevertheless finds time to plan and to offer generous encouragement to Colonial development.'

This Act superseded that of 1929. It provided £5 million a year, plus £500,000 a year for research, for the ten-year period 1941–51, and at the same time cancelled loans owing to Her Majesty's Government to the amount of £10 million. The expenditure was no longer linked directly with the economic interests of the United Kingdom, and the Act enlarged the scope of assistance to include 'any purpose likely to promote the development of the resources of any Colony and the welfare of its peoples,' thus covering all the social services and enabling help to be given towards meeting recurrent charges. The separate provision of £500,000 a year for research was an innovation. Some research grants had been made under the 1929 Act, but the fact that funds were now assured for the future made it possible to undertake research on a much greater scale and for a longer term.

On the administrative side the Act laid down the procedures for the control and disbursement of funds which are still in operation. It extended the 'fair conditions of labour' clause in the 1929 Act and made it a condition of assistance to any territory that the local law should provide reasonable facilities for the establishment and the activities of trade unions.

One of the objects of the Act was to provide money to carry out the recommendations of the West Indian Royal Commission (Cmd. 6174) and much of the expenditure was devoted to West Indian projects. War-time difficulties inevitably prevented the Act from having its full effect. Nonetheless, much was done. By 1946 schemes totalling £30 million had been approved, of which £10·4 million had been spent – £5·3 million in the West Indies.

Colonial Governments had meanwhile been encouraged to examine their long-term requirements as a basis for post-war planning. The information thus obtained showed that a provision of £5 million a year would not suffice if assistance from Her Majesty's Government was to meet the needs foreseen. Also experience had shown a defect in the working of the Act. Under its terms any money unspent at the end of one year lapsed and could not be carried forward. This had meant the loss of much of the benefit of the Act in the war years, and, as expenditure rose, was leading to serious problems in planning ahead. It was extremely difficult to fit long-term projects into a tight annual budget, and the temptation was to plan hurriedly from year to year.

By the end of the war it was seen that more money and a new approach to planning were required. The 1945 Act met both needs. It provided a total sum of £120 million for the ten years 1946–56, including £20 million carried forward in commitments under the 1940 Act. It also overcame the planning difficulties by allowing the money to be drawn upon at any time within the period subject only to a ceiling – set high enough for all practical purposes – of £17·5 million a year. Of this an amount of up to £1 million a year could be devoted to research and expenditure on research schemes was permitted to run beyond the statutory time limit of the 31st March, 1956. But its most important advantage was that it enabled the Secretary of State to make to Colonial Governments firm allocations of money in advance which could form the nucleus of their development finance. This gave a great impetus to the planning of development, even in the territories where C.D. and W. funds were to be only a small part of the total finance available.

After allowance had been made in the new provision for the needs of research and other central services, £24 million, and a general reserve, £11 million, the balance, £85 million, was allocated to the various territories on the basis of need. The research and central allocations were established to cover subjects which from their nature required central handling and direction or to which the Secretary of State wished special attention to be paid. Allocations were also made to the East Africa High Commission and to the Comptroller of the Development and Welfare Organisation in the West Indies for regional needs.

The purpose underlying the Act was described as follows in a circular despatch dated the 12th November, 1945, from the Secretary of State to Colonial Governments (Cmd. 6713):

'This increase in the total sum to be provided and the lengthening of the period of such assistance by a further five years mark an important turning point in the development of Colonial productive resources and the improvement of human well-being. It comes at a time when a gradual easing of the war-time shortages of materials, equipment and skilled technical and scientific personnel may be hoped for. There are great possibilities in the years that lie ahead for raising the standards of health, education, social welfare, and general well-being of Colonial peoples if these expanded services are based upon improved economic efficiency and increased production. The primary requisite still is an improvement of the economic position in the Colonial dependencies, the utilisation of their natural resources to the greatest extent possible, and the widening of opportunity for human enterprise and endeavour. As a contribution towards improvements in Colonial development and welfare the present Act provides a substantial sum of money, but it is not intended that this sum should be taken as indicating the total Colonial need for development expenditure in the next ten years. The total cost of development that can be embarked upon may be expected to be considerably greater than £120 million according to the extent to which Colonial Governments can supplement the contemplated grants whether from public funds or with the assistance of private trade and enterprise. The new Act will, I am confident, enable Colonial Governments to draw up plans of development over the ten-year period, and to achieve steady and sustained progress towards the great goal of raising the standards of living and well-being of their people.'

Colonial Governments were asked to submit their programmes to the Secretary of State for approval, showing the development proposed by broad categories with priorities and the sources of finance. These included the C.D. and W. allocations, surplus balances and the estimated contributions from future revenues and loans. Governments were expected to make the maximum use of their own resources, increasing taxation where appropriate. They were encouraged to set their sights high, even though finance for the full programme could not be foreseen at the outset. It was recognised that the standards of the social services had to be raised; that social and economic development were inseparable; and that the improvement of health and education was a necessary concomitant to economic advance. But Governments realised that priority would have to be given to projects which would strengthen their economies and enable them to bear the increased charges arising from the expansion of the social services. The responsibility for drawing up the programme and for deciding priorities lay with the Colonial territories, and to arouse the interest of the local people and to associate them directly with the work, Development Committees were set up which included representative unofficial members.

The programmes did not mean a wholly fresh start. They stemmed from the work already done or in progress. Although large capital projects formed an important part of the plans, much of the work, to quote the Governor of Uganda in 1949, consisted of an 'intensification of a great number of activities in a great number of directions. Development can, perhaps, best be described as planned evolution. It involves a speeding-up of normal processes; the doing at once and the doing quicker of some work which would otherwise have been done later or more slowly. Those who complain that they see little development in progress do not always grasp the fact that every time they see a new house being built, a new officer appointed, a new bore-hole being sunk, more trees planted, or a surveyor surveying the course of a new road, they are watching development in progress and the execution of a work chargeable to the development programme. If all these individual efforts are added together, a good deal is being accomplished. It may not be spectacular – it is not intended to be – but it represents solid progress.'

Statement of Colonial Policy (1951)

The following declaration of policy was made by the Secretary of State in the House of Commons on the 14th November:

'Certain broad lines of policy are accepted by all sections of the House as being above party politics. These have been clearly stated by my predecessors from both the main parties.

'Two of them are fundamental. First, we all aim at helping the Colonial territories to attain self-government within the British Commonwealth. To that end we are seeking as rapidly as possible to build up in each territory the institutions which its circumstances require. Second, we are all determined to pursue the economic and social development of the Colonial territories so that it keeps pace with their political development.

'I should like to make it plain at the outset that His Majesty's Government intend no change in these aims. We desire to see successful constitutional development both in those territories which are less advanced towards self-government and in those with more advanced constitutions. His Majesty's Government will do their utmost to help Colonial Governments and Legislatures to foster the health, wealth and happiness of the Colonial peoples.

'I hope that, however much there may from time to time be disagreement between us on details, all parties will be with me in agreeing on those ends.'

Mr. James Griffiths said that the Opposition would fully support this policy and he asked Mr. Lyttelton to make it clear that in multi-racial communities the first fundamental he had mentioned must include participation of all the people in the territories, irrespective of race, creed, or colour. The Secretary of State replied, 'I think I can, in general terms, accept that.'

The Colonies and
the United Kingdom Budget

1953/54 ESTIMATES OF FINANCIAL AID TO THE DEPENDENCIES

(The net totals are reached by the deduction of appropriations in aid which are not shown.)

COLONIAL SERVICES

Grants in Aid of Local Revenues £

St. Helena	41,500
British Solomon Islands Protectorate	135,000
Somaliland Protectorate	650,000
British Honduras	43,750
Antigua	151,000
Montserrat	65,000
Virgin Islands	42,000
Dominica	113,500
St. Lucia	189,000
St. Vincent	89,000
Cyprus	92,000
Malta	747,000
Falkland Islands Dependencies	116,010
Nyasaland	15,050
Aden (loan)	1,000,000
Hong Kong (loan)	125,000
Malaya	2,391,666
North Borneo	300,000

Far Eastern Territories:

War damage compensation schemes (grants)	6,000,000
,, ,, ,, ,, (loans)	4,000,000
Jamaica (grant)	857,000
,, (loan)	453,000
St. Kitts-Nevis (grant)	20,000
U.S. Bases in Bermuda and the West Indies	6,000

Grants for Special Services

Christmas, Hull and Canton Islands	6,500
Tonga: Services at Suva	3,000
New Hebrides: Services at Honiara	4,000
Cyprus: maintenance of distressed British subjects of Maltese origin	12,400

Contributions to Various Organisations

Bureau of Hygiene and Tropical Diseases	3,000
Imperial College of Tropical Agriculture, Trinidad	35,000
International African Institute	1,500
National Institute of Oceanography	10,000
Caribbean Commission	42,650
South Pacific Commission	25,000
Hong Kong University	300
Commission for Technical Co-operation in Africa South of the Sahara	2,400

Internal Security Measures

African Territories	3,508,600
West Indian Colonies	250,000

African Development

SOME HARD FACTS

by RONALD MILLER

Now to examine ourselves in relation to the task we have set ourselves in Africa and, if possible, to strip away the sophistications which, though comforting to us, are assuredly no concealment of weaknesses or foibles to the eyes of that great majority of Africans who are so near to nature.

Here we are in our islands, blessed with as good a position, climate and natural resources as any comparable area in the world. We started from just as primitive beginnings as the African, but with the help of a vastly superior climate (which we generally deride, possibly in order to take all the credit upon ourselves) developed our primary industries, agriculture and fishing until they yielded a surplus that permitted security and time for thought for at least a section of the population. A proportion of our labour force, too, was liberated from the simple task of winning a subsistence from the soil and was free to go – or forced by necessity – into trading ventures, leading ultimately to our penetrating every part of the globe. As the technique of manufacture developed, the labour force was there to operate the machines and in brief, we became, last century, the wealthiest country, at least in the material sense, in the world. Then came a new development. Those who had amassed fortunes during the Industrial Revolution saw that in spite of financial credits they lacked something that the older wealthy class, the landowning and therefore hereditarily wealthy class, possessed. Call it culture, polish, social prestige, what you will. As a result, the types who developed Britain at the Industrial Revolution did not use their experience and wealth to set their sons off on similar lines overseas, where alone fresh fields were to be found. They sent them to the schools and universities that had formerly been the preserves of the landowning class and the great boom in English public schools, so characteristic of the latter half of the last century, followed. At these schools, of course, the traditional studies, the humanities, were followed and there was great emphasis on the creation of a hall-mark, with its insistence on 'good form' and the cultivation of what were regarded as typical English virtues. At their best these, of course, produced very fine types, probably second to none, and at their worst the absurd conformity to a rule which could prescribe a dinner-jacket for a lonely meal in an African bush rest-house and question whether the Prince of Wales really did speak the King's English.

However, the main point is that men of great competence, with just that thrust and enterprise (plus capital) that might have developed colonial territories as effectively as they did the United Kingdom, bred not their like but liberally educated gentlemen who, if they did work, entered the Church, or medicine, or law, or public service but rarely became engineers or foresters or agriculturists. Without attempting to assess the position as a whole, there can be little doubt that it was not the best for colonial development. While it was the missionaries and traders who opened up Africa, the men set in authority over them were, as a rule, products of this liberal, classical education. Can it be wondered at, then, that their preoccupation was not with practical matters like soil erosion or clean drinking water, but with the perfection of the political and legal system? After all, government at home at the time was regarded as being responsible only for law and order. It set the stage and held the ring while our grandfathers struggled for existence on their own resources. A very brief examination of the history of the colonies up to recent years shows that, apart from establishing the *pax Britannica*, we did little else in the colonies. While the *pax Britannica* is no doubt a good thing on the whole, it has its disadvantages when enjoyed neat. It can, for example, as pointed out by Bertrand Russell recently, be extremely boring.

The application of strict British standards of law, too, has not always been an unmixed blessing. Our law has evolved in the British environment and does not transplant without loss to the African soil. Petty crime, particularly theft, has reached alarming proportions and most Africans will insist that the penalty meted out is no punishment. Formerly mutilation and/or beating was the penalty: now a man goes to prison. Whatever our views on the function of a prison in the United Kingdom, we are all at least agreed that it is better not to be in one, and many of us would find incarceration a crushing blow to our self-respect. It is not generally so in Africa. The element of disgrace is normally completely absent and, on the contrary, it is often felt to be a distinction to wear the uniform.

Again, the interminable procedure of our law, adjusted to a culture far more complex than that it is made to serve in Africa; the presence of lawyers and possibilities of appeal all lead to endless wrangles and divert capable Africans into the law at the expense of productive work.

This whole question of emphasis is illustrated by the precedence officially accorded to Departments. In the case of Nigeria at least, this was Administration, Law, Finance, Medical, Education, Marine, Customs, Railway, Public Works, Agriculture. These Departments had seats on the Legislative Council. Agriculture, on which the fortunes of the country overwhelmingly depended, was the least of those present. Forestry, Geology, Veterinary and the rest were not represented on Legislative Council. They were, in fact, 'outsiders,' or came in only by the back door – the 'tradesman's entrance.' And this in a continent where, above all, the help of scientists is required.

In our favour much is to be said that need not be catalogued here. At the same time it would be as well to remember that the proper person to make such a catalogue would be an African, who might not only gratify but surprise us. Once, in Nigeria, the writer, having more or less gained the confidence of a Village Head who had been brought up under German rule in the Cameroons, asked him (before he had heard of Hitler) whether he preferred British or German rule. The answer came frankly but with no great enthusiasm, 'The British.' 'Why?' he was asked, and the reply, given after appreciable thought, was, 'Because the Germans oppressed us all day long with their education and their improvements, whereas you English go to bed in the afternoons and leave us alone.'

But, perhaps, this has become ancient history: science and technology have, as a result of the war and the subsequent social revolution, gained ground at the expense of the classical studies. It is, however, too soon yet to assess the position in this respect.

Turning to capital, we find again that an overburden of prejudice has to be cleared away and the fundamental fact brought to light, that capital goods in Africa are grossly inadequate. Little development is possible without capital for railways, roads, harbours, power stations and the like and, of course, if wealth is to be exchanged for commerce, mining and manufactures. Before the European contribution began, Africa had pitifully little in the way of capital goods productive of wealth – a few hoes and axes, but practically nothing in the way of bridges, boats and other transport necessities. We therefore had to start practically from scratch in this respect and we may, therefore, perhaps, be excused to some extent for the poor progress we had made until recently. Not only has Rhodes' dream of a Cape-to-Cairo railway not yet materialised, but there is not yet even an all-weather road over the British part of the route. Many other glaring omissions could be cited – the great harbour of Freetown, of vital strategic importance, is only now acquiring a deep-water quay – but our purpose here is rather to seek the underlying factors.

Colonial Economic Development

ITS PURPOSES AND SOME AS ITS PROBLEMS

The two chief criticisms which are being made of Britain's policy are, first that the planning is not matched by achievement and, second, that Britain is, in fact, exploiting the Colonies. How far are these justified?

We can be frank. There is not much doubt that at the moment achievement is falling well behind the programme. The rate of expenditure from Colonial Development and Welfare funds on approved schemes is nothing like the annual average of £12 million or the maximum permitted in any one year of £17 million. At the moment it is only between £5 million and £6 million.

Even allowing for the amounts colonies are spending from their own revenues and surpluses, it is still true that things are not yet going ahead in the way hoped for. This fact is, of course, reflected in reports that education, health, road building and works programmes generally are well behind the plans. Nor, of course, in view of the short time that the Colonial Development Corporation has been established are many concrete results of its work yet to be seen. Even the East African Groundnut scheme, though it has made progress, is not yet bearing its full fruits. The reason for this state of affairs is not far to seek. Allocations of funds are not the same as allocations of materials and men to carry them out. As a result of the Colonial Development and Welfare Acts and the Overseas Resources Act, Britain has, we think, gone a long way towards solving the problem of financing colonial development, but this does not of itself, produce the *physical means* of development.

At the time the plans were drawn up – in many cases 1945 and 1946 – it was still thought that the main problem, failure to solve which had held back development before the war, was finance. It was expected that physical supplies would, as normal peacetime conditions were restored, become easier and that finance would once again, as between the wars, become the governing factor. But this is not how things worked out. Firstly, the fuel crisis of February, 1947, and the priority directives issued to British industries thereafter and then the repercussions of the balance of payments crisis of August, 1947, and the bilateral agreements with other countries into which that crisis drove the United Kingdom – all these things pressed heavily upon the margin of physical resources available from the United Kingdom for the colonies. The result was that in many cases schemes which were due to have started were held up for lack of the necessary materials such as steel and cement.

Strenuous efforts are, however, being made to remedy this situation. As soon as the effects of the events described in the preceding paragraph began to show, special arrangements were made to ensure that colonial needs should be fully taken into account and that, in future, supplies should come nearer to requirements. These efforts have met and are meeting with not inconsiderable success. To quote but one example, steel: the present programmed supply is more than double the level of six months ago. The result of these efforts will, of course, not always be immediately apparent owing to time lags, but they do give rise to hope that the main material bottlenecks can be broken and a real spurt in actual development made.

Another shortage is that of technicians, and this is a more difficult problem for they are not something which can be 'allocated.' Nevertheless there should be some improvement as those who began their training after the end of the war begin to be available. As to the second class of criticism, that the plans so far as the Colonial Development Corporation is concerned, involve exploitation, it is a fact that the Corporation is by statute required to pay its way, taking one year with another. This means that it is bound, over all its transactions, to earn enough to pay gilt-edged rates of interest on its capital. This in turn means that, as not all its operations can be winners, some may have to earn rather more.

The answer to such criticism of the principles on which the Corporation is to work is that it would not really be of benefit to the colonies if the Corporation were a sort of charitable organisation. What the colonies want in the field of productive enterprise is not subsidies for uneconomic industries but finance for undertakings which, if suitable to the conditions of the various territories, have a reasonable chance of being economic, at any rate in the long run. Moreover, there is this very important difference between the Corporation and a private undertaking – namely that any profit over and above the interest which the Corporation has to pay on its advances from the Treasury, has, under the statute, to be disposed of in accordance with the instructions of the Secretary of State. This means that it can reasonably be assumed that such profits would be 'ploughed back,' in one way or another, into the business of Colonial development. Taking into account also the fact that the Corporation cannot operate in any Colonial territory except with the consent of the Government of that territory, the answer to the critics on this score is complete.

The answer to the charge that the development of the Colonies, as new sources of particular foods or raw materials, is exploitation is that the benefit is mutual. No territory, whether sovereign or dependent, can develop in isolation. Countries of the southern and western hemispheres, which have developed in the past century or two, owe their progress to their ability to supply the world with what it needed. The colonies now, through the worsening of the world situation, have their opportunity to contribute in the same way. If the contribution is made on fair terms and with careful safeguarding of the interests of the local peoples, there can be no justifiable talk of exploitation. The careful way in which the chosen instruments of economic development on the economic side have been constructed shows Britain's firm intention to rebut any charge of this nature.

This, then, is an outline of the nature of the policy now being followed and of some of the difficulties with which it is faced. If the policy is successful the benefit to millions of individuals both in the colonies and in Britain and elsewhere will be immense. Yet it is essential that the policy should be understood and believed in by all the millions of individuals concerned and one of our most difficult and important tasks is to convince those who question Britain's sincerity.

In Tanganyika, the immediate benefits of regular employment, good wages, training in skilled work, schools and dispensaries will presumably soon be obvious to every African helping groundnut development. It is, however, of the greatest importance as a matter of principle, rather than expediency, that from the start, wherever practical and in all cases as soon as possible, opportunities should be made available to the local people to have a *direct* interest in as many of the new economic projects as possible.

How this can be achieved is a matter for each Colonial Government to consider in the light of its particular circumstances. In some colonies, though not many, the people may be prepared to invest in a local loan or a government-sponsored industry. The co-operative method of agricultural production can perhaps be expanded and the system might be extended to industrial undertakings. More capital might be made available to local business men or manufacturing concerns of known enterprise and integrity to extend their activities or to build and operate new secondary industries. Native Authorities can be helped to develop bus services, markets and their own local industries. The importance of this particular aspect of the development policy will not be underestimated. There must be many other ways in which the people can be given a stake in development from the start and an exchange of ideas on this might be of considerable value.

Economic Co-ordination in East Africa

The Commission headed by Sir Jeremy Raisman, Deputy Chairman of Lloyds Bank, recommended in its report that the Common Market between Kenya, Uganda and Tanganyika should continue but that owing to inequalities in benefits derived from the participating territories (which was one of the sources of discontent with the working of the Common Market) there should be a redistribution of revenue between them. An attempt should be made to negotiate a code of agreed general principles of inter-territorial trade and marketing policy in order that the policies of the territories might be brought into greater harmony and the interest of East Africa as a whole asserted. The Commission indicated that in general it had been difficult to develop an East African view of the interests of the region as a whole and that centrifugal tendencies had been becoming more apparent. It recommended that inter-territorial co-ordination of policy in matters of trade and price, preferably within the framework of a general agreement on principles, should be sought by regular meetings of the relevant Ministers; and that these meetings should be assisted by an Economic Adviser and Secretariat free of territorial affiliations, and that the scope and staffing of the Department of Economic Co-ordination in the East Africa High Commission should be expanded for this purpose.

The report advocated the provision for the East Africa High Commission of an independent service of revenue for the financing of the non-self-contained services (i.e. those which, like the research services, depended for their financing upon funds provided by Governments). Such a service could remove the disadvantages of the cumbersome and inflexible system whereby funds were voted annually by each territorial Legislature – a system which might subordinate finance for High Commission services to individual territorial requirements with inadequate regard to the best interests of East Africa.

The provision of an independent source of revenue to cover the non-self-contained services, as well as the redistribution of revenue recommended to offset inequalities of benefit from the Common Market, could be achieved by the creation of a distributable pool of revenue, drawn from a portion of the yield from the income tax charged to companies on profits arising from manufacturing and finance, and a portion of the yield from customs and excise duties. The pool would be administered by the East Africa High Commission and would have credited to it 40 per cent of the income tax charged to companies on profits arising from manufacturing and finance, and six per cent of the annual revenue collected by means of customs and excise duties. The actual sums to be paid into the pool would be less the costs of their collection; one-half the annual receipts into the pool would be distributed to the High Commission as a source of finance for the non-self-contained services as specified by the Commission, and one-half would be distributed in equal parts to the three Territories.

In an illustration of the actual working of the pool the report estimated that Kenya would have £675,000 less available for her own expenditure than she would have under the present system, and Tanganyika, Uganda and the High Commission £310,000, £245,000 and £120,000 more, respectively.

The Commission gave a warning on artificial impediments at variance with the Common Market system, such as import (and some export) prohibitions in the separate territories. 'Not a few of the criticisms levelled at what is thought to be the working of the Common Market ought in fact to be directed at those impediments. They are, however, in many cases part of the established structure of the East African economy, and it would be unrealistic – as well as in many cases unjustified – for us to recommend their abandonment. But if they are not to endanger the maintenance of the Common Market it is important that they should be made subject to some discipline and control in order that the policies of the territories may be brought into greater harmony and the interests of East Africa as a whole asserted.'

Community Development

'You cannot educate people for citizenship unless you give them the chance of exercising their citizenship.'–*Education for Citizenship in Africa.*

All of us in the Colonial Service have heard of 'Mass Education.' Some, indeed, have no doubt felt that they have heard too much of it, and that it is a 'stunt' evolved by air-borne theorists. We understand, however, that all Administrative and technical officers, and others in the African colonies who may be concerned, are likely now to receive information and guidance on the whole subject which should do much to clear the air and to remove doubts and misunderstandings. This is very necessary because Mass Education, or Community Development, as it had much better be called, has now been adopted as one of the central features of the African policy of His Majesty's Government.

There is nothing new about the principle of Community Development. Many Administrative and departmental officers in all parts of the Empire have, from the earliest days, started and often successfully carried through a very great variety of schemes which would now all be called Community Development. All good officers have always had their pet projects of this kind and have always known that it was much better to encourage the people to do a thing for themselves than to do it for them. It is precisely on this kind of initiative and on this principle that the tradition of the Service and the finest achievements of our colonial administration have been founded.

But the policy is not entirely empirical. Its parents were, on the one side, the Advisory Committee on Education in the Colonies and the Colonial Economic and Development Council and, on the other, Administrative and technical officers working in the field. At Cambridge last summer theory was married to experience and their child is a practical, constructive policy which can be adapted to the needs and circumstances of any kind of community anywhere in the Colonial Empire.

Most of the previous mistrust of 'Mass Education' was due to the use of those two words, and one of the most valuable contributions of the Cambridge Conference was that it gave us a proper definition. It begins:

'We understand the term 'Mass Education' to mean a movement designed to promote better living for the whole community, with the active participation and, if possible, on the initiative of the community, but if this initiative is not forthcoming spontaneously, by the use of techniques for arousing and stimulating it in order to secure its active and enthusiastic response to the movement.' This is the key to the whole matter. 'Mass Education' methods can be used to promote all kinds of development and all kinds of improvement in the life of any community. They can lead to better soil conservation, better livestock management,

better sanitation and water supplies; to schemes for infant and maternity welfare, and to the spread of literacy and the improvement of schools. Furthermore, full use can be made of all suitable organisations already in existence, such as the Co-operative movement and Local Government bodies.

If the key to the movement is the co-operation of the people, the wide variety of possible objectives suggests another equally important feature which should, in our view, be incorporated in any local scheme. Everybody will not be interested in the same thing. More than one objective should, therefore, be chosen and a properly co-ordinated range of activities be organised, designed so as to make the best use of available staff and facilities and so as to arouse and sustain the interest of as many of the people as possible. Once, in fact, enthusiasm has been aroused, and no scheme will be successful if it is not, the very most should be made of it.

'Mass Education,' then, does not merely mean mass literacy and many people will be glad of this reassurance. A mass literacy campaign, however, will nearly always form an incidental part of any communal project, because there will be a demand for it and for the fundamental reason that the achievement of literacy is essential to progressive citizenship. As Mr. Hodgkin says in an article in this issue: 'To learn to sign one's name instead of thumbing it is a great achievement for any illiterate and, to him, well worth the effort.'

Nevertheless, in our experience, it is useless and dangerous to teach more and more people to read if this results only in widening the influence of bad newspapers or bad books. This does not mean that people who want to learn to read and write should ever be discouraged, but rather that, at the very start, steps must be taken to provide them with enough good reading material. The stream of good, cheap books from London and the East and Central African Literature Bureaux, specially written to meet this vast potential need, is growing, but for many reasons, including language problems, it will not for a long time be big enough. The writing, printing and publication *locally* of human, entertaining, and informative booklets, including news sheets, pamphlets and broadsheets giving full explanations of government policy, must, we suggest, be undertaken on a scale not yet attempted or even contemplated by most Colonial Governments. Unless this is done, few officers will feel like launching mass literacy campaigns themselves and those who are being urged to do so by their people will be placed in a very embarrassing position, and may even find the pitch altogether queered for the rest of their plans for Community Development.

A point which we were particularly glad to find so strongly emphasized at Cambridge was the necessity for team-work at all levels. We have always felt that the difference between good and bad administration in any province or district has depended on whether there has or has not been proper team-work between the various officers concerned, and now team-work from the village level upwards is made the corner-stone of the whole organisation of Community Development. The Community Development Officer, moreover, is not to usurp or interfere with the most important function of the Administrative Officer – creative administration – but will be there to give technical advice and to train specialist staff.

We do not think that those who will have to carry out this policy will find much to criticise in the proposed organisation. On the contrary the plan will, we believe, give particular personal satisfaction to a large number of individual officers. They will feel that their efforts have now been recognized and that the plan would assure for them official backing, a properly trained staff, an adequate organisation, and easily accessible funds.

But there must be no delay. The success of our efforts to prepare the African peoples, either to govern themselves or to take a full and responsible share in the government of their countries, depends, more than anything else, on the development of their own initiative and public spirit, and there is so little time. The pace of Africa may be the pace of the ox, but in some colonies we are more like cowboys trying to control a galloping herd than *voorlopers* leading the plodding span, and even the span may soon begin to tread upon our heels.

It is probable that *Corona* may be able to help a little. In this issue we are including some articles which may be useful. We make no apology for publishing once again the story of the Udi project in Nigeria. There are still hundreds of Administrative Officers and others who are not familiar with it and, because it can so easily be adapted, it is a most useful model. We could have gone to Northern Rhodesia for a blue-print of a mass literacy campaign, but, since we are always glad to learn from others, we have gone to the Sudan instead.

At Dueim mass literacy was the sole objective, but this does not affect the value of the technique. Mr. Hodgkin, incidentally, has some very useful things to say on what to do and what not to do in the production of cheap reading matter. We have included also a description of the work which has been done in the training of ex-Servicemen and their wives at Kabete in Kenya. The suitability of this undertaking as a model for the institutional training of specialist workers in Community Development has already been recognized.

If, however, *Corona* is to stimulate ideas, as we hope it may, we too need team-work. You want to know what others are doing in the way of Community Development and they want to know what you are doing. If you have been successful, others might like to copy. If you have failed, you might save others from making the same mistakes. You have problems, others may have the answer – and modesty can always use the cloak of anonymity. Nor need this be an exclusively African affair. The articles in this issue happen to come from Africa but many of the ideas they offer could surely be used elsewhere.

Community Development in Udi

Mass Education, or Community Development, in the Udi Division of Nigeria grew naturally out of the ordinary work of administration. It may, in fact, be said to have started as far back as 1927 when the Native Authority system was first introduced into the Eastern Provinces. The only things that are new about it are the introduction of the title 'Mass Education' and the injection of Mass Literacy into the work of developing the people towards a fuller and better life.

When the system of Native Administrations was first introduced it was necessary in the Eastern Provinces to find out on what basis the people were likely to be able to manage their own affairs. Until 1935 the social organisation of the Ibos was carefully studied in detail and in the main it was found to be based on the exogamous unit, or 'the extended family.' Usually villages were ruled by a council of the heads of these exogamous units, or 'Family Heads,' and though, most villages were virtually autonomous, many of them recognized clan relationships or agreed that their local administrative affairs should be run by a Clan Council of representatives from the village councils. It was these Clan Councils which became the Native Authorities.

At first these Councils found that after collecting their taxes there was more revenue than was needed for the amenities expected by their people. But as the people gradually became educated to higher standards of living they wanted such things as dispensaries and roads and schools, things which were more costly than their revenues could provide. This was bound to happen as instruction in matters of Native Administration has always been given to the Councils by the Administrative Officers and as it has not been given privately, but in meetings open to the public, meetings either of the Clan Council or of village councils when the District Officer has been on tour. The villagers themselves were encouraged to put forward their requests to the Councils and the position has now been reached in most if not all the Native Administrations in the East that public services are taking up all the available revenue. Any further advance is therefore out of the question unless some new source of revenue can be found. This is hardly possible – so the people must be encouraged to help themselves.

To quote an instance. The people of the Owa sub-Clan of the Abaja Clan were so keen to have a road from their Native Court to their dispensary that they were eventually persuaded to build it by voluntary labour. The expenditure of 12,000 man-days of voluntary unpaid labour on this road, and of another 5,000 man-days on a similar one at Affa, showed that the people of the Abaja Clan had the spirit and the power to improve their lot by their own efforts if they were given the right kind of encouragement. This voluntary work on roads, which opened up the remoter villages, was really the beginning of the whole scheme of Mass Education in its present form in Udi Division.

The six sub-Clans of the Abaja Clan then undertook to provide the land and to build by voluntary labour six villages in which to segregate their lepers. That scheme was dropped later for technical reasons but the Nkanu Clan was persuaded to set aside two square miles of land for the same purpose. The Chief Commissioner requested the Senior Leprosy Officer to provide the necessary medical supervision if the administration would be guaranteed by the District Officer. There was no trouble in persuading the Nkanu Clan to clear the site and build the village by voluntary labour and the growth of the settlement has been proof that such a scheme can be wholly successful.

It was after these roads had been built and the Leper Village was in use, that the Colonial Office paper *Mass Education in African Society* reached the Division. Now it is clear that 3,000,000 Ibos could not be taught to read and write except by the aid of voluntary teachers. Since the people in Udi Division had shown already that they were able to unite for voluntary labour to build roads and leper settlements, it seemed worthwhile to experiment with the idea of getting the few literates to teach their illiterate compatriots. As a result four communities, living under very different conditions, were chosen for experiments in Mass Literacy. One of these was the village of Ogwofia which soon raised by voluntary subscription a fund of £30 to buy reading and writing materials. Although some financial assistance came from Native Administration funds to purchase such things as cement and corrugated iron sheets, the people themselves by voluntary labour cleared the bush to make a village centre and connected this centre by road to the Native Administration road. They then built, in this order, a temporary Village Hall, where Mass Literacy classes could be held, a handsome Reading Room, the first co-operative consumer's shop in Nigeria, a temporary house to contain hand-machinery for processing palm fruit, a sub-dispensary, an incinerator, and lastly, and most costly of all, a village Maternity Home of brick with a 3,000 gallon water tank, and a midwife's quarters attached. They built a house for their shop-keeper's chickens as part of an attempt to improve the local breed of fowls; bought a sewing machine so that the midwife could teach mothers to make and mend clothes and especially those of their children; and they agreed to a leprosy survey, a hookworm survey and to mass treatment for hookworm, if that were found necessary. They also agreed to set aside land for a forestry plantation, but this came to nothing as a result of rumours reaching them from Lagos political circles that they would lose their land to Government if they went on with it.

It is most important to note in this that the suggestions came from the people themselves. They came through the normal administrative channels – but they were not put to the people by any government officer, Administrative or otherwise. For instance, at Ogwofia the clearing of the Village Centre, the erection of temporary buildings and the creation of a small market were done without even consulting the District Officer, just as the village fund was started before he was informed. The idea of a village sub-dispensary came from the village council, and at that time it was against official policy, but when permission came it was built in less than a month. The idea of a Maternity Home came from the women, who were told that the services of a trained midwife could be secured if the village would put up the building and meet the recurrent charges.

At first there was some suspicion that there might be a 'catch in it' but in 1946 there was a rapid outburst of development generally, going hand in hand with Mass Literacy, and by the end of that year no less than thirty communities were started on their own development plans.

One of the objects of the introduction of a Mass Literacy experiment had been to find out whether it stood any chance of success in Ibo Communities and, if it did, what the main difficulties were likely to be. The first step had been to ask the members of the African Staff at the Government Station at Udi whether they would be prepared to help voluntarily in their spare time to teach the inhabitants of a hamlet, or quarter, of Udi and sufficient of them agreed. Then came the first snag; many of the Elders thought that this step was the thin end of the wedge to abolish their *ju-jus*, from which they derived some of their perquisites. They were easily reassured.

But then came a much more difficult problem: where to get cheap materials for reading and writing? At first the people had to trace their letters in the sand with their fingers. A small grant of money had been made at the start, £20, but with this it was impossible to provide simple reading books, slates at 2s. 9d. each and chalk for two hundred people. At once someone had the idea of sawing up planks into boards twelve inches square, then planing and blackening one side. These cost five-pence each and were still far too expensive for general use, so many of the people who came to the first classes could not be provided with them. Then one day a child brought its own home-made wooden 'slate': it was just the size and shape of the shingles with which the village Reading Room was being roofed. The problem of slates was solved. The Native Administration was able to buy thousands of machine-sawn shingles made from rejected railway sleepers. These, when planed on one side, made a 'slate' for less than a farthing, six of them made a 'blackboard' for less than two pence – as compared with the genuine article from the bookshops at 10s. each or those made by the village carpenter for about 3s. 6d. each. The Public Relations Department in Lagos made free, by its Government-owned Process Engraving Section, a large number of blocks for reading charts prepared locally on the Laubach principle. From these blocks thousands of leaflets were printed at small cost, then these were distributed along with the shingles free of charge to all who attended the classes.

Another problem was the method of teaching. Although the Laubach method leaflets were useful initially, the system could not be followed throughout as the scheme had to rely on hundreds of untrained instructors, many of whom had, as their only qualification, the fact that they were literate. The charts had the merit that they showed the pupils that literacy was not a difficult or mysterious subject and they were something for them to take home and study with the help of some literate neighbour. But for the main part instruction at the classes had to be on the lines which the instructors had themselves experienced at the Mission Schools. A simple and inexpensive primer and a few simple booklets for reading were produced locally and each village was given a notice board for news bulletins in Ibo, but these had to be prepared as the people, for some reason, would not use them for their own news items.

Before starting the experiment at Udi it was necessary to take the Native Administration into the picture. This was done at one of the monthly meetings of the Council so that there should be no false impressions allowed to get abroad. It was at this meeting that other Elders asked for their villages to be included – and one of the keenest of these was Ogwofia, which I have mentioned above. At that village the Elders made all the school-children teach their parents in the evenings: 'We pay their school fees, so they must tell us for nothing what they are taught.' The adults agreed. In Udi, classes were held every other day (except week-ends) but in most of the villages they were only on market-days (every fourth day) when all the people had come in from their farms or did not go to them. Naturally classes had to be timed not to interfere with marketing or the preparing of the evening meal.

Four communities were chosen for the experiments. The first was Udi where there was some available educated staff to volunteer and where the District Officer could more closely supervise the work. The second was Ogwofia, which was so very keen and had a progressive leading village Elder, a village only eight miles from Udi where the District Officer could visit fairly frequently, but which had little teaching talent. Third was a large quarter of Okama Oyo, which had an ex-school teacher Elder, a man of personality, but a place which the District Officer could only visit infrequently. Lastly there was a quarter of Nze, furthest of all from Udi, and which could not be visited more than once in about two months, but the people were keen though there was little teaching talent. It must be remembered that the Administrative Officer was doing all this Mass Literacy work in his spare time.

So far as could be seen in these villages, as well as in others which took it up later, there was no rule about the relative proportions in which men, women and children attended the classes, though in most cases a large proportion of the children did attend. Six months after the start of the work some twenty people in Udi were fully literate in Ibo, about forty had made good progress, another hundred had made little progress and a few had proved keen but unteachable. At Okama Oyo about a dozen were fully literate, another hundred had made some real progress and some three hundred had made no progress worth mentioning. Ogwofia had made some real progress but the figures were doubtful – though it must be remembered that here events had taken the remarkable turn mentioned before, which probably turned their main activities into development works, and in any case there was hardly any teaching talent. At Nze some twenty people had progressed about one third of the way to full literacy. Six months later the more advanced people were ready to take lessons in English. At Ogwofia the people had engaged, through their village fund, a full-time instructor, but in the main adults had ceased to attend the classes and only children were attending, about sixty regularly; and the adults had provided them with desks and all the paraphanalia of a vernacular school.

Tanganyika

THE SUKUMALAND DEVELOPMENT SCHEME

by JOHN T. PURVIS

At the Cambridge conference in 1949 Mrs. Elspeth Huxley gave a very stimulating address which she called 'Must Africa Starve?' and possibly a brief description of what is being done in Sukumaland in Tanganyika may be a useful contribution to that very pertinent problem.

Sukumaland is the name given to the country lying south of Lake Victoria and occupied mainly by Basukuma, with some Banyamwezi to the south and Bazinza to the west. Its total area is approximately eighteen thousand square miles, of which about nine thousand are occupied; two thousand at present lie within the Serengeti National Park, and the balance is unoccupied bushland, mostly infested with *tsetse* fly.

In the occupied part of Sukumaland there are now approximately one million people, who own two million head of cattle and a similar number of sheep and goats; in the more densely settled areas, surveys show densities of up to five hundred persons to the square mile. Stock are unevenly divided amongst individuals and their distribution throughout the area is dictated by available water supplies and grazing.

Sukumaland is semi-arid; the rainfall ranges from thirty to forty-five inches a year but the seasons are erratic and precipitation is usually in the form of tropical storms with consequent high run-off. The topography is gently undulating, with granite hills or kopjes near the lake. Drainage is mainly into Lake Victoria, except on the east where the flow is through the River Manonga system to the land-locked Lake Eyassi. None of the rivers of Sukumaland flow throughout the year. Soils derive chiefly from the granites and have proved to be reasonably stable and able to stand up, for long periods, to the burden of over-cultivation and over-stocking and to primitive methods of African husbandry. There is less spectacular gully erosion than in some other parts of Tanganyika but the more insidious sheet erosion naturally follows over-grazing, excessive trampling by stock in search of water, and flat cultivation on the tougher soils.

Sukumaland is often described as a 'Cultivation Steppe,' where increases of humans and stock, together with wasteful and destructive methods of husbandry demand a new approach and an overall plan for development and rehabilitation.

Officers of the Administration and technical departments have long been aware of the problem and dangers which inevitably arise with an increasing population and a steady decrease in land fertility, but it is only recently that federation of all the Sukuma Native Authorities covering the administrative districts of Shinyanga, Maswa, Kwimba and part of Mwanza made a concerted effort possible.

Federation of all the Native Authorities which now go to form Sukumaland was mooted by the Chiefs as far back as 1932; the idea was spontaneous but it made only a little progress during the periods of depression and war. A survey was made, chiefdom by chiefdom, by a Senior Administrative Officer in 1945, during which it was ascertained that all the fifty chiefdoms wished to form a Federation of the eight local federations which previously existed. The first full Federation meeting was held in October, 1946, and in order to expedite business an advisory council of fourteen Chiefs, representing the original federations, dealt with the agenda before the full council met.

The full Federal Council now sits bi-annually, preceded by sittings of the Advisory Council. A recent innovation has been the admission of so called 'people's representatives' to the Federal Council in an attempt to make this governing body less autocratic, but, in the absence of any regular system of elections, it is yet too early to decide how far these 'Bagunani' will prove to be independent of the influence of the Chiefs.

The new Federation naturally needed a headquarters and this was sited at Malya, on the Tabora-Mwanza railway, approximately at the centre of the area.

Various development plans for the whole of Tanganyika were being drawn up by the Government during the early war years against the time when money and staff would again be available to carry them into effect. A plan for the development and rehabilitation of Sukumaland gradually took shape as a result of the 'Malcolm Report.'

During the war years, the Government controlled the price to the producer of various kinds of agricultural produce such as cotton and coffee. The difference between the price paid to the producer and that realized for the produce on the open market was placed to the credit of the Agricultural Development Fund, and it is mainly from this source that finance for the scheme has been derived. An initial plan, estimated to cost about £230,000, grew, with further contributions from territorial housing and water development votes, until the approved expenditure finally amounted to £472,000 to be spent over a period of ten years beginning in 1946.

When the scheme was started it was agreed by Government that its detailed planning and execution should rest in the hands of a team specially selected for their experience and knowledge of the people and their land; this team was to consist of a Senior Administrative Officer as Co-ordinator, with technical officers seconded from the Departments of Agriculture, Forests, Veterinary and Water Development. The team came together in April, 1948; it is now housed at the Federation headquarters at Malya, where already quite a few buildings have grown up round a new four hundred and forty million gallon dam. These include the Council Hall and houses for Chiefs and subordinate African staff; offices, stores, and workshops; a dispensary and a village hall; African shops and a railway station.

The Chiefs do not reside permanently at Malya, but collect there for Advisory and Federal Council meetings twice a year. It is at these meetings that the members of the team present their progress reports, discuss plans with the Chiefs, offer advice, answer queries, or put forward formal requests for Native Authority Rules and Orders to enforce such things as improvements in methods of husbandry.

The team idea is something new in Tanganyika. It is in addition to, and does not replace, the ordinary district and departmental staffs, who carry on with their normal programme of propaganda and extension in the occupied areas. To avoid any departmentalism and foster team working, officers seconded to the scheme are divorced from departmental routine and direction and become answerable to the Provincial Council, but appeal on a matter of policy may be had through the appropriate Provincial departmental officer to the Head of Department.

The organisation also has its own subordinate staff consisting of Mechanics, Field Officers, Storekeeper, Office Superintendent Accountant, African Engineer, Clerks, Instructors, Forest Guards, Veterinary Guards, Lorry and Tractor Drivers, Dam Foremen, Road Foremen, Surveyors, Carpenters, Masons and Labourers.

Before the team came into being, the Provincial Agricultural Officer prepared a map of the whole of Sukumaland showing parish boundaries (where they existed), main roads, rivers, hill masses, bush edges marking the limit of settlement, and other details; this parish boundary map was supported by a soil map and a gazetteer showing the gross area of each parish in square miles, the number of people and stock in every parish and the density of each. In addition to this fundamental survey of the occupied lands, numerous other crop, stock, soil, water and population surveys have been taken from departmental records and made available to the team. The unoccupied lands present a much more difficult problem, as, in many cases, no detailed maps are available and often those which do exist have proved to be inaccurate and misleading.

At a very early stage it became clear that if there was to be any rehabilitation of the occupied lands, the development of new lands must proceed as quickly as possible in order to provide room for surplus population and stock; and the surplus stock is undoubtedly the more dangerous of the two.

It may well be asked why, in view of this over-stocking, the people have not moved to new lands of their own accord. The answer is that the undeveloped land is more or less waterless and is infested with *tsetse* fly, game and vermin; and that for many years indiscriminate penetration has been actively discouraged or forbidden because of a past history of sleeping sickness.

It is well known that desert-like conditions favour, up to a point, rapid increase in stock mainly because the incidence of tick-borne diseases such as East Coast fever is reduced. Records show that in spite of endemic rinderpest the cattle population of Sukumaland doubled itself between the years 1928 and 1948 and that the herds had multiplied to a point where the land could no longer support them. In the 1949–50 dry season severe drought caused the death of some 600,000 head of cattle and, although this alleviated the position for the time being, it did not provide any permanent solution, as experience has shown that the herds will have increased to their original size in a period of two or three years.

There always has been on the part of the cattle-owner a marked reluctance to move his stock into the long grass country, where ticks abound, until such time as these areas have been tamed by pioneer cultivators. In a bad season, however, stock owners are being forced more and more into the bush and *tsetse* country in an effort to save their cattle from death by starvation (e.g. the heavy mortality mentioned above), when losses amounted to thirty per cent of the livestock population in the more heavily stocked areas.

Over-grazing is responsible for most of the erosion so evident in the occupied country and in many areas the indigenous system of grazing reserves is disappearing under the constant pressure of hungry herds. When the land is kept so bare of cover, run-off, particularly at the beginning of the rainy season, becomes excessive, water ceases to penetrate the soil to any depth, the water table is seriously lowered and springs dry up.

A permanent solution of over-stocking can only come through education. For this purpose a stock farm of two thousand five hundred acres has been established at Malya where improved methods of animal husbandry and mixed farming can be demonstrated. The short-term policy must be the removal of the stock to new lands which, fortunately, are available. But there remains the immediate problem of so reducing the stock in the occupied country as to enable the rehabilitation of the pastures and the land generally to be undertaken; this cannot await the opening up of the new land, although nature has allowed a short breathing space as a result of the recent drought and the heavy losses.

The long-term policy towards solving the problem must be to change the attitude of the people towards their stock and this, unfortunately, has remained almost static during the last twenty years. Stock are the African's bank, his bride price, his barometer of affluence and social standing. Quantity and not quality is his aim and few, if any, look upon their herds as economic assets. True, sales have increased slightly on local auction markets since the war but until the African can be persuaded to regard stock as he would an economic crop, there must be provided some method of limiting his herds to numbers which bear some reasonable relation to the size of his grazing lands.

Culling of all unproductive and undesirable types of cattle has already been discussed as perhaps the only measure likely to produce results, but compulsion in this direction would hardly be popular with the influential cattle owners.

Private Enterprise in Uganda

In his speech at the opening of the Uganda Legislative Council at the end of 1952, the Governor, Sir Andrew Cohen, had this to say: 'May I take the opportunity of defining beyond doubt this Government's attitude to private and individual enterprise? We believe in a positive and constructive approach to all our problems. We aim at giving the greatest possible encouragement to everything that makes for initiative, energy, vitality and imagination. We want to create a climate here where confidence in the future of the country, in the wisdom of the Government and in the good relations between the different communities will produce the best possible atmosphere for vigorous and constructive action by individuals, companies and societies generally. It is the business of this Government, like other Governments, to protect and help forward those who are most in need of help, to raise their standard of living and to stimulate and assist their economic progress. At the same time we must make sure that the country derives full benefit from the energy of those members of the community of all races, who are most vigorous and most able to contribute to the public good by their individual and joint efforts. It follows that we believe in private enterprise and the contribution which private enterprise can make to the wealth and well-being of the country. We are not, however, dogmatic believers that private enterprise is the only solution in all circumstances, as is shown by the existence of publicly financed bodies like the Uganda Electricity Board and the Uganda Development Corporation. We believe our task to be to develop the resources of the country to the best advantage of its people and to use or encourage whatever agencies are best adapted to that purpose.'

Later in his speech the Governor gave prominence to the newly-formed Uganda Development Corporation which is designed to take over the existing commercial investments of the Government (apart from the Uganda Electricity Board) to conduct research into new fields of development, to give advice to those wishing to invest capital in the country and where necessary to join with private investors in development projects. The Corporation will work in close co-operation with African interests and whenever possible encourage investment by or on behalf of Africans.

Sir Andrew had this to say on the Africans' part in the country's economy: 'The aim of this Government, and this Council, is the comprehensive development of the Protectorate. That means that all must take part in the process of development and all must benefit from its results. If any part of the country or any section of the community is left out of the process our plans will be incomplete and our achievements will fall short of our aims. With this object in view I know that all honourable

Members are agreed that every assistance must be given to Africans to take a greater part in the economic life of the country. There is a great demand among Africans wherever I have been to play a bigger part in trade and commerce – a demand which often underestimates the difficulties involved. There is wide recognition among the European and Asian commercial community of the importance of doing everything possible to assist Africans forward in commerce. A special officer has been appointed for this purpose in the Department of Commerce and the advisory committees of business men which assist the Department have given much thought to the subject. Already Africans are playing a substantial part in retail trade. The Department of Commerce is carrying out a trade survey district by district. We hope also that it may be possible next year to undertake a wider economic survey of the potentialities of the country as a whole ...'

The Volta Scheme

The idea of a Volta River Authority to develop the great bauxite deposits of the country, to manufacture aluminium, to provide power and irrigation, to open up the Volta for water transport and to create a new deep-water port, has fired the imagination of the Gold Coast people for many years; and now it looks as though it may become a reality within the next decade.

The plan, as set out in a recent White Paper (Cmd. 8702, H.M.S.O., 9d.), is to be carried out by a very sensible combination of public and private enterprise. The Gold Coast Government is to be responsible for the new port, railways, roads and townships; and it will contribute to the cost of the dam at Ajena and the hydro-electric plant below it, though H.M.G. is to carry the major burden of these two projects. The development of the bauxite mines and the building of the aluminium smelter are to be the share of the British Aluminium Company and Aluminium Limited of Canada. The proportions of the final cost to be borne by the three partners are: H.M.G. £56,800,000, Gold Coast Government (and private investors) between £39 and £44 million, and the Companies between £42$\frac{1}{2}$ and £48 million. This division is an example of the principle that Governments should bear the cost of basic development and private enterprise that of the economic projects which this development makes possible. It also shows that no one is really afraid of the appearance of a Gold Coast Mossadeq, though the United Kingdom investment, which will be in the form of a loan to the Volta River Authority and subsequently to the Volta Electricity Board, secured on assets and repayable over 80 years, will be safeguarded by a power contract for sixty years.

The White Paper estimates that the United Kingdom demand for aluminium will be three times as great as at present by 1975 and total about 900,000 tons a year. The annual output from the Volta plant should be 210,000 tons, and United Kingdom consumers are to be offered 75 per cent of this output for 30 years. The scheme involves the creation of a new port at Tema, east of Accra (which is needed anyway and will be built regardless of the aluminium project), new townships, four railway extensions and one of the biggest dams in the world. The effect of the dam will be to create a lake in the Volta basin 2,000 square miles in area and to make possible the irrigation of much of the Accra coastal plain, which will bring thousands of acres under cultivation. It is estimated that it will take about eight years to complete the construction work and to bring the smelter and power station into production. All this preliminary stage will be the responsibility of the Volta River Authority, which will co-ordinate the work of the Railways, the Aluminium companies, the (public) Tema Development Corporation, the P.W.D. and the Agricultural

Department. The Volta Electricity Board will be created when power becomes available. The Chairman of the V.R.A. would be appointed by the Gold Coast Government with the concurrence of H.M.G. Most of the power produced will be needed for the aluminium smelter, but some will also be available for other uses. It is recognised that a lot still remains to be done before this great organisation can be set up, and it is therefore proposed to appoint a Volta River Preparatory Commission to press on with all the preliminary work.

Here, then, is another spectacular project in colonial development which, like that in Uganda, will not be held up for lack either of capital or of confidence in the political future of the country. It is, indeed, particularly gratifying that a great economic undertaking such as this should follow so soon upon the equally bold political experiment in West Africa. Not only will it add great strength to the essential economic foundations of the new democracy in the Gold Coast and set the country well on the road to full industrial development, but it should give confidence to private investors both in Britain and the United States.

The Colonial Cinema

by C. Y. CARSTAIRS, C.M.G.

I t will be very plain in my remarks that I do not speak as an expert but as a layman, one with some official responsibility for the development of undeveloped peoples, to use the fashionable phrase, and some connection with the use of film and of other media to that end. There is therefore, I imagine, little that I can say that is both true and novel about the use of the film.

But I take it that those responsible for organising this Conference have asked me to speak, knowing all this. At least part of the purpose of this Conference, as I see it, is to consider the relation of the film-maker to his paymasters – to discuss the question 'Sponsors, are they human?' To the extent, therefore, that I am a member of a sponsor department, I may perhaps serve to illustrate the nature of the sponsor in general, his possibilities, and his limitations.

This I can perhaps do best by describing how we stand as regards the colonial cinema, what we think about it, and where we think we are going and ought to go.

The question is put – how can films be better used to raise standards of living and of education in what are now elegantly called undeveloped territories? There is no single answer to this question. The first and overruling one is – provide more money. This, under the pattern which has evolved for the colonies, means not only the provision of funds by this country, and not even chiefly that. It now means the provision of funds by the various Colonial Governments themselves. In twenty-six years, since the colonial cinema, if I may so call it for convenience, first came into being to help to kill rats in Lagos, we have seen several changes of organisation and control. These are of more than purely administrative interest. In its origin, the colonial cinema was a local response to local needs. Up to the war it developed on a shoestring, largely in West Africa under the leadership of William Sellers, who is still with us as head of the Colonial Film Unit in London. Shoestring or no, the value of his work was by 1939 sufficiently realised to cause him to be brought into the Ministry of Information to run the Colonial Film Unit there, whose purpose was to use the film to help colonial peoples to meet the strains and bewilderments of the war years. This was the period of centralised operation and control. Besides making films in this country for showing in the colonies, the Unit maintained from first to last some twelve production units in the colonies themselves, making films on behalf of local Governments. Between 1940 and 1950, the organisation produced some 339 reels and distributed upwards of 12,300 show copies.

But since then the wheel has come full circle – or perhaps it would be more accurate to say that we are one turn further up a spiral staircase. The general tendency of British colonial administration has reasserted itself, and the responsibility for actual production has reverted to units working for and under the direct control of Colonial Governments themselves. Yet not reverted, for there are more of them than there were before the war, and they are much stronger in every way. In addition the Colonial Film Unit itself remains in being, now an agency of the Colonial Office itself. It makes no films, and it gives no orders, but it performs a whole series of services without which the colonial cinema as a whole would certainly suffer. It edits films, attends to titling, sound dubbing, the recruitment of staff, the ordering of equipment and stock, the running of the 'raw stock scheme,' and training; it collects and disseminates information, and sponsors research.

This is not a discourse about the Colonial Film Unit, but it may help to illustrate policy if I describe and give the underlying reasons for some of its activities. First, the 'raw stock scheme': it is a tenet of the colonial cinema that accessible audiences are not ready-made but have to be created – an interest in the medium and a disposition to be influenced by it have to be built up. To this end it has been found essential to start by showing the people – themselves, and their surroundings. Therefore, during the war and since, the Unit has supplied numbers of cameras, and raw stock, to territories without full-fledged film units so that interested officers, with little training, can make and show films of local interest, something between newsreels and film magazines. So great is the relative importance of local content, as compared with technique, that such films are still generally the biggest 'draw' and constitute the sugar that coats the pill of better drains, maternity centres and all the rest.

This leads on to training. I said earlier on that the colonial cinema needs more money. But however much money it gets, it will always have to spin out its resources as far as possible. I am not sure that that isn't healthy – that it isn't better to have rather more on one's plate than one can easily deal with, than to have the opposite trouble of how to justify the existence of lavish resources. However that may be, the point is academic, and the colonial cinema does not suffer from idle resources and is not likely to. One important economy is imported staff. The European staff of colonial film units do not live soft, but they are still a relatively costly item, and while some will be needed for many years to come, it is important on cost grounds alone, even if there were no others, to train likely local lads for the work.

Apart from training on the job, which always goes on, the Colonial Film Unit has embarked upon a series of one-year training courses. Three have been held so far, one in the Gold Coast in 1948–49, one in Jamaica in 1950–51, and one in Cyprus in 1951–52. There have been those who contended that one cannot impart really useful training to complete beginners in so short a time. Certainly the courses do not turn out, and do not aim to turn out, experts who could walk into jobs in Pinewood, or Hollywood or any other wood. But the proof of the pudding is in the eating. Trainees are turning out a type of straightforward film, eschewing frills, but strong in content and local touch, which very closely fits the stage of film education which their audiences have reached. And moreover, such is the importance of local settings that even the more sophisticated audiences, accustomed to the commercial cinema, find them very much to their taste.

Turning again to the main question of how the film can be more effectively used for colonial betterment, I think that, so far as subject-matter is concerned there is no limit that need worry us. I have become very chary of saying, or even permitting myself to think, that any given subject cannot be illuminated by film. I thought at one time that juvenile delinquency seemed a bit unpromising, and then saw 'The Boy Kumasenu,' as many of you will have done, last week. Incidentally this, the work of the Gold Coast Film Unit, powerfully helped by friends in this country, some of whom are here in this room, is hardly typical of the work of local units. But perhaps it is a portent. It has commercial ambitions, and I hope that it may achieve them. However that may be, it has already had an uproarious success in the Gold Coast.

Given funds, the problems are to choose the right subjects from among the endless possibilities, and to make the best possible use of the finished product. That means that film production and use must be intimately integrated with the work and thinking of the administration as a whole. That in our view is one of the strongest reasons for having films under the control not of some remote central organisation but of the local government. Otherwise it will come to be considered, or continue to be considered, an apparently costly frill, and will indeed be in danger of being one.

This integration itself raises questions which are not all easy. The film makers may have a good idea of what the film can do to forward public policy, but what if the other parts of the administration have not? This is not, I think, an academic question, even in this country. I do not think that there is a simple answer to this one – it is the central problem of the relation between the film-maker and the sponsor. Often have I heard wailing and gnashing of teeth from frustrated film people, and often they have had my sympathy. But the problem is there, and has to be dealt with, and, while it is a duty of the administrator to try to grasp what the film, together with all the other media, can do to forward the common cause, I think that the main responsibility lies with the film people to show and persuade the administrator. It can be done, and it has been done. Film people are past masters at putting ideas across their primary audiences. This they do not do by regarding them as perverse and obstructionist, but by taking them as they come. Why not try the same approach with officialdom? Why not assume that they are good fellows at heart, and open to persuasion if it is well put to them, even if they start off by being ignorant and seeming contrary? Above all, show them – and show them in their own time, and in a way related to their interests and responsibilities.

The goodwill and intelligent co-operation of the administration at large is indeed not merely a convenience for the film unit – it is quite essential if the film is to approach its potential usefulness. To put it at its lowest, it is not much good showing the Nigerian film 'Smallpox,' and enthusing your audience about vaccination unless the Medical Department is at hand to vaccinate the new enthusiasts. An impulse not acted upon, or left in the air, is I think worse than none at all – it breeds frustration, and acts as a stopper against the next one.

There is no one way of achieving full co-operation, and controversy rages on how best to use film. But one thing seems clear – it cannot be used in a vacuum – it must lead to useful action, and possible action.

Again, I think it necessary to recognise, or at any rate affect to recognise, that the film has its limitations. I do not think that there is any fundamental difference of objective between the administration at large and the film-maker. But there is a necessary difference of approach. We – that is officialdom – are concerned to forward colonial betterment by any and every means that comes to hand. You – that is the film-makers – are concerned to do it by films. I know that I am treading on dangerous ground, and if I am wrong I am sure someone will tell me – but it does seem that whereas the film is an excellent, if not an ideal medium for arousing interest for broadening the mind and touching the emotions, it is rather a cumbrous means of imparting exact information. It seems to me better at convincing people that something needs doing than at telling them precisely how to do it. If I am right, the film needs to be followed up and supplemented by other media, notably the film-strip and illustrated pamphlet, not to speak of lectures, demonstrations and all the rest. For this reason, the Colonial Film Unit training courses give prominence to the design of film-strips, with heavy emphasis on planning and treatment. Here I must digress and say that I have seen film-strips that have been so designed and edited as to be more exciting than many a movie, almost to the extent of making one wonder whether it is worth the trouble of having moving pictures at all. Anyhow, it has been found that good film-strips can hold the attention even of audiences well used to the cinema, and their advantages for imparting detailed information – and of cheapness – are obvious.

I have said nothing about research, or about the great debt of the colonial cinema to its big brother the British documentary movement, or about the possibilities and value of making entertainment films, let us say, in Africa for Africa. But if I have given some idea, however limited and scrappy, of how we see the problems and potentialities of the film as applied to British dependent territories, I think I have done something of what was asked of me.

Development of Colonial Broadcasting

by O. J. WHITLEY

Many of those who are concerned with the colonies must at one time or another have 'pipe dreams' about broadcasting. A medium which travels with the speed of light must surely have much to offer to territories over most of which travel is at the speed of bare human feet. A medium which can beat the printed word in range and intimacy, as well as speed, must surely be enlisted by Governments whose officers in the field complain that they are losing personal touch with their people through preoccupation with the inevitable paraphernalia of increasingly complex administration. But why should it be necessary to speak of 'pipe dreams'? Why is broadcasting, this peerless purveyor of information and ideas, not universally established throughout the colonies? Why can the United Kingdom boast that there is a receiver to every three or four of its people, while the colonies must admit that they have not one to every hundred?

There are two main answers, which include all the others. First, broadcasting is technically much more difficult to develop in large tropical countries than in compact, temperate countries. Second, the level of incomes of many colonial peoples is too low to support a broadcasting service, always an expensive amenity and made more so in the colonies by the technical difficulties which have to be overcome.

Consider the technical difficulties. First European countries rely on long and medium wavelengths for their domestic broadcasting services. In the tropics long waves are useless. The range of medium waves, unless transmission were to be with a power higher than any colony could supply or afford, is measured not in hundreds of miles, as in Europe, but in tens or less. Medium-wave stations, therefore, will only serve small areas and it is only economic to use them for fairly closely populated places. For rural areas there is no alternative to short waves. But short waves are hard to come by, since nearly every nation in the world competes for the use of the strictly limited total number available. They require a rather more elaborate receiver, which costs more and is not so easy to tune. Nor do they normally serve the immediate neighbourhood of the transmitter. A colony of any size, therefore, must instal a short-wave transmitter for general coverage and, probably, several medium-wave transmitters or wire rediffusion systems for local coverage.

As if this, and the considerable recurring costs of producing programmes and maintaining equipment were not enough, it is then also necessary to consider the problem of reception, for the best broadcasting service is useless if it is not heard. When broadcasting began in the more advanced

68

countries the broadcasting authorities hardly needed to concern themselves with facilities for reception. They created the demand. The demand created the supply. This may not necessarily be so in many colonies, for the cheapest suitable receiver produced anywhere in the world may cost more than the average annual income of their inhabitants. And how is the power to be supplied for receivers in areas where there is no main electricity supply, where accumulators cannot be recharged without impracticable portage and where the heat and humidity bring dry batteries to a premature demise?

These are not all the difficulties. Even so they are a formidable array, and they have to be tackled, for the rewards of success and the cost of neglect, are both too high to countenance inactivity. How is it being done?

Several salient facts have first had to be recognised. Technical difficulties and comparatively low standards of living combine to make it almost impossible, for a considerable time, for broadcasting services in most colonies to pay their way from the proceeds of receiving licences, as home broadcasting services in Britain have paid their way almost from the beginning. As an aspirant for a subsidy from local funds, broadcasting has not generally been given a high place among other social services by Colonial Governments faced, as they always are, with the task of squeezing a quart of development from a pint of money.

Some colonies have allowed commercial broadcasting to provide a solution to this impasse by granting a concession to a private company to operate a broadcasting or a wire rediffusion service. Several companies have shown themselves very ready to do this at no cost to the local Government, provided that they are given the right to derive revenue from broadcasting advertisements. It became clear a year or two ago that, left to their own resources, most Colonial Governments would before long probably accept the terms, attractive in many ways, which commercial broadcasting companies are able to offer. But His Majesty's Government does not believe that the need to make even a modest profit out of broadcasting can be compatible with the full use of the medium for the information and enlightenment of colonial peoples, which, as distinct from their entertainment, must be financially unremunerative. Nor does it expect that commercial broadcasting can ever be relied upon to serve any but the more closely populated, and therefore remunerative, regions.

Thus the conclusion has been reached that if broadcasting in the colonies is to be used as the Government would like to see it used, generous contributions must be made from United Kingdom funds specifically for that purpose. A decision to this effect was taken recently and Colonial Governments were informed that a substantial sum is available subject to the submission and approval of schemes for its use to the best effect.

It has been suggested to Colonial Governments that the main immediate effort in most territories should be directed to the development of transmitting services. Funds likely to be available in the near future could hardly be stretched to include expansion of transmitting services as well as the formidable sums which would quickly become involved in any wide subsidisation of receiving facilities. Just how formidable such sums would be can be seen from the fact that to reduce the commercial retail price of the

cheapest suitable receivers now available to an actual selling price in the
colonies of £3, in quantities large enough to supply one in every ten people,
would cost at least £12,000,000. It is not, however, intended that this
preference for the development, in the first instance, of the transmitting
side of a broadcasting service should be carried so far as necessarily to
exclude altogether any participation by Governments in the distribution
or maintenance of listening facilities. Such participation might take
various forms; for example, a limited initial purchase of cheap receivers,
the collection of defective receivers for central repair and replacement,
the transport of batteries, or any other ways of helping or encouraging
commercial agencies to overcome their formidable difficulties. There is
good reason to believe that new transmitting services will give an effective
fillip to the supply of cheap receivers through the ordinary commercial
processes; but manufacturers and distributors can be greatly encouraged if
Colonial Governments show themselves willing to co-operate in any of
these ways or by the reduction or removal of import duties on receivers
below a certain price. This applies particularly to the smaller manufacturers.
For a variety of reasons they tend to be the ones most interested in the
colonial radio market; but they naturally have little, if anything, of a ready-
made sales or maintenance organisation in the field.

While these general conclusions were being reached efforts have been
made, both in the colonies and at home, to solve the most important and
least tractable of them all – the problem of cheap reception. Every now and
then, as in the search for perpetual motion, someone claims to have found
the solution. It may be the distribution of programmes by wire, requiring
only a small monthly subscription from the listener. But the high capital
cost of installation restricts wire rediffusion to towns and closely populated
places. It may be the installation of unattended sub-stations for wire or
wireless rediffusion in scattered or remote villages and areas. But, in the
absence of a mains electricity supply, a generator is required, which will not
run unattended for long: and, apart from the electrical supply, there is no
close prospect of stations, proof against excessive heat, wild animals and all
other obstacles, being produced at an economic price.

Again, crystal receivers have been hailed by some as the key to these
problems. They need no batteries and virtually no maintenance. They could
be mass produced for less than £1 apiece. But, unfortunately, they are no
good for short-wave reception. They only give effective reception within a
very few miles of any but the most powerful and therefore prohibitively
costly medium-wave transmitter, and that only with an aerial which would
be a dangerous electrical conductor. Nor will the crystal stand up against
the severe electrical storms which are an almost daily occurrence in many
colonies. If it were possible to produce a crystal receiver proof against all
these disabilities, it would cost more per listener from every aspect than a
small battery receiver of more conventional type.

Experiments have been made with receivers with printed circuits and
components mass produced and mechanically assembled, which might sell
at a retail price in the colonies of £2–£3. Receivers thus produced were tried
out in several colonies, but proved a failure.

It has often been suggested that a large number of community receivers of more elaborate design should be produced and distributed to places of assembly and be maintained from public funds. This has indeed been done on a small scale in several territories. But it has been found in some territories that casual community listening, as distinct from listening in schools or elsewhere as part of an organised activity, has a short-lived popularity. Colonial Governments have therefore hesitated to devote large sums to a form of listening whose value may depend upon its novelty.

In dealing with all these possibilities, the Colonial Office has throughout acted upon two main assumptions: first, that it is unlikely that any single solution to the problem of cheap receiving facilities will apply to the varied conditions of all colonies, and, second, that, in consequence, every seemingly practicable possibility or suggestion should be followed up until proved otherwise. At an early stage, therefore, the help of the Radio Industries Council was enlisted. Information was circulated to British radio manufacturers showing what types of receiver seemed most likely to be needed in the colonies and giving detailed technical specifications of their basic performance and design. Several different prototype receivers, whether or not specially built for the purpose, have been put through their paces by Information Officers and broadcasting staff in the colonies.

At the present time, largely as a result of the initiative of the Governments of Northern Rhodesia and Nyasaland and of the enterprise of a British radio manufacturer, several thousands of dry battery short-wave receivers are being marketed in Central Africa at a retail price of about £5. This low figure is possible only because the local distributors have agreed to handle the receivers for a negligible charge – they will have a more substantial share in the proceeds of sales of batteries – and because the two Governments have agreed to waive import duties on receivers below a certain price level. These receivers had previously been tried out in Central Africa and modified in the light of the experience gained there. They are accompanied with full and simple instructions in the vernacular, specially designed for people who have never before handled a wireless receiver. These instructions vary from advice on tuning to a warning that brute force creates more problems than it solves. Written exhortations to remember not to waste the batteries are to be backed up by announcements to the same effect at the end of each transmission.

In the course of a general broadcasting survey, other receivers have been tested in West Africa, including a specially built prototype of a rather more elaborate one, costing about £10, which might appeal more to Africans of the middle income level. In addition a considerable extension of community listening in Singapore and the Federation of Malaya, where conditions favour it, is under consideration.

The development of broadcasting in the colonies is a stubborn problem, but some progress is being made.

The Saucepan Special

by HARRY FRANKLIN

B roadcasting to six million Africans scattered thinly over Northern and Southern Rhodesia and Nyasaland, an area of half a million square miles, is the task of the Central African Broadcasting Station at Lusaka. Starting from scratch, and in wartime, it was a task that bristled with so many difficulties, that there were times when it seemed almost impossible and we nearly gave up. To programme for fifty or sixty different tribes speaking as many different dialects (though fortunately nearly all of them can understand one of the six main languages) is not easy. To give adequate short wave coverage over such a vast range in one of the worst areas for electrical disturbances in the world is not easy either.

To overcome these troubles after years of patient work and then to find that only one African in every thousand is able to listen to the broadcasts is really quite depressing. Yet that was the situation last year. We knew of course long before that that would be the situation unless we could find some solution to the listening problem in time. We hoped two years ago (and now we know we were right) that we had the answer to the problem. But before that we pursued our doubtful course with a Micawber-like faith that something would turn up.

We knew that community receivers were largely a failure. We knew that asking European employers to let their African employees listen to the household set was, naturally enough, producing hardly any result. We knew that one day we should be able to reach some of the industrialised population through wire broadcasting, which we are in fact starting in Lusaka now. But wire-broadcasting has its difficulties too, and anyway we wanted to reach the rural population; the townee always seems to get the best of everything. The only solution to the problem was to produce and market a strong, simple, cheap, dry battery, short wave receiver, and we had to find somebody in either Britain or the Dominions (dollars were 'out') to do this for the past two years and failed.

When I went on leave in 1948, I told the broadcasting staff that I would find a manufacturer to take the job on or bust. But for a stroke of luck I should have had to bust. Sitting, in some desperation, in front of a telephone in the Northern Rhodesia Haymarket office, towards the end of my leave, I decided, as a last chance, to try the headquarters of a firm, a branch of which, in another part of world, had turned the proposition down before. I asked the voice at the other end of the 'phone for the name of the Managing Director, got it and hurriedly put the 'phone down. I then looked up his private number and home address.

Fortunately he did not throw me out, and I should very much like to conduct the negotiations which followed again. So I think would the then B.B.C. Adviser to the Colonial Office and a B.B.C. Engineer who both gave me invaluable help at subsequent meetings. The negotiations were almost entirely carried out over pre-lunch gins and post-prandial brandies and I had my first rides in a Rolls Royce not owned by a Governor.

The Managing Director had a keen sense of adventure and was prepared to take a chance on producing a receiver at a very small profit in the hope that it would ultimately sell on a very big scale, not only to the African peasant, but all over the world.

In a few weeks he had several prototypes ready and we had chosen one which filled all the specifications that we had got so tired of repeating over the last two or three years. The cabinet was a mass-produced saucepan and we nicknamed the receiver the 'Saucepan Special' on the spot. It was strong, simple to operate, impervious to white ants and looked a good deal more attractive than one would have imagined an ex-saucepan could look. There were no secrets about it. It was of a formal four valve superhet design operating from a compact 300 hours dry battery, on a wave range of from twenty-five to ninety metres. The set and battery weighed fourteen pounds.

A few weeks after my return from leave forty hand-made prototypes were flown out for testing in the field. The factory manager flew out soon afterwards. He was not at first impressed. Investigations into African population figures, wage rates, cash earned by sales of native produce, and other sources of income, revealed the fact that in a country of only a million and a half men, women and children, the average cash earnings per family were barely a pound a week! It was difficult for a merchant, not knowing the African's increasing thirst for knowledge, his need for some brightness in a life largely deprived of the old primitive excitement of cattle raids and hunting, and his self-sufficiency, without cash expenditure, in food, housing and other essentials of life, to realise that such a poor population could and would buy radio sets.

Fortunately we had sold, and not given away, to Africans the sample prototype sets at £5 each. The visits we paid to the African owners of these first sets were equally a surprise to the Africans, the Manager and myself. The sets were in operation as we walked into the huts, they were well set up and being properly used and the enthusiasm of their owners was obvious. The manufacturer's emissary was impressed. It was in fact the Africans' own enthusiasm for something which the strange Europeans thought would be good for them, which obtained that thing for them – a unique experience in my twenty-one years' service, and none the less refreshing for that.

Everything was arranged to keep the price of the 'Saucepan Special' to the purchaser as low as possible. A wholesale and retail firm which has the widest network of stores in the country agreed to accept a very low profit margin, and was appointed distributor for Northern Rhodesia. The agreement fixed the retail price at £5 for the set and 25s. for the battery, and the distributors had to make the 'Saucepan Special' available to any other traders at a small discount.

Government agreed to suspend customs on receivers of not more than £4 f.o.b. United Kingdom value and on dry batteries of over 30 v. capacity. The Information Department (which controls broadcasting) agreed to undertake the checking and trimming of sets on arrival and to service the receivers at a flat rate of 2s. 6d., provided the seal was unbroken and the set had not been obviously misused. This undertaking was for the first year of the scheme only.

A leading motor transport firm showed great public spirit in agreeing to transport the sets free, off the line of rail.

It was twelve months after the factory manager departed, before the first mass-produced 'Saucepan Specials' arrived, and we were all on edge until we could get them out to the stores and see if they would go. They went.

In the first four months from the launching of the 'Saucepan Specials' they have been bought by Africans in Northern Rhodesia alone at the rate of nearly three hundred a month and a lot more would have been sold if supplies had not run out. The Government has now decided to allow African Civil Servants to buy the radio on an advance repayable on instalments from salary, and our present difficulty is to get supplies fast enough from the manufacturers. Southern Rhodesia and Nyasaland, after waiting a little to see how the sets would go in the North, ordered their first consignments early this year and have since ordered more.

The 'Saucepan Special' is now selling, not yet in great numbers, in Singapore, Malaya, the Belgian Congo, Basutoland, Bechuanaland, Nigeria and Kenya. Africans are writing to us, some even sending cash to include air freight charges, from South Africa, Tanganyika and Uganda. Broadcasting authorities seeking information on the 'Poor Man's Radio' have written to us from Pakistan, Mexico, New Guinea and Samoa. Sample sets have been sent to them and, at the request of the Colonial Office and the Foreign Office, to almost every British colony and to most of the countries of the Middle East. The 'Saucepan Special' is becoming almost famous and is getting a press varying from a paragraph in *The Times,* to Ripley's 'Believe it or Not' strips in the *Sunday Express.*

The popularity of these cheap receivers with the Africans of Northern Rhodesia is reflected in hundreds of letters which the Lusaka station has received from 'Saucepan' owners or from literate friends on their behalf. Radio has opened up a new world for them. One correspondent wishes the Saucepan radio to be christened 'The Great Teacher.'

Webster Kmombo writes from the Mines:– 'I am pleased to have this opportunity in which I wish to thank the Government of Northern Rhodesia for the fine work they have thought to do for the Africans to enable them to have cheap wireless sets to listen to in their own houses. I have bought my own set and I have fear perhaps the shopkeeper who sold it to me will come and snatch it from me.

'If you have had bad thoughts in you or are fond of fighting others when you get your own set and listen in you can forget and stop all your bad ways. Nowadays I will be enjoying a lot if I don't die quickly.'

The Senior Chief of the Lunda, who wears a wristband of dried human flesh, handed down by his ancestors, writes through his Court Clerk from

Balovale, the most primitive district in the Territory:– 'We are writing to thank the Northern Rhodesian Government for the greater work it has done in providing cheaper wireless radios for the African peoples of this Territory... Many Africans in this district bought them and I also bought one and brought it to my capital at Mukandakunda. Many people, men, women and children come in larger numbers, as if they were entering a Church, all desirous to hear the news. You can see them wagging their heads. Then they say– "These Europeans are wonderful people and the wisdom which God gave them is incomparable".'

I wish the Managing Director with the sense of adventure could have lived to read these letters. He died just before the 'Poor Man's Radio', which he created for Africa and the world, reached its first market in Northern Rhodesia, but the 'Saucepan Special' is doing him justice.

Mandates and Trusteeship

U.N.O. VISITING MISSIONS

We are inclined to regard the Trusteeship system as merely a continuation of the old Mandate system without recognising the important differences between them. The most important difference is that, whereas the Permanent Mandates Commission was composed of experts appointed in their own right, the Trusteeship Council consists of representatives of member-States who voice the views (and prejudices) of their Governments. A second difference is that, unlike the Permanent Mandates Commission, the Trusteeship Council has the right under Article 87 (*c*) of the United Nations Charter, to 'provide for periodic visits to the respective Trust Territories at times agreed upon with the Administering Authority.'

Our first experience of this innovation was not altogether a happy one. The territories visited were Ruanda-Urundi (under Belgian administration) and Tanganyika. The Mission chosen by the Council consisted of a Frenchman (as Chairman), an Australian, a Costa Rican and a Chinese. Throughout their visit they were accompanied by six members of the United Nations Secretariat. The French Chairman has had long experience of administration in French territories in Africa, the Australian representative has a wide knowledge of primitive peoples in the Southern Hemisphere, but no member of the Mission had any practical experience of Tanganyika. It was therefore to be expected that after only six weeks in a territory of some 360,000 square miles, where communications are not easy and where social conditions vary enormously from one tribal group to another, any conclusions reached would necessarily be tentative. They would be based largely on memoranda received and on interviews given to representatives of the African, European, Asian and Arab peoples in the territory. An international Mission visiting the United Kingdom would find it difficult to write a balanced, comprehensive report on this country from such sources after only six weeks acquaintance!

But, in spite of the widely diverse experience of the members of the Mission and the vast field they had to cover, they submitted a unanimous report containing a number of far-reaching recommendations. In the Introduction to the report, there is a revealing passage which runs as follows: –

'The observations and conclusions do not necessarily reflect the precise views of each member of the Commission. The desirability of submitting a unanimous report to the Council may have resulted in the formulation of an average opinion on particular points to which the Commission as a whole finally subscribed.'

In these circumstances, it was only reasonable to expect that the report would need the most careful examination before its findings were accepted or broadcast throughout the world. But it was submitted to the Trusteeship Council in November, 1948, and circulated to members of the Council as an unrestricted routine document. Inevitably it leaked to the Press, with the result that quotations from it, many of them isolated from the general run of the Mission's recommendations and observations, hit the headlines in New York, London and East Africa before the text of the report was generally available for study. This caused a good deal of misunderstanding and adverse criticism.

To make matters worse, the Trusteeship Council met in January, 1949, and embarked on a 'preliminary' discussion of the report and even to the formulation of resolutions endorsing some of the Mission's recommendations, without waiting for the considered comments of the men on the spot who had given years of study to the problems raised in the report. The protest of Sir Alan Burns, the British member, was not heeded, and one resolution – on racial discrimination – was actually passed by the Council.

A full 'running commentary' on the report, prefaced by a restatement of His Majesty's Government's policy in Tanganyika, was handed in to the Secretary General of the United Nations on the 10th May and made available to the Press on the following day. This document emphasises the size of the territory and the fact that it has been under British administration for only thirty years, of which ten were war years. It regrets that the report gave currency to statements on white settlement which could only be described as 'gross and misleading exaggeration'; it rebuts, for example, the Mission's criticism that too much land was being alienated from the African population by pointing out that the area of cultivable land is many times greater than the 4,487,772 acres under cultivation at any one time by Africans, quoted by the Mission. The 1,846,278 acres alienated to non-Africans are, in fact, only a minor proportion of the total area available.

On the need for the expansion of education and medical services the Administering Authority expresses entire agreement with the Visiting Mission, but points out that they did not deal with the all important question of the means of financing this expansion.

The report will be further discussed in conjunction with the British comments during the Fifth Session of the Council, starting this month. If the technique of inspection by Visiting Missions is to be saved from ridicule, some heed will need to be paid to the views of the responsible Administering Authority, which has long and close connection with the questions raised and pronounced upon in the report. A second Visiting Mission is due this year – to the West African Trust Territories, in November. Its first resolve should be to confine its recommendations to practical questions and to comment adversely only where it sees and can point out a way of making an improvement. It should also realise that any individuals or groups who present memoranda are speaking from their own point of view and that it will be necessary to check from other sources the facts presented to them, before basing their recommendations on them.

And it is hoped that this time some means will be found of withholding garbled or fragmentary accounts of the Mission's report from the world until proper consideration has been given to it in the light of the observations of the men on the spot, who are in a position to say, from long experience, what other factors should be taken into account before judgment is pronounced.

West Africa

U.N. VISITING MISSION REPORTS

The Visiting Mission consisted of four representatives, a Chairman from Iraq, one member from Belgium, one from Mexico and one from the United States, and it was accompanied by six members of the staff of U.N.O. It visited the British and French Togolands and Cameroons during November and December.

The Commission finds that most of the people of northern Togoland want their country to be absorbed into the Northern Territories of the Gold Coast and that the people of Krachi in the centre want to be brought into southern Togoland, but that the majority of those in the south favour the unification of the whole of British Togoland into a separate administrative unit, as a first step towards unification with French Togoland. The report describes in detail the present political situation and, while making no specific recommendations, suggests that British Togoland will probably fare much better if it continues to be associated with the Gold Coast than if it were separated from it. Those sections of the report which deal with economics and the social services are in the main descriptive; praise is given to the cocoa marketing organisation, the complete freedom of speech which is everywhere allowed and, in particular, to the mass education campaigns in southern Togoland. Criticism is reserved mainly for roads and water supplies, and the report as a whole is reasonable and sympathetic. It is also short and to the point.

The report on the Cameroons is written in the same helpful spirit. Here again the Mission is impressed by the sharp difference between the northern and southern parts of the Territory; it commends the steps being taken in both areas to promote political evolution and does not think that the administrative separation of the Cameroons from Nigeria would be of benefit to the people. It does, however, consider that, in framing the new Nigerian Constitution, the desirability of giving some measure of internal administrative, legislative and budgetary autonomy to the Cameroons should be carefully examined. It adds a warning that the problems created by the Anglo-French boundary may, before long, become of more importance than they are today. The Mission regards the decision to vest the ex-German plantations in the people through the Cameroons Development Corporation as 'an example of good will and constructive and enlightened land policy,' but points out the need for making the true position clearer to the people. It approves the measures proposed for the rehabilitation of the Bakweri tribe in the plantation areas, and suggests a more intensive development of education and social services in the area. So far as the remainder of the Territory is concerned, the Mission also commends the efforts now being made, but deplores the shortage of staff, and stresses the need for more rapid development of education, particularly in the north. Finally, in considering some petitions about allegedly harsh marriage customs, the Mission listened to protests against such libels on the polygamous state, not only from the Fon of Bikom himself but also from many of his 110 wives, and wisely decided that reforms must be left to time and education. The Mission came to the conclusion 'that polygamy in Africa has been the subject of some misconception in other parts of the world,' and wisely emphasises that it is 'a type of social security which will have to remain until western civilisation through education convinces the Africans that other ways are better and preferable.'

These reports are now being examined by the Trusteeship Council in Geneva and the Council's final reactions are not yet known, but it is certainly gratifying that on this occasion a Visiting Mission should have approached its task with sympathy and confined itself to modest and realistic suggestions.

Malaya (1952)

STATEMENT BY THE SECRETARY OF STATE

T he following is the text of a statement made by Mr. Oliver Lyttelton in Singapore on Tuesday, December 11:–

'I've tried to see as much as I could during the short time I have been in the country. It had to be a short time because action was required at once. I've been in the States of Johore, Pahang, Selangor, Negri Sembilan and Perak and in the Settlement of Penang. Now I'm back in Singapore, I've given the problem of the emergency intense study. First let me express my admiration for the courage of many ordinary people – Malay, Chinese and Indian – growing rice, tapping rubber or mining tin, who go about their daily life not knowing what may befall them. Amid them all, Europeans have set their own splendid example of continuing courage. Nor can anyone who has recently been in touch with what I may call the front line help saying a word of gratitude to the women who are steadfastly suffering all these anxieties and dangers.

'I've tried as far as possible to see everybody I could. I've seen representatives of all communities. I've talked to District Officers, planters and miners, policemen, soldiers, Resettlement Officers and Home Guards. I've listened to many voices, but the problems are many and there is no one answer. I've seen something of British, Gurkha and Malay troops and their commanders, the Royal Navy and R.A.F. with its Australian contingent. This is warfare which makes heavy demands upon troops, especially those used to northern climes; yet day by day they are showing to the inhabitants of this country and to the world an example of discipline, courage and humour. The National Serviceman has proved himself beyond all expectation. In short, I've been engaged, so to speak, upon reconnaissance. This must be followed by plans, and plans must be followed by immediate action. When I get home I shall address a State document to the Prime Minister and the Cabinet to obtain their agreement and their help. I must therefore excuse myself from going into detail now, but there is much that I can say. I shall report that the main headings under which the immediate problem should be attacked are these:–

'First, the overall direction of our forces, military and civil, against the enemy. It is not an easy problem. Let me put it this way. War is a matter of violence, the art of administration is a matter of reflection and of check and counter-check. These two widely different activities have to be geared so that they move in concert and express themselves in immediate impact upon the enemy. I cannot go into the measures which I shall propose to secure this end. They will not be long delayed.

'Second. The reorganisation and training of the police is urgent. They are doing a stouthearted job in the face of trial and difficulties, but we must now achieve a much higher state of training in the special constabulary, and create a reserve of trained police.

'Third. Education. Too many do not have a clear enough idea of what they are fighting for. They must be taught, and one of the ways in which it can be done is by pressing forward with the project for compulsory primary education. It is not only the war of arms that must be won, education must help us to win the war of ideas. Of course, the effects of education are most striking in the long term but, even at the beginning, children who go back to their parents from school are living evidence of another way of life to set against that which is being whispered to them from the jungle.

'Fourth. A much higher measure of protection of the resettlement areas must be achieved and achieved quickly.

'Fifth. The organisation of a Home Guard. We must move now to enlist in the Home Guard a large number of Chinese in towns and in resettlement areas to defend their homes and their fellow countrymen. I've seen such a Home Guard working in Pahang and I am encouraged to think from this small instance that the object can be achieved.

'Sixth. We must tackle the problem of the great strain under which the Civil Service is at present suffering. We must review their terms of service and strive to maintain the high standards which have always been set. We must recruit the best here and at home.

'These are the main subjects upon which we must concentrate our attention and our energies. There is a host of smaller but highly important details which we must tackle at the same time. My report to the Cabinet will contain a massive appendix and I cannot go through all the subjects, but I can only mention a few upon which action must be taken at once. For example, armoured vehicles. There must be sufficient armoured vehicles to enable both civil authorities, police, planters and miners to move about upon their duties in vehicles which enable them to hit back if they are attacked. I cannot subscribe to the theory that protecting a man from rifle fire reduces his fighting spirit.

'Another subject is the officering of the Malay Regiment. This will require consultation with my colleagues. There is also the important matter of increasing, and rapidly increasing, the number of Government officers who can speak Malay and Chinese. There is the question of appropriate weapons for issue to planters and tin miners. The propaganda system appears to require careful scrutiny.

'These are a few instances among many. On my return to England, I shall wish to be kept in close touch with all these important matters and shall closely watch their development in solving these problems. We must look for help to the great Colony of Singapore. We must look to all races here and particularly to the enlightened and educated Chinese. We must look to those who are proud to call themselves King's Chinese, who have been here for many generations and whose descendants will be living here long after the present problems are forgotten. I've already said that this is a war of ideas as well as of arms. We have to see that our philosophy opens up to the peoples of Malaya a prospect of a finer and freer life than that which our enemies are now trying to instil. The ideal for which all communities in Federation of Malaya must strive is a United Malayan nation. When this has been achieved that nation will carry the responsibilities and enjoy the advantages of self-government. Then, we confidently hope, Malaya will add strength to the British Commonwealth, the greatest association of free peoples of which history tells. Political advancement, economic development, social services and amenities are rungs in the ladder today. However, we have to place emphasis on the immediate menace. We must ask who are the enemies of those ideals? Who are the enemies of political advancement? What is delaying progress towards it? The answer is Communism. The answer is the terrorists. The answer is the Min Yuen and those who, partly from fear and partly from sympathy, create a passive but no less serious obstacle to victory. All these in greater or lesser degree betray our ideal and upon them we must unite in visiting under the law the full severity which their betrayal merits. Only so will victory be gained. Without victory and the state of law and order which it alone can bring, political advancement becomes a hollow mockery to everyone, and not least to the worker in the field, in the mine and in the factory. The first duty of every government in every country is to ensure and protect liberty. Freedom from fear is the first human liberty. The pursuit of the ideal of a United Malaya will demand great political wisdom and the exercise of those rarest of human virtues, patience and forbearance.

'The British believe they have a mission in Malaya and they will not lay it aside until they are convinced that terrorism has been killed and buried; and that the future partnership of all communities can lead to true and stable self-government. The road to this partnership will certainly be long; it may well be very long. It runs through jungle and ravine but we will protect it. We will stay; we will never quit until our aims – and they are common to all races – have been achieved. I believe, too, that when self-government has been attained, the British have a place and a part to play in Malaya. Together with their fellow citizens of the other races let all Britons know therefore that there is a future open to them in Malaya, first in bringing about a partnership of all communities and thereafter in a united and self-governing Malaya which will emerge.

'In conclusion, I want to turn back to the subject of the emergency. I cannot promise you speedy success; I can and do promise you speedy action. Only with your help can the war be won. But I end by saying that if we act together, my confidence and my faith is that law and order and freedom from fear can be regained and restored.'

Self-Government and the Gold Coast

T he White Paper recently published in the Gold Coast completes a stage which began in October, 1952. Then, the Prime Minister invited views on constitutional reform from political groups and Territorial Councils. The following summary gives some of the main Government proposals based on the representations received in answer to that invitation.

1) The Government agrees to seek revision of the Gold Coast (Constitutional) Order in Council to an extent which will ensure that all Ministers should be representative Ministers, and that there should be no ex-officio Ministers. Special consideration must be given to subjects included in the United Kingdom Government's responsibility, e.g. Defence, Foreign Affairs, the Trust Territory of Togoland.

2) There should be an Economic Adviser to the Government, responsible to the Cabinet through the Prime Minister. There should be an independent Auditor-General. The Minister of Finance should receive advice on financial matters from the Permanent Secretary of Finance.

3) To avoid political control of criminal proceedings, the same person should not hold the offices of Minister of Justice and Attorney-General. A representative Minister of the Interior and Justice should have administrative and financial responsibility for such Departments as might come under him, and should formulate policy on such Departments' affairs. This Minister would be responsible for dealing with such affairs in the Cabinet and the Assembly.

4) The Governor, assisted by a Deputy, who will act as Governor when the Governor is absent from the country, should be responsible for Consular Matters, External Affairs and U.N.O., with special reference to Togoland; Naval, Military and Air Forces, Defence and Internal Security, and Police where special responsibility exists in connection with internal security and the maintenance of public order.

5) The Prime Minister should be appointed by the Governor from the members of the Legislative Assembly. Other Ministers and Ministerial Secretaries should be appointed by the Governor with the advice of the Prime Minister. The Northern Territories should be represented in the Assembly in proportion to their population and adequately in the Cabinet. Special Regional representation in the Cabinet is not considered justifiable.

6) The Governor will retain the right to summon a special meeting of the Cabinet if he sees fit and shall then preside. Otherwise the Prime

Minister shall preside and exercise functions similar to those of Prime Ministers in other countries.

7) The Government intends to recognise an official parliamentary Opposition and to provide remuneration for its leader in future estimates.

8) The Legislative Assembly should be composed entirely of members elected directly by secret ballot. A Commission is to be set up to enquire into representational and electoral reform.

9) Until full self-government is achieved, appointments to the public service, promotions, dismissals, transfer and disciplinary control should remain vested in the Governor advised by the Public Service Commission, but in filling certain higher posts the Governor would consult the Prime Minister, as also would be done in making appointments to the Public Service Commission. The Establishment Secretary should be responsible for the administration of the Public Service and should be attached to the office of the Prime Minister who will deal with Civil Service matters in the Assembly. Existing safeguards of the Public Service are under urgent consideration. In accelerating the Africanisation of the Public Service, the necessity for an efficient service and the continued need for the services of experienced overseas officers will be taken into account.

10) The United Kingdom Government should he informed of the general demand for the Gold Coast to achieve Dominion status and be requested to make a declaration regarding the grant of Independent Status within the Commonwealth. It is suggested that the Gold Coast Government should request the United Kingdom Government that Gold Coast affairs should be dealt with by the Secretary of State for Commonwealth Relations.

Of the above, paragraphs 9 and 10 are most likely to attract general attention, and since the publication of the White Paper, events concerning them have moved fast. Speaking at Accra, on 8th July, Dr. Nkrumah, the Prime Minister, made an important announcement regarding the Gold Coast public service. Previously, Mr. A. R. Thomas, Assistant Under-Secretary of State, Colonial Service Division, had visited the Gold Coast to discuss the future of that service and the Chief Secretary's office had declared, 'It may be stated that the aim of the Gold Coast Government is to retain and not to dispense with the services of oversea officers.' Now Dr. Nkrumah endorsed the principle that the responsibility towards expatriate officers must be fully discharged. The Gold Coast, he said, had more than laid the foundation for a future African Civil Service, 'but the fact must be faced that for some years we shall have to continue to rely on the services of oversea officers ... a fully self-governing Gold Coast will need their services.' Accelerated Africanisation should not be achieved, said Dr. Nkrumah, at the expense of efficiency, nor should promotion in the service be on a colour basis. A scheme in two stages would be introduced by July, 1954, to enable officers who so desired to retire before their time with compensation in addition to the normal pension. Officers for whom the Colonial Secretary was responsible and who joined the Gold Coast local service during the period of transition to self-government should still be eligible for transfer elsewhere within the Colonial Service, though without the compensation awarded to those who elected to retire.

In London Dr. Nkrumah's words were welcomed by Mr. Lyttelton as a ready recognition by the Gold Coast Government of its responsibility in ensuring satisfactory conditions of service for overseas officers.

Two days after his announcement about the public service, Dr. Nkrumah in the Gold Coast Assembly tabled a motion for self-government, based on the White Paper. Dr. Nkrumah was confident of Britain's attitude to the request for the Gold Coast to become a self-governing unit within the Commonwealth and he saw no conflict between the Gold Coast's claims and the expressed policy of all parties in the United Kingdom (and here perhaps it will be pertinent to remind readers that, by themselves, the Gold Coast White Paper and Dr. Nkrumah's motion cannot bring about constitutional change: the decision rests with the United Kingdom Parliament).

The Assembly passed the Prime Minister's motion by an overwhelming majority and rejected an Opposition amendment asking for the British Government to be told that independence should be declared by March 6th, 1954. The Ministers of Commerce and Industry and of Education spoke strongly against the amendment, and were forthrightly supported by Dr. Nkrumah, who called the amendment fantastic and irresponsible. 'By the impracticable proposals of the Opposition,' he said, 'we should have withdrawn from our position of strength and forfeited good will.'

Ghana Resurgent?

An interesting feature of the many representations from Territorial Councils and political groups which led to the recent Gold Coast Government's White Paper on constitutional reform is the frequent use of 'Ghana' as a name for the Gold Coast, and the evidence of a desire that the country should be so called in the future.

Why 'Ghana'? The name is one of long historical association with West Africa, deriving from rulers so called, and subsequently transferred to the capital of an early West African kingdom ... one of many in West Africa's history. The Ghana rulers founded their state early in the 4th century A.D and it covered that area of the present French Sudan which lies north of Bamako. It was a rich kingdom: gold came from south of the present river port of Kayes; copper was worked and textiles produced. Crops seem to have been excellent, thanks to better water supplies, either from nature or by irrigation, than now exist. The capital city was made of stone and its remains were excavated in 1914.

A likely theory is that the founders of Ghana were Syrian Jews who intermarried with indigenous peoples and hence brought the Fulani to birth ... the Fulani themselves, spread widely from the Senegal to the Upper Nile, are one of Africa's ethnological mysteries. Whoever founded

Ghana, the state flourished and reached its highest prosperity in the 9th century.

In 1076 the Marabouts from Morocco pillaged Ghana and established an empire from Senegal to Spain. In 1203 the remnants of Ghana were swallowed by the Sosso empire and finally disappeared thirty-seven years later under the flood of the Mangingo, founders of Mali, the greatest of all Negro African empires.

Now the name has been reborn, in connection with a part of Africa to which, it seems, it could not have been related in the past. For Ghana was well to the north of the Gold Coast; moreover, it existed and fell into ruin while African settlement in the Gold Coast was still in its infancy, for only about the time of the Sosso empire did the first Africans enter what is now the Gold Coast. Perhaps there is a link here; the first comers to the Gold Coast were the Akans, a Sudanic people, and Ghana was Sudanic. The entry into the Gold Coast began in the early 13th century, the time when Ghana was finally crumbling ... for despite its rape by the Marabouts, the name and state lingered on another 130 years. For the despoiling by the Marabouts, perhaps, was a reason for Ghana dwellers to seek new lands, and the Volta river which became the first settlers' route to the Gold Coast had its origins in Sudanic lands, northwards towards the old Ghana kingdom. This is speculation, it is true, but it derives from recorded facts; is it too much to hope that from the Gold Coast itself will come an authentic explanation of this interesting glance into West Africa's past?

Kenya

A STATEMENT OF POLICY

T he following statement was recently issued by the Kenya Government:– Since the Council of Ministers was established on the 20th April, 1954, Ministers have been examining their responsibilities and planning afresh particular projects to give effect to this broad outline of policy. A point has now been reached at which this policy can be interpreted in rather more precise and practical terms and a public declaration made of the Kenya Government's intentions. The speed at which the Kenya Government can achieve its objectives will depend upon the extent of co-operation received from all races and classes, the final defeat of the terrorists and the restoration of security, and the availability of finance, the necessary manpower and material resources, and upon the rate of economic progress. The Government, however, will not be deterred by the sedition of one section of the population from pushing on with schemes for the advancement of loyal members of all races in Kenya.

Many development projects for agriculture, industry, education, housing, health and communications are already in hand in accordance with the Development Plan for 1946–53, and further plans are now being made to cover the period up to 1957. The Kenya Government is encouraged by the success of this Development Plan to hope steady progress can be made towards realisation of its intentions. But ability of the Government to do more than it is now doing must depend on an early end to the Emergency followed by a period during which its exhausted financial reserves can be restored and it can build up economic strength necessary to carry through these plans.

The Governor and the Ministers of the Government have agreed upon the following objectives which have the support of Her Majesty's Government:

1) to use all the resources at their disposal to end the Emergency; but at the same time to ensure that in spite of the Emergency, development plans of all types are undertaken as rapidly as finance, manpower and the operational situation permit;

2) to ensure by the following means the effective maintenance of law and order throughout the country, and thus a solid foundation for continued development and reconstruction:

    (*a*) the intensification of closer administration by the establishment of additional administrative teams in both the African Reserves and the Settled Areas;

    (*b*) the progressive build-up of the Colony's Police Force to a point where the Provincial Administration and the Police can assume full responsibility for the maintenance of law and order without assistance from military forces;

(c) the education of African men, women, and children to accept the citizen's responsibility to assist the forces of law and order; and the improvement of relations between the police and the public;

(d) the rehabilitation of as many as possible of those who have been misled by the Mau Mau doctrine so as to fit them to take their place once more in society;

Economic Progress

3) so to improve husbandry and land use generally that the value of crops and livestock and the human carrying capacity of the land are increased as speedily as possible, while at the same time preserving and improving the fertility of the soil;

4) to continue the development and support of European farming and agricultural settlement, taking into account the recommendations of the Troup Report for European farming; and vigorously to accelerate the development of African farming on the lines of the Swynnerton Report. This is relevant not only to the rehabilitation and re-absorption of Africans displaced from their normal way of life by the Emergency but more especially to the acceleration of the economic advancement of the African peoples by the encouragement of cash crops, the consolidation and enclosure of holdings in African areas and the issue of appropriate forms of individual titles, which is an essential part of this plan;

5) to preserve and protect in perpetuity sufficient areas of Crown forests to ensure protection of climate, conservation of water and soil, and to provide adequate sustained supplies of forest products; at the same time, by accelerated development to provide in Crown forests employment for a part of the African population with their families; and to assist African Local Authorities in the preservation and development of their forest areas;

6) to complete the Colony's geological survey as a high priority, so as to exploit the mineral wealth of the country;

7) to encourage the rapid development of commerce and industry so as to absorb the growing population into useful economic activity and, at the same time, to increase the wealth of the Colony, thus enabling it to support and progressively to expand the social Services which are so urgently required; to provide large-scale opportunities for Africans in trade by means of technical education, and skilled occupations and, where necessary, to facilitate the importation of skilled persons from suitable places;

Social Advancement

8) to improve the quality of education for increasing numbers of all races, and in particular to expand African and Arab education at all levels; to insist on a spiritual basis for education through active co-operation with the Churches, the Missions and other religious bodies; to provide additional facilities in trade and technical education; to increase the

output of qualified Asian, Arab and African teachers; to increase the strict supervision of schools; and to move as rapidly as means permit towards compulsory education for the children of Africans resident in urban areas;

9) to institute adult literacy schemes, with particular emphasis on English, for Africans, Arabs and Asians with the object of helping them to raise their general standard of living;

10) to encourage the development of Young Farmers' Clubs, other youth organisations, and Women's Institutes;

11) to provide a measure of social security for employed persons in their old age;

12) to pursue towards Labour a progressive policy, including conditions of service and wages;

13) to improve the general standard of health, especially amongst the African population;

14) to improve the standards of housing in all areas, and especially for the least advanced sections of the Colony;

15) to provide housing, including home ownership schemes, and improved amenities for African family life in urban areas, recognising the special needs of the more advanced members of the African community; such facilities would apply in appropriate cases to coastal Arabs;

16) to encourage the creation of villages, with their attendant communal activities in appropriate areas.

Political Advancement

17) to appoint as soon as possible a body to study and advise on the best method of choosing African members of the Legislative Council;

18) to increase the effectiveness of Local Government in all areas particularly at the locational levels in African Districts, and to proceed with the progressive devolution of responsibility for appropriate services from Central to Local Government.

Kenya's Target

The statement of policy made by the European elected members of Kenya's Legislature is important to the whole of East Africa. European unofficial opinion in Tanganyika and Uganda has already given expression to the need Legislature in Uganda, those thoughts and discussions had a solid background of non-official opinion. In Kenya, with political progress temporarily checked by the Emergency, it appeared possible that, for all the liberal European thought available in the Colony, opinion might not be solid on the best means of putting that thought into practice; that, when the time came, the European elected members might be unready to give a lead and might, indeed, split among themselves on vital questions of constitutional reform in the interests of all races. A split would have been bad enough for Kenya alone; in fact, its results could hardly have been confined to Kenya when the African throughout East Africa (not to mention Central Africa) tends increasingly to pay more attention to nationality than locality. It is, therefore, encouraging to find that the Kenya non-officials' statement of policy is not only liberal but unanimous. It gives as its clear target the promotion of friendly co-operation between all groups and races in the Colony, and the building of a nation based on the interests of all its different peoples. Both Tanganyika and Uganda should welcome the Kenya aim. The former will find it akin to the views of its own settlers, who have much in common with their neighbours over the border. In Uganda the statement may go some way towards allaying African fears of the adverse consequences that might arise from any future East African federation (the Kenya statement, indeed, envisages such a federation).

The policy statement takes as a foundation nine principles enunciated by the Elected Members Organisation last August. At the time, Mr. Blundell, leader of the elected members, said, 'The principles will be lifeless unless they can be translated into policy which makes them realistic and active ... I hope that by the end of the year we shall be able to place before you ... a realistic, live policy to translate those principles into action....' The translation has now been made and the following are the main points of the policy statement:

1) Whatever changes there may be in Kenya's Constitution, British guidance and control must be maintained. It will be desirable for all groups to participate in the Government.
2) The transition from existing delegated government to national government is a desirable object, but only a gradual process of development can bring about a national Parliament with sovereign authority. Kenya's Government must for the immediate future continue to derive its authority from powers delegated by the British Government, while constitutional advance must grow from the present system whereby non-officials join the Government in a policy acceptable to them and their electorates. Constitutional changes must only be made after discussions between the Governor and leaders of all racial groups.
3) 'Partition' is rejected. Economically a partitioned state is unsound. Mr. Blundell, maintaining that partition substituted isolationism for leadership, said partitionists reminded him of a man retiring to the top of the Eiffel Tower to avoid the Parisians.
4) The existing policy of land tenure must be maintained, the best use of land must be ensured by law, Africans should be encouraged to grow cash crops and individual tenure by African farmers should be extended.
5) Posts in the Public Service should carry equal pay for persons of equal qualifications and ability, and salaries should be in accordance with responsibility, regardless of race.
6) The youth of all races should have a chance to serve their country in the armed forces of the Colony.
7) The European community must accept the responsibility of guiding African development towards maturity, with special consideration for those who have actively assisted in the struggle against Mau Mau.
8) In social relations, the status of all must be based on standards of behaviour.

Mau Mau into Citizens (1956)

(We give a special welcome in *Corona* to the three African officers in Kenya whose names appear below, and are glad to publish their joint article, sent through Major Breckenridge, who as a member of the Department of Community Development and Rehabilitation is closely concerned with their work.–Ed.)

We were extremely interested in the article published in *Corona* for December, 1955, and January, 1956, entitled 'Medicine for Mau Mau.' We, Wilfred Thimba, Jeremiah Gitau and Benjamin Wangendo, are Rehabilitation Assistants stationed in Works Camps for detained Kikuyu, and all three of us left our previous employment to undertake this work which we consider vital to the future of our tribe. We want to mention some of our experiences and some of the activities which we consider 'medicine for Mau Mau.'

It has been argued that rehabilitation of detainees is a waste of time and money, and critics have alleged that only physical force could be effective in quelling Mau Mau, and detainees would resuscitate Mau Mau after some time. The Kikuyus have a traditional belief that if one is defeated judicially one never returns, but if defeated with a club, one has to go and prepare for a further struggle. Rehabilitation defeats a man judicially.

It is realised in Works Camps that an idle mind is easy prey for the devil and detainees are sent out, after prayer at 6.30 a.m., to work on a land-development scheme. They return at two o'clock and rehabilitation takes over at three. This is where, under the guidance of a European Officer if we are lucky enough to have one, or with the help of our African staff of evangelists and elders, we begin to play our part. For the rehabilitation work to be really successful the staff must work as a close team (rehabilitation assistants, evangelists, classification team and European officers).

Selected detainees who have made good confessions and are known co-operators are instructed by us in the mornings in desirable subjects and we supervise their teaching of the other detainees in the afternoons. They are known as pupil teachers. Attendance at lectures and classes in literacy is voluntary and at least 90 per cent of the detainees come to them and understand that education is very important to them.

As the land question was the corner-stone of Mau Mau, our task is to teach the detainees how the Kikuyu land was alienated through error, how this was rectified by providing other land and cash compensation, and how the Government is developing Crown land for Kikuyu settlements. A comparison is vividly made of the benefit derived from British rule, economic progress, better communications, school services, hospital services and better methods of agriculture. They are informed that everybody, irrespective of his physical constitution, is entitled to possess property through *pax Britannica*. They are taught how their country is governed, how the taxes are spent for their benefit and how they participate in the government of their country, beginning with African District Councils.

Lectures are also given to illustrate how Mau Mau has cut across Kikuyu land and custom, as it was considered taboo to administer oaths to women and children, and how the movement has manifested its vice, defeating its own ends by the murder of babies, innocent people and aged ones. These lectures supplement simple literacy, geography, history and hygiene lessons.

Resident evangelists in each camp are supervised by an African Anglican clergyman who covers all camps in our district. He was sent by the Christian Council of Kenya to help us and he arranges religious instruction for all those who wish to have it. Periodical cleansing services for those who have confessed, baptism services and Holy Communion are held when required in the camps. Recently this clergyman conducted the christening of Jeremiah's son, which was attended by the whole camp. The God-parents were members of the European staff. Arrangements are made for Roman Catholics to have regular services and classes, and many camps have a Catholic catechist resident to take charge of this work.

A lot of rehabilitation time is taken up with religious instruction, because after the detainees have voluntarily disgorged the terrible Mau Mau oaths, the vacuum created must be filled with something durable. We and the evangelists spend a lot of time outside the allotted rehabilitation time talking to the detainees, encouraging them to confess and throw off the weight of Mau Mau. We lead and help them, and they come to us with any problem they may have. We have to deal with people of all ages – with the old man as much as the difficult adolescent. Benjamin is 23 years of age, Jeremiah is 27 and Wilfred is 40, a responsible man whose age enables him to be particularly successful with the older man as he understands the old Kikuyu traditions.

Following on the lectures, comes a very important section of rehabilitation machinery – the classification of detainees. A detainee who feels repentant goes to the classification team, and records his oaths and Mau Mau activities. It should be mentioned that no attempt is made to force the detainee to go to the team: it is entirely voluntary. The team may put a few questions to the detainee, partly to ascertain his sincerity, and partly to help him in his confession, but they try to convey as much as possible that they are the detainee's friend, and have been appointed to witness his confession and not to cross-examine him. At first this process is slow but it gradually gathers momentum. When a detainee makes an important confession, he is asked to make a public denunciation in front of all the detainees, and this makes many brave enough to come forward and confess. Confessing has the same effect as the traditional Kikuyu vomiting ceremony, whereby a witch-doctor would utter incantations, saying: 'Vomit the oath concealed. I extract it from you. Vomit the abominations that are in you.' Unless a man confesses, the Mau Mau oath is a disease he has concealed within him that will gnaw him inwardly until he dies. It is helpful to relate confession to a traditional ceremony of the Kikuyu people.

After confession, the people are divided into three main groups: those who showed great willingness to confess, those who are keeping something back from the team, and those whose names have been mentioned in various confessions, and deny all knowledge of the activities in which they are alleged to have taken part.

Committees have been formed in all the camps with a Rehabilitation Assistant as chairman and one man from each hut of 50 detainees in the compound as members. They are selected by the detainees themselves, and meetings are held once a week on a purely unofficial basis to decide points of interest. Sports, plays and allotment of rehabilitation time are discussed.

Jeremiah has organised a vegetable garden to encourage a practical interest in agriculture, and he also coaches sports teams. Benjamin has organised a scout troop, selected from a large group of volunteers of about the age of 20, and feels that the scout laws give the young men a practical guide on which to base their lives.

Short propaganda plays are sometimes written by Rehabilitation Assistants, and a terrorist, acted by a confessed detainee, only makes Mau Mau appear ridiculous. We feel we are a long way towards the cure when a man learns to laugh at Mau Mau and himself. Other plays may show the advantage of modern ways of agriculture, dipping of cattle to kill ticks and the unwillingness of backward people to agree to this, which are both entertaining and instructive.

Life in the camps is not without its funny moments. A tremendous team spirit is developed in a happy camp. One evening at about six o'clock a meeting was held to discuss whether detainees would like to work in rehabilitation time to build a church of mud bricks and grass, for services of all denominations. On being asked to discuss the project among themselves, the whole camp got up and asked if they could start building straight away. In the same way, when we attempted to form a small choir, all 900 detainees in our camp attended the rehearsals.

We believe that if the facts are imparted to the detainees and sincerity to serve them is shown, this will be a sure cure for Mau Mau. We think it important that they should be followed up after their release so that they may maintain what they have learnt in the camps and so be useful to the community in which they will live.

Up the Pipeline

by J. B. W. BRECKENRIDGE

In 1956 an article written by three of my African staff in the Kenya detention camps described some of the methods we were using at that time to rehabilitate the 70,000 men and women of the Kikuyu, Embu and Meru tribes detained as members of Mau Mau. A few comments on how the work has been carried out since then may be of interest.

A number of the more intelligent detainees were quick to see the value of rehabilitation, and in 1956 many of them were found to be acceptable again in their home districts, and were then released. This encouraged others, and for a time we went along surprisingly well, considering the nature of the work, and the human material involved. But soon we began to notice that a different type of detainee was coming through our hands – not necessarily a worse Mau Mau, but a much less intelligent *man*. It was obvious that such a type would require a much slower approach.

Whereas our classes had been voluntary and had had a bias towards literacy, we now had to slow down the whole process. The staff and myself had to re-group our teaching, and concentrate on the simplest lectures, making a point of reaching the slowest member of a slow group, through easy talks on farming, civics, and general knowledge. This went well, particularly a patient exposition of taxation, where your money goes, and how to improve the farm. These men had taken in Mau Mau doctrines slowly, and could only let them go slowly. At the same time we made every effort to stimulate a sense of enjoyment of life, with entertainments, singing, puppets and, of course, our primary work of patient teams interviewing and reinterviewing the man until he reached the stage of voluntary confessions.

A point of great importance here is that among those coming through, there were a fair proportion of what we call the intractables, as there had been all along. But, whereas the intelligent detainee, once on our side, ceased to fear the power of these intractables or agitators, the stupider man remained frightened and half in the hands of the agitator, and we had much more difficulty in isolating the agitators, and sending them to a special camp. This also slowed up the general process of large scale rehabilitation.

We removed the intractables and sent them to the special camps to await attention later. This was called sending them 'down the pipeline', while the man who did well went 'up the pipeline' to his own district, where the District Commissioner had camps through which he could pass to final release. At this time the energy and determination shown by the African staff was most encouraging; hardly a day passed without a new scheme being thought of to help or interest the detainees, and keep them from falling under the spell of the intractables.

It is hard for those not connected with the work to realise how vital it is to keep the detainees busy after the day's work is over. We enlisted their interest by offering prizes for the best hut, the best team in games, singing and dancing, and the hut with the best record of confessions and co-operation. Through the steady use of these tactics, a large number of men moved through the camps, and on towards eventual release.

At this time – about April, 1956 – I moved to Athi River Camp, near Nairobi, and still keeping up with the other camps in various parts of Kenya by visits, I concentrated my own efforts and those of a carefully chosen staff on the men I may perhaps call the intellectual intractables. These men had been arrested during the first days of the Emergency, as suspected Mau Mau leaders and organisers, and very few had taken more than the initial oaths, or had much direct connection with the later brutalities perpetrated by the forest gangsters. In fact, most of them had never seen a real gangster with his long hair and beard. On the other hand, they had been in detention for three years, and had not been rehabilitated at all. They were a group of clever men; some were well educated and the rest had been influential Kikuyu business men, with great power in the tribe. They were a most interesting study. My staff and I found that they regarded us with surprise and amusement rather than with dislike. My attitude was one of complete frankness. One was able to tell these men clearly what was wanted, and we held meeting after meeting in the compounds, at which numbers of my staff who were themselves ex-Mau Mau told their stories, and gave their reasons for coming over on to the Government side. This affected the Athi detainees very much, as most of my ex-detainee staff had been known to them *as* Mau Mau prior to their detention. At the same time, of course, we were carrying out a strong programme of our routine activities, and giving them a real chance to laugh – once a Kikuyu is laughing his best side is forward.

Among these detainees was a B.A. (Fort Hare) who had been caught by Mau Mau and oathed on his return from the University in South Africa. He was considered a very dangerous man, and had never confessed to anything of value. I sent for him and appealed to him, as an educated man, to help me to teach others, and to head my educational programme. He agreed, helped in a steady way for a week or two, then he went completely to pieces, could not eat or work, and looked terrible. After a few days of this, he suddenly came forward, made a full confession, which he repeated in front of the whole camp, and from then on never looked back. The ice was broken, and confessions began to pour in much faster than I had hoped. The awful nervous strain was often a necessary part of a detainee's determination to throw off Mau Mau, and was very marked in the clever, highly strung types.

At this camp we were able to establish a long cherished idea, that of a camp newspaper. We printed once a week, in Kikuyu with some English copies for official use. The paper contained news of detainees, camp affairs, a serial story, agricultural notes, jokes, and so on. It was intended for Athi only, but the men began sending it to their friends in other camps, and home to their families, and contributions poured in. We were given permission to extend it to other camps, and were always short of copies, for demand far exceeded supply. My wife began a series of articles on a young, progressive Kikuyu couple, and their plans for their home and future, and this became so popular that the courting couple in question became real Frankensteins to her, and she only got rid of them after a huge Christian wedding which took three weeks to describe.

After many of the detainees from the camp had been sent up the pipeline, it was decided that we should take the real intractables, who were being held on Mageta Island, where they had shown themselves hostile to any form of discipline. These men were put through Athi River in small batches. This was quite the hardest piece of work we had undertaken, but the co-operating Athi detainees rallied round us, and we planned the whole thing with their help. The Mageta men were brought in and sorted into small groups, each of which was sent to one compound, under the direction of a detainee co-operator acting as compound leader. Prison staff were, of course, standing by in case of trouble. The Athi men then began to talk quietly to the Mageta men, and pointed out how much better it would be to co-operate and join in things willingly. The Athi men were kind and friendly, and I remember their very sensible handling of a rather tough Mageta man who declined to work. Six hearty smiling co-operators picked him up, placed him in a wheelbarrow, and wheeled him off to the garden where he arrived a much quieter man, climbed out and got to work amid laughter.

A surprising number did co-operate, but we did have occasional bursts of rage from some of these men. After each such affair, we were able to spot the leaders of that sort of behaviour, and send them off in the normal way, to await attention later. Very often after a violent fit of rage, a man would suddenly come round.

These men were hardly normal people – they shambled as they walked in an animal way, with their mouths half open and their eyes narrowed to a slit. Dr. Carothers has mentioned this fact in his report on the psychology of Mau Mau, and has also dealt with the fact that oathing and confession or vomiting of an oath, is traditional among the Kikuyu people. It will therefore be easily understood what a vast change took place in such a man after he had confessed, and how his whole facial expression changed. The fear of confessing the oath was dreadful, and it was not surprising that we had some attempted suicides. All of these made confessions after their recovery, and made every effort to help others to confess.

The strain of their work on the staff was considerable, and that is an understatement, but slowly and surely we were getting results with the intractables and gradually, with many setbacks, we got them on the road to release. After these five years of work, there now remain only a handful, compared to the original number detained, who are yet to be dealt with. I should like to make it clear that of those released, almost 100 per cent have remained completely satisfactory where their local authorities are concerned, and this I consider the greatest proof that rehabilitation can turn a man or woman out to face the world again.

The Future of the
High Commission Territories (1953)

An issue in the coming general election in South Africa is expected to be a proposal to address a petition to the British Crown by both Houses of the Union Parliament for the transfer of the High Commission Territories (Basutoland, Bechuanaland and Swaziland) to South African administration.

Dr. Malan's statements and intentions on this matter have popularly acquired a more sinister tinge than they merit. There is nothing new in the desire to take over the Territories. During the last war the matter was held over, but South Africa has been raising it for forty years.

Geographically all three Territories are, in effect, enclaves in the Union, although Swaziland has some eastern boundary with Mozambique, and Bechuanaland marches with the Rhodesias to the north and north-east. (Southern Rhodesia has approached the United Kingdom about its claim to parts of northern Bechuanaland.) Economically all three Territories are most closely linked with the Union.

But it is in the political field that the greatest interest lies. The presentation of a petition would be constitutionally correct. Under the South Africa Act of 1909 the King in Council is empowered, if addressed by both Houses of the Union Parliament, to transfer administration of the Territories to the Union, subject to the safeguarding of certain native rights and interests which the United Kingdom Government has undertaken to observe. Repeated assurances have also been given in recent years that no transfer would take place without previous consultation with the inhabitants. There must also be full discussion in Parliament in London of proposals for transfer.

A point which will need much consideration is how far the provisions of the South Africa Act have been affected by the change in the status of Commonwealth countries since the Act was passed, as a result of the Statute of Westminster of 1931, and how far South Africa is now free to amend the Schedule of the 1909 Act which was framed to meet the United Kingdom's view of its obligations to the native inhabitants of the Territories.

The progress of the Territories under the United Kingdom's administration will also, no doubt, be cast upon the political waters in any future discussion, and much can be reported.

The basic policy has been the same for all three territories, namely to increase their own economic prosperity to a condition under which they will themselves be able to provide greatly augmented and improved services for their inhabitants.

But each territory has different problems to overcome before its economic level can be raised. In Basutoland an absence of minerals and little prospect of industrial development has thrown the burden of economic progress on to agriculture. A surplus for export is the target. But agriculture has been vitiated by soil erosion and consequently a formidable campaign has had to be undertaken; over three-quarters of all lowland, and half of the mountain, arable land has been dealt with by anti-soil erosion methods which world experts have described as outstanding. The defeat of erosion is opening the way to modern, mechanised farming and co-operative systems.

Bechuanaland's main problem is water supplies for the fine cattle which support the country's economy. The hope and the intention is to develop new cattle-raising areas from which greatly increased exports can be obtained, not least to meet the rising demand caused by the Rhodesias' mounting industrial expansion. The plan includes an abattoir and cold storage.

Swaziland is lucky in having no water problem ... the country has been called the 'hydro-electrical engineer's dream.' The possibilities of developing a quarter of a million kilowatts power are being examined, but the Territory has other strings to its bow. Private enterprise and the Colonial Development Corporation are involved in great forestry projects covering 200,000 acres. Under the present ratio of prices and costs these schemes will alone, when they mature in ten to fifteen years' time, produce as much revenue as Swaziland receives at present from all sources. Coal and iron exist in the Territory and large-scale production of ferro-silicates and manganese are potential industries of more than local importance.

The sums involved in this development are impressive. Since 1945 twelve million pounds (equivalent to twelve pounds per head of population) have been set aside, including Colonial Development and Welfare funds and Colonial Development Corporation expenditure, to initiate the progress which will eventually achieve the aim of providing first-rate services for the Territories from their own resources. But in the meantime social services have not been neglected and a considerable part of the Colonial Development and Welfare funds have been spent on them.

This brief survey is, for considerations of space, pared to the bone, but it will bring into prominence one important issue which must be in the forefront of any negotiations for the Territories' future: an improved economy depends largely on the building up of exports which will be of increasing value to the countries receiving them, and which can be assured only by long-term schemes. If the ships now launched on the tide of progress are checked in mid-stream, the consequences will not be confined to the Territories alone.

Central African Federation I

The London conference ended on the 5th May with the adoption of a resolution of sincere loyalty and devotion to Her Majesty the Queen and the Royal Family. The conference reached agreement on a draft constitutional scheme, which will be published as a White Paper as soon as possible and will, for the first time, provide an opportunity for the fullest explanation and discussion of a definite draft constitution, both in the United Kingdom and in Central Africa.

'The conference has agreed' – it was stated in a communiqué issued on the 5th May – 'on all important matters of principle, including the setting up of a Federal Legislature and Executive; the maintenance of the Protectorate status of the two Northern Territories and of the self-governing status of Southern Rhodesia within the federation; the composition of the Federal Assembly (including two elected Africans from each of the three territories); the financial implications of federation; the appointment and functions of a statutory African Affairs Board; the establishment of a Federal Supreme Court, and the procedure for amending the Federal constitution. The conference re-affirmed and gave effect in the draft scheme to earlier assurances on the subject of African land rights.

'It was decided to appoint fiscal, judicial and public service commissions to fill in the details of certain parts of the draft Constitution in the light of principles accepted at the conference. As soon as the reports of these commissions are available it is intended that a further conference shall be held to put the draft constitutional scheme into final form. It is hoped that this conference will take place in the last quarter of this year.'

'The conference recorded its regret at the absence from the discussions of African representatives from the two Northern territories, and paid tribute' to the contribution of the African representatives from Southern Rhodesia.'

'The conference believes it has devised a draft federal scheme which will work and will safeguard the essential interests of the three territories and of all the inhabitants.'

A draft statement on partnership, prepared by the Government of Northern Rhodesia as a basis for local discussion, was published in April. The full text is as follows.

The Policy

1) The ultimate political objective for the people of Northern Rhodesia is self-government within the British Commonwealth; self-government must take full account of the rights and interests of both Europeans and Africans, and include proper provision for both.

2) The only satisfactory basis on which such provision can be secured is economic and political partnership between the races, and this is the approved policy for Northern Rhodesia.

3) The application of such partnership in practice must ensure that Africans are helped forward along the path of economic, social, and political progress on which their feet have already been set so that they may take their full part with the rest of the community in the economic and political life of the territory. Africans for their part must be willing to accept the responsibilities, as well as the privileges, which such advancement entails.

There can be no question of the Government of Northern Rhodesia subordinating the interests of any section of the community to those of any other section.

The application of the policy of partnership is not in any way inconsistent with, and does not in any way interfere with, the territory's present Protectorate status. It imposes on each of the two sections (Europeans and Africans) an obligation to recognize the right of the other section to a permanent home in Northern Rhodesia.

4) In the political sphere, partnership implies that any constitutional arrangement must include proper provision for both Europeans and Africans and proper safeguards for their rights and interests.

5) Generally, partnership implies that Europeans and Africans will pay due regard to each other's outlook, beliefs, customs and legitimate aspirations and anxieties.

Putting the policy into progressive operation

6) In the political sphere, Africans will be able to advance until ultimately (so long as representation on racial grounds remains) they have the same number of representatives as the Europeans in both the Legislative and Executive Council, when they are fit for this. It is hoped to make early progress towards this end, and it is proposed that there should be an increased number of representatives of African interests in the next Legislative Council.

7) In the economic field every individual must be free to rise to the level that his ability, energy, qualifications and character permit. In accordance with its declared policy, that Africans in Northern Rhodesia should be afforded opportunities for employment in more responsible work as and when they are qualified to undertake it, the Government will continue to provide more and better facilities for the training of Africans for such work.

8) In the educational field the Government will, in co-operation with Native Authorities and missions, continue to work steadily towards universal literacy for all African children of school-going age and it will, in accordance with long-term plans already made, provide

expanded facilities for both secondary education and vocational training. The question of building in Central Africa a higher college for Africans is being actively pursued in consultation with the other two governments concerned and expert advice on the subject is being sought.

9) In the field of Local Government, the Government is training Africans to take a larger and a more effective part in the administration of rural areas. In the towns, African membership of African Affairs sub-committees of municipal councils and township management boards is extending, and it is to be expected that as Africans gain the necessary knowledge and experience, they will become members of such councils and boards.

10) In the Government service, Africans are being trained for and promoted to more responsible positions as they show themselves capable of assuming heavier duties and increased responsibility.

11) At the present state of development of Africans, repeal of all differential legislation would not be in their best interests; much of it is designed to protect them, and some of it grants them special privileges. It has been the policy of the Government to remove or relax the differential provisions in legislation as the advancement of the Africans renders such provisions no longer necessary. The Government will keep this matter under close review and propose to the Legislature, from time to time, such further amendments as it may consider appropriate.

12) As regards discriminatory practices based on racial distinctions, these are incompatible with the policy of partnership, and the trend of public opinion in Northern Rhodesia is towards a clearer recognition of this fact. Such practices are diminishing in Northern Rhodesia and will diminish still more rapidly as Europeans and Africans recognize each other's needs as well as their own obligations in this matter. The Government has taken and is taking steps to encourage, in both races, a sympathetic and helpful approach to this problem.

Central African Federation II

The draft scheme published as a White Paper (Cmd. 8573) on the 18th June represents the conclusions of the London Conference and both elaborates the recommendations of the original officials' Conference and differs from them in the strengthening of the safeguards for African rights. The Federal Assembly is to consist of 26 Elected Members (Southern Rhodesia 14, Northern Rhodesia 8, and Nyasaland 4), 7 Elected Members for African Interests (3 from Southern Rhodesia, one European and two Africans, and 2 from each Protectorate to be elected by the Territorial advisory councils), and 2 Appointed Members for African interests, one from each Protectorate. This arrangement will give a total Territorial representation of 17 for Southern Rhodesia, 11 for Northern Rhodesia and 7 for Nyasaland, and a total representation of African interests of 9 out of the 35 seats.

The principal safeguards for African interests are (1) the provision that the power of the Federal Government to acquire land shall be subject to the existing Orders-in-Council in the Protectorates and existing laws in Southern Rhodesia, which are to be specified in the Constitution (land legislation will, moreover, remain a Territorial responsibility); (2) an African Affairs Board, and (3) the safeguards in regard to amendment of the Constitution. The African Affairs Board, it is now suggested, should be an extra-parliamentary body of six members (one European and one African from each Territory) and a Chairman, none of them officials and all appointed by the Governor-General and responsible to him, but with access to the Federal Prime Minister. The Board will have the constructive duty of making representations (of both a legislative and executive nature) on any matter which it may consider to be desirable in the interest of Africans, and of scrutinising all Federal Bills and Regulations to see whether they are 'differentiating measures,' i.e. those by which 'Africans are made liable to any conditions, restrictions or disabilities disadvantageous to them to which Europeans are not also subjected or made liable, or which might in [their] practical application have a like effect.' Any measure so 'certified' by the Board must, subject to the agreement of the Governor-General, be reserved for Her Majesty's pleasure. Amendments to the Constitution may be made by Federal law, but (a) they will require a two-thirds majority of the Federal Assembly and (b) they must be reserved for Her Majesty's pleasure. Further if either a Territorial legislature or the African Affairs Board objects, an Order-in-Council will be required, the draft of which must be laid before Parliament and so made available for debate. It would, as Lord Salisbury said at a Press conference, be difficult to devise any safeguards more complete.

The composition of the Territorial legislatures is not subject in any way to Federal authority and the prospects of African political advancement in them are not, therefore, altered or endangered; the Protectorate status of Northern Rhodesia and Nyasaland is specifically confirmed, and in their Territorial affairs the Secretary of State's responsibility remains. In Federal matters, as Lord Salisbury has explained, the channel will be the C.R.O. but he will naturally consult with the Secretary of State for the Colonies and, in the event of disagreement, the question at issue would be referred to the Cabinet.

The draft contains two lists of Legislative powers: those which are delegated to the Federal Government, and those which can be exercised by both the Federal and Territorial Governments, provided that in case of inconsistency Federal Law shall to that extent prevail. All other powers are to remain with the Territorial Governments. The Federal ('Exclusive') list covers external affairs, public utilities, and the like, and, notably, immigration, broadcasting, all non-African education and Higher Education for Africans. The second ('Concurrent') list covers other subjects of predominantly local interest, such as National Parks, census and town planning; others which affect both European and African interests – such as health, produce marketing, industrial development, and films – and others which, according to circumstances, may be either of Federal or Territorial concern, such as roads and water development. Everything else, including African political administration and local government, African primary and secondary education, agriculture and animal health, and (because of the present differences in policy) Trade Unions and industrial conciliation, remain the sole concern of the Territorial Governments (and, in the Protectorates, of the Colonial Office) exactly as at present. It is, in fact, clearly the intention that in matters affecting Africans, including those on the Concurrent List, there shall be the least possible interference with the *status quo*. Flexibility is, however, provided by giving both the Federal and Territorial legislatures power to delegate authority to each other within certain limits and to revoke such delegation. The financial structure of the Federation, the constitution of the Federal Public Service, and of the Federal Judiciary have still to be settled and three special Commissions have been set up to draft proposals. The first Commission is required to have regard both for the existing rights and prospects of serving officers and to provide for retirement on 'abolition' terms. The policy should be to work towards uniformity in terms of service between the Federal and Territorial Services to encourage interchangeability. The rights of retired and transferred officers of the Colonial Service are also to be preserved. And the site of the Capital is left unsettled.

It is hoped that this short and incomplete analysis of a complicated, 38-page document will be found helpful and reasonably clear. The scheme is now to be submitted, with the full support of H.M.G. and all three Territorial Governments, to public opinion both here and in Africa, and, when the three special Commissions have reported, it is proposed to hold another Conference, this time in Africa. Only after that would the issue be put to the statutory Referendum in Southern Rhodesia and to the northern legislatures. Meanwhile none of the Governments is committed.

It is now the duty of our colleagues in Northern Rhodesia and Nyasaland to explain the scheme to the Africans and the reasons why H.M.G. supports it. One of the functions of this Journal is to try to help officers in the Service in their work and what follows has that intention.

The moral dilemma which confronts many people on this issue, at any rate in Britain, may perhaps be summed up in the question 'Is Federation so urgent and desirable that it must be achieved even if African opinion cannot be won over to it?' The first thing to remember is that a decision on this will not have to be made unless all efforts to change African opinion fail. Secondly, if they succeed, there will be no dilemma left, except perhaps on other grounds for some Europeans in Southern Rhodesia, because the great majority of people accept the Federal solution as being in itself right. Those who have prepared the scheme have obviously tried to incorporate into it every political safeguard that can be devised, and by so doing to resolve the potential dilemma. Nevertheless, there are certain very important aspects of the matter which were not sufficiently emphasised in all the premature arguments before the White Paper was published and it may help if they are mentioned here and at this stage.

First, there is the argument of realism. All of us who have served in West Africa since the war know that the policy followed there, which was condemned by a section of British public opinion as weak and sentimental idealism, has been above all things realistic. The issue now in Central Africa is similar except that those who favoured the realistic course in the first case are reluctant to pursue it to its apparently different conclusion in the second, because that conclusion may conflict with the democratic principle that the will of the majority must, regardless of the consequences, prevail. All of us share this reluctance in varying degrees, but we must face the facts of the political situation in Southern Africa just as frankly as we did those in West Africa. In the face of them this scheme is not put forward as a design for Utopia but as an inevitable compromise designed to achieve a great and urgent purpose and, in the process, to protect the interests and to allay the fears of both Europeans and Africans.

This federation is indeed a great purpose, in no way less important than those other federations, of Canada and Australia for example, on which the foundations of the great nations of the Commonwealth were laid. It is also urgent because, as Lord Salisbury also said, this may be the last chance we shall be given to build up a multi-racial society north of the Limpopo based on the British way of life. The formation of the Union of South Africa itself gives strong negative support to the historical argument. The racial and constitutional difficulties which now endanger it result not from the Act of Union, which has made a powerful and prosperous country out of a collection of petty states, but from the fact that the growth of South Africa took place before western thought awoke to its true responsibilities in race relationships. South Africa is entangled in its past and is trying to solve its difficulties with a philosophy which is ill-attuned to that of the rest of the free world. And these are precisely the factors which make the federation of

Central Africa, based on the principles of inter-racial co-operation, so urgently desirable. The prospects of possible discontent among a few Europeans and many Africans in the next few years are not so important as the future verdict of their grandchildren. There were similar divisions of opinion in Canada and Australia all those years ago, but they proved to be ephemeral in the face of the progress and prosperity which federation brought. Little has been said of all this except in Sir Godfrey Huggins' speech in the Southern Rhodesian Parliament on the 24th June and recently in the House of Lords.

Those who are honestly trying to face the situation as it is must also ask themselves what may happen, both immediately and in the years to come, if federation is abandoned or delayed? It is becoming increasingly clear, since the feelings of the local Europeans are just as sensitive as those of the Africans, that the rejection of a federal scheme specifically founded on an offer of inter-racial partnership by the Europeans may well be the greatest danger of all to race-relationships and the future happiness of both Europeans and Africans. It is also worth considering whether there are in fact any greater political safeguards for the Africans, at any rate in Northern Rhodesia, under the present constitutional arrangements than those proposed in the White Paper, and does not the threat just mentioned give this an additional importance? Some people discount this offer of 'partnership' because they do not believe that it is genuine or, if it is, that, in the face of the formidable difficulties of carrying it into obvious practice in daily relationships, it cannot be made effective. But, again, there is no tolerable alternative. The *only* practical, constructive course for responsible European and African leaders is to assume that those who say they accept the principle of partnership mean what they say and will, if given the opportunity, prove their honesty by their conduct – but they must be given both that opportunity and leadership and

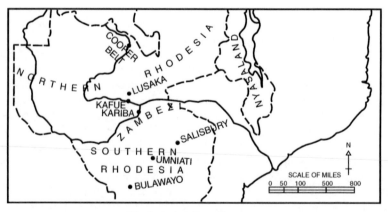

The Central African Territories

this may call for some difficult and courageous decisions. In any case the potentialities of the present situation in Central and Southern Africa are surely such as to induce any responsible person at least to take a constructive attitude towards the proposals and to try to win African support for them.

Meanwhile the first fence confronting Administrative Officers in Central Africa is how to persuade Africans to discuss the details of the scheme at all. It is fair to say that in it an honest attempt has been made to meet every concrete expression they have given of their vague and very understandable fears, and it may be that this first obstacle may prove to be the highest of all. Let us hope that it is even now being cleared.

Malta

SOME PROBLEMS OF SELF-GOVERNMENT

An interesting study in the responsibilities of self-government and in the constitutional relationship of a self-governing colony with the British Government is provided by a non-Parliamentary White paper (Col. No. 253. H.M.S.O. 4d.) which has recently been published, setting out the details of the negotiations which took place last summer with the Malta delegation to London.

Since 1942 the taxpayers of this country have, both in recognition of the gallantry and sacrifices of the people of Malta during the war and as part of the policy of colonial development, given or allocated nearly £34 million to Malta, made up as follows:

	£
War Damage and Reconstruction grant	31,000,000
C.D. & W. Allocation	1,000,000
Additional C.D. & W. grant to the Royal University	125,000
Contributions towards food subsidies in 1946–47, 1947–48, and 1948–49	1,650,000
	£33,775,000

From the first two of these grants considerable sums still remain to be drawn by Malta. The Island has virtually no public debt and at the 31st March, 1949, the reserves of its Government stood at nearly £2 million.

Malta's economic problems are, however, very serious because it has a population of over 300,000 which is increasing by about 8,000 each year, and relatively little productive capacity. Its economy has always rested to a disproportionate extent on employment provided by the Admiralty in the dockyard and by the other two Services, and the announcement by the Admiralty that for financial reasons and following the reduction of the size of the Mediterranean fleet from its war-time strength, it would have to reduce the number of its dockyard employees by 1,200–1,300 caused the Malta Government very grave concern. The average employment in the dockyard before the war was about 7,000, rising to over 8,000 in 1938. In July 1949, before the reductions began to be made, the labour strength was 12,500, and even after the reductions the annual wages bill will still be £2$\frac{1}{4}$ million as compared with £800,000 before the war.

There is no need here to go into the details of the negotiations, the salient point being that, whereas the Malta Government thought Britain had a historical responsibility for maintaining the high level of employment in the dockyard, His Majesty's Government could not accept such an argument, which implied bolstering Malta's economy by asking the Admiralty to pay, from moneys voted for Defence, men whom it did not need for work which did not exist.

Similarly the delegation asked that Britain's contributions to the Island's food subsidies should be continued in order to keep down wages, although it had previously been made clear that the contribution for 1948–49 was positively the last. The reply to this was that a subvention of this kind was also inconsistent with Malta's constitutional position.

The third claim made by the delegation was that Malta was not receiving its rightful due under Marshall Aid. The negotiations on this point served to emphasise that Malta has, so far as dollars are concerned, exactly the same privileges and responsibilities as any other colony.

Broadly the Malta Government considered that Britain had moral responsibilities for the people which had not been fully discharged by the grants already given. The problems of over-population and the worsening economic situation of the colony were stressed by the delegation. In the absence of more information than was made available by the Maltese to them, the United Kingdom Government, in the light of the present financial position of Malta, did not consider that an economic crisis was imminent but, from the long-term aspect, there was admittedly a serious problem to be faced. The grant of self-government implied, however, full financial responsibility because without it self-government could not be a reality.

In the outcome it was suggested to the delegation that it would be worth their while to have an expert enquiry made into the long term problems of Malta's economy. The United Kingdom would gladly help in finding a suitable expert, but it was constitutionally the duty of the Malta Government, and not of His Majesty's Government, to take the lead and institute such an enquiry.

In this brief note we have not tried to set out the details of the discussions nor to assess the merits of the argument, but merely to show, for future reference elsewhere, the kind of problems with which a colony may be faced when it attains self-government and how the constitutional principles underlying self-government are likely to be applied. And, of course, none of this has made one iota of difference to the admiration and affection which this country and all the other members of the Commonwealth have for Malta.

Malta's Immediate Future

After the visit of the Maltese delegations to London and the resulting failure to devise a Constitution for Malta generally acceptable to the political parties there and to Her Majesty's Government, it became necessary to make special interim arrangements for the island's government.

An official statement was published simultaneously in London and Malta, and the Governor of Malta amplified the statement in a broadcast to the people.

The statement recalled that Malta had had no elected Government since April, 1958, when Mr. Mintoff resigned and Dr. Borg Olivier declined to form a Government. Disturbances at the time necessitated the proclamation of an emergency, and since then the Governor had governed under his emergency powers.

Against that background, and regarding earlier negotiations for Malta's integration with the United Kingdom under which Malta would have enjoyed far-reaching self-government, it was hoped that the political parties of Malta would have been able to agree at the Conference in London with Her Majesty's Government on a new Constitution which would have given Malta self-government in most fields. Although the integration negotiations had not borne fruit, there had been a substantial measure of agreement and the Secretary of State for the Colonies was prepared to discuss with the Maltese delegations a new Constitution drawing its inspiration from those agreed measures.

It was not possible, however, to arrange a plenary conference with all three delegations. The Malta Labour Party, at meetings and in correspondence by Mr. Mintoff with the Secretary of State, took the view that future constitutional arrangements must be based on immediate independence or independence by 1962, and persisted in that view after the serious consequences to employment in Malta and to the island's economy had been pointed out. Although there were valuable exchanges of view with the Nationalist Party delegation (which required assurances beyond those which Her Majesty's Government were in a position to give on Malta's eventual position in the Commonwealth) and with the Progressive Constitutional Party's delegates, the attitude of the Labour Party made it fruitless to discuss constitutional arrangements with that Party's delegation.

Her Majesty's Government had no alternative, therefore, but to revoke the present Constitution and to make special interim arrangements necessitating legislation which would shortly be introduced into Parliament.

It was proposed that the Governor should he assisted by a Council on which there would be Maltese representation. During this interim period the Governor would press on with economic development, with a main aim

110

of attracting new industries. An important step, already taken, was the decision to convert the Naval Dockyard to a commercial ship repair yard and to develop associated industries.

In his broadcast in Malta the Governor, Sir Robert Laycock, said that the new Constitution which it had been proposed to offer would have been much more liberal than the existing Constitution and would, in effect, have given elected Ministers full powers and responsibilities for the affairs of Malta subject only to satisfactory arrangements being made for defence and external affairs, and for the independence of the police and public service. At the conference Malta's many economic problems – most importantly the dockyard issue – could have been discussed.

'But what happened? The conference was wrecked by Mr. Mintoff's insistence from the start on demanding immediate and full independence for Malta. He was asked whether by this he meant that all ties between Malta and the United Kingdom should be severed, that British aid to Malta should cease, that all British forces and defence installations should be withdrawn and that Britain should in future treat Malta as a foreign country. In reply he requested immediate and full independence in the *full* knowledge of the economic consequences of this decision and, as he said, with the full support of the majority of the Maltese people ... In the course of the many letters Mr. Mintoff sent to the Secretary of State during the talks he never altered his demand for full independence. He did say that he was prepared to discuss an interim Constitution to run until the grant of full independence in January, 1962, provided that, during the time, the Maltese Government could negotiate defence and any other agreements with any country it wished. These agreements would take effect from the date of Malta's independence. This would simply mean postponing the economic disasters for Malta for two years.'

Sir Robert explained some of the ways in which Malta and its people would be hard hit by independence and mentioned the strings likely to be attached to any aid which any foreign Power might have reason to give to Malta. 'Mr. Mintoff,' he said, 'no doubt believes that full independence is the best thing for you ... I think it would be a terrific gamble, with your livelihood and welfare at stake and with the dice loaded against you from the start.'

Saying that he thought it wrong to continue the present state of emergency and that there must be interim constitutional arrangements the Governor said: 'I intend to do all I can to ensure normal conditions and, equally important, the free expression of public opinion ... My first responsibility is to the ordinary law-abiding people. I shall continue to do my utmost to ensure that they are not subjected to disturbances by anyone – whether it be actual physical disturbance or incitement to violence and disaffection in the Press. I shall have no hesitation in invoking the law firmly and deliberately in order to achieve peace and good order in Malta ...' Referring to certain remarks attributed to Mr. Mintoff about the loyalty of the Civil Service to the present Government and about the police, Sir Robert paid a warm tribute to the Service and added: 'As for the police, they are in great heart and they remain as always the defenders of peace and good order in these islands.'

Public Services in the West Indies

FIRST STEPS TOWARDS UNIFICATION

P ublished simultaneously with the Closer Association Committee's report is the report of the Commission on the Unification of the British Caribbean Public Services. This Commission was also appointed after the Montego Bay Conference in 1947, under the Chairmanship of Sir Maurice Holmes, G.C.B., formerly Permanent Secretary of the Ministry of Education. It included one representative from each colony. The report, like that of the Closer Association Committee will now be discussed by the West Indian Legislatures.

The Commission make it clear that they had to deal only with proposals for Unification of the Civil Services of the West Indian colonies. At present certain senior posts can be filled by the Secretary of State appointing to them members of the Colonial Service from other colonies; otherwise the great majority of Civil Servants in the West Indies spend all their careers in their 'home colony.' In a unified Caribbean Civil Service its members would be liable to serve in other West Indian colonies. This would give them better opportunities, and do something to foster the growth of a 'Caribbean' sense of citizenship. The position of a member of a Unified Colonial Service as regards promotion and transfer to and from the Caribbean would not, of course, be affected by the present proposals.

The Commission consider these branches of the Service as suitable for unification: Administrative, Agriculture, Civil Aviation, Forestry, Legal, Medical, Police (Commissioned ranks), Postal and Prison. Clerical and executive personnel would continue to serve in their 'home colony.' Promotions and transfers within the region would be made by a Caribbean Public Services Commission of four.

Chief among the problems which the Commission examined is a means of securing entrants of good educational qualifications who could eventually attain to the highest posts. In 1946, all but 287 out of 11,318 posts with salaries of £600 a year or more were held by West Indians, but of these the great majority had entered in the lowest clerical and even messenger grades. The Commission recommend that a new Cadet grade in the Administrative Service be created, to attract young men with University degrees, and look forward to the West Indies University College proving a most valuable source. They do not, however, wish to prevent higher posts in the Administrative Grade being filled by promotion of experienced clerical officers, or by promotion of young clerical officers at an early stage in their career to the Cadet grade.

The Commission admit that the existing differences in practice among the West Indian Governments are so great that it is at present impossible to prescribe common conditions of service and basic salaries for a Unified Service. They maintain, however, that this state of affairs should not prevent a fair measure of effective unification. The Commission make it clear that they were not asked to plan for the 'Federalisation' of the West Indies' Civil Services. While the creation of a Federal Government would solve most of the difficulties, even such a measure of unification as could be achieved beforehand could be a valuable stepping-stone towards Federation.

The Enugu Report (1950)

The report of the Commission of Enquiry into the riots which began at the Enugu colliery on the 18th November, 1949, and, spreading to other places in the Eastern Provinces, eventually resulted in the death of 21 people and the wounding of 51 others, was published on the 10th June together with despatches exchanged between the Secretary of State and the Governor. The Commission consisted of Sir William Fitzgerald, K.C., Mr. R. W. Williams, M.P., Mr. Justice Quashie-Idun of the Gold Coast and Mr. Justice Ademola of Nigeria. Their report is unanimous.

The introduction, which sketches the political background, contains a clear warning that no time must be lost in impressing upon the people that 'a civilised government cannot be carried on by the mere drawing up of a document containing a statement of the rights of man, followed by a draft constitution.' The people must first have their economists, engineers and doctors.

The Enugu colliery has a long history of declining output per man, from 63.5 cwt per shift in 1941 to 33.5 cwt in 1948, whereas hewers' wages rose from about 3s. a day to over 6s. during the same period, while the labour force had also doubled. All this is the result of suspicion, mistrust and industrial disputes. In order to restore productivity a Joint Production Committee, containing workers' representatives, should be set up as soon as possible.

Against this background the Report then sets out the depressing story of the continual friction over wage-rates and the 'go-slow' strikes which culminated in the bloodshed of last November. The Commissioners describe this period as marked by the continued unscrupulous behaviour of Ojiyi, Secretary of the mine-workers' union, who tried to bolster up his own position with the workers and against his rivals by fomenting trouble with the management, and also by some ineptitude on the part of the latter, as a result of which the workers gained the impression that 'go-slow' tactics paid. In addition to exposing the 'worthless and dishonest Ojiyi,' the Report accuses the newspaper *New Africa* of lying when it said that £80,000 was due to the Enugu miners and was being deliberately withheld from them, and then says that 'the major part of the press of Nigeria discloses a degree of irresponsibility that bodes no good for the people of the country or for the furtherance of their political aims.'

The 'go-slow' strike of hewers which began on the 7th November, 1949, was concerned with wage-rates and arrears of pay. The report says that if the efforts of Mr. Ojukwa, a Nigerian member of the Board, had been properly followed up there might have been some response, and that to post up on the next morning 50 notices of summary dismissal instead was a 'major blunder.' The Governor, however, in his despatch, points out that similar action had been effective before, that the November strike was merely the continuation of a series, and that the men all knew exactly where they stood. Moreover, there was no one with whom to negotiate except Ojiyi and that was useless. In recounting the story from 16th November onwards, the Commission criticises the Chief Commissioner on three grounds: that he did not call the newly arrived Senior Labour Officer to his daily consultations, that he wrongly treated the dispute as political rather than industrial, and that he should not have instructed the police to remove the explosives from the mine 'at all costs.'

The Governor considers that the Commission has been 'less than fair' to the Chief Commissioner and his advisers. He points out that Commander Pyke-Nott's daily meetings were concerned with security, and maintains that he did not treat the situation as political but as industrial and, after a certain point, as a problem of law and order and public security, which is not the same thing as a political dispute. He further states that no order was in fact given to remove the explosives 'at all costs,' and takes the opportunity of paying tribute to the Chief Commissioner's 'devotion to the people of Nigeria and the passionate sincerity of his desire and determination to help them to progress.' The Secretary of State agrees with the Commission that it would have been better if the Chief Commissioner had not refused to continue negotiations lest that be construed as 'a sign of weakness,' and that use should have been made of the Senior Labour Officer; but he accepts the Governor's view that the Chief Commissioner was not thinking in terms of a political dispute, and also that he did not give the order to the police in the words which the Report had criticised.

From the story of the shooting at Iva Valley it emerges that no labour was provided for removing the explosives from the mine to the police lorries and that the quantity to be moved was found to be six times as great as had been stated by the Management. The Police were kept hanging about for hours waiting for an engine and truck and for labour while tempers were frayed and tension was rising. As a result Mr. Philip, the Senior Superintendent in charge, decided to move his 125 men across a bridge on to a hill and away from the crowd. He had got all except 35 of them across when he decided that the attitude of the crowd was menacing and that he must open fire. He intended than only three men should fire, but in fact firing took place from ranks all down the line and from the hill and, when the cease fire was given, it was only 'the prompt action of Mr. Brown, Superintendent, in knocking up the rifles of individual policemen that made them stop.' Mr. Brown is commended for this. The Commission concludes that the crowd was not armed, in that they only carried their usual sticks, picks and other implements; that, although it was 'noisy and screaming and getting worked up,' it was not attacking the police and would not have done so unless they had tried to move the explosives, which they were not, in any case, proposing to do themselves. The conclusion is that Mr. Philip made an error of judgement, that he 'did not appear to have complete control over his men' and that, while he acted in all honesty, he 'fell short of that standard that might be expected from one of his rank and seniority.' The Governor, in his despatch, accepts this finding and has since announced that Mr. Philip will not be returning to Nigeria.

The subsequent riots at Aba, Port Harcourt, Onitsha and Calabar are then described. In every case the actions of the Administrative Officers and the Police are either commended or approved. The conclusion is that the tension was exploited in the Eastern Provinces by political extremists.

The main recommendations of the Commission aim at isolating industrial disputes from political agitation. All Government industries should be run by independent statutory Boards; within these industries and in large private undertakings, Conciliation Boards should be set up, operating in two stages, a Negotiating Committee and a National Reference Tribunal. The former should have equal representation of management and workers; the latter should consist of three permanent members from outside the industry appointed by the Chief Justice, and would deal with questions referred to it by the Negotiating Committee or by the Government. All questions relating to industrial disputes should also be removed from the sphere of the Administrative Service, and a Central Government Ministry of Labour should be established. Sir John Macpherson says that the Minister will, in fact, be a Nigerian Member of the Central Legislature. The Secretary of State is sending out experts to help the Governor to establish the new machinery, particularly and as quickly as possible at Enugu.

Political Evolution in African Territories

by THE RT. HON. VISCOUNT CHANDOS, D.S.O., M.C.

One of the most fruitful sources of error is to regard the racial problems of Africa as one. The mere use of the term 'African' starts by putting discussion on the wrong foot. The African of the Mediterranean littoral differs from the African in Nigeria or the Union of South Africa more than an Englishman differs from a Rumanian.

The face of the great African continent, like that of all great land masses, shows the marks of many migrations and changes which have come upon its inhabitants over the centuries. The Nile Valley was the birthplace of one of the oldest civilisations, the North African littoral bears the marks of Carthaginian and Roman domination. In Central and East Africa those who speak the Bantu language form about two-thirds of the whole of the population of Africa south of the Sahara; in West Africa we find negroes who speak the Sudanic languages, and from the North and North-East the sons of Ham, the pastoral Hamites, penetrated into the rest of Africa and inter-married with the inhabitants: the half-Hamites, the Masai and the Baganda are typical examples. Thus the racial problem is not susceptible of a comprehensive, uniform discussion or analysis.

If the Europeans fall into these initial errors, it is hardly surprising that the Africans themselves, particularly in the Central African Federation, are apt to regard constitutional changes in other parts of Africa, perhaps in Nigeria or the Gold Coast, as strictly applicable to their own territory.

The first essential, therefore, in discussing either constitutional or social changes, is to realise that they must be very different in almost every African country. From the constitutional aspect, the proportions of the indigenous population to the European are of the first importance. These are often determined by Nature – that is, by climate and not by design or man-made influences. In other cases, economic causes are at work which increase the proportion of immigrant Europeans. The great gold-mining industry of the Rand and the Orange Free State, and the Copperbelt and Wankie Colliery of Northern and Southern Rhodesia are the obvious examples.

To these differences must be added the great differences that are found within the African population itself, to which some reference has already been made. For example, among the 31 million inhabitants of Nigeria there are nearly 17 million Northerners, who are predominantly Mohammedan in religion and who, racially, differ from the Ibos and Yorubas of the South as much as the Latins differ from the Teutons.

On the other hand, in the Gold Coast there is less of a racial problem among the Africans: it is racially a far more homogeneous country than Nigeria.

It is, therefore, necessary largely to isolate these problems and never to imagine that constitutional or social experiments in one territory have necessarily any significance for any other African territory, merely because they happen to be carried on within the continent of Africa.

Two subjects touched upon above require further explanation: first, the climate of these countries and, secondly, their economy.

The racial problem between Europeans and Africans will obviously become most acute in those parts of Africa, such as the Rhodesias and the Union of South Africa, where the white man can make his home, generally enjoy a climate that is far more agreeable than the misty islands or western coast of Europe from which he has sprung, and where, above all, he is able to educate his children and see them grow up as citizens of the country of his choice and not of his birth.

There are others, such as Sierra Leone and the Gold Coast, where the wonderful advances of medical science have, it is true, expunged from our vocabulary such phrases as 'the white man's grave,' but where, nevertheless, the heat and humidity of the climate make permanent settlement by the European almost impossible. These two are territories in which young white children cannot thrive after early age, and from which they have to go home to be educated, or be sent to schools situated in more temperate parts of the African continent. It is thus most unlikely that the racial problem of the Gold Coast will ever present itself in the same form as it is presented in (say) the Union. On the other hand, in the Central African Federation the problem may easily grow to the size and importance which it has there assumed.

The beginning of any survey of these questions must be to examine the racial proportions. In the Union of South Africa there are 9 million Africans and over $2\frac{3}{4}$ million Europeans. In the Gold Coast there are 4 million Africans and 7,000 Europeans. In the Central African Federation there are $6\frac{1}{2}$ million Africans and something over 200,000 Europeans.

The second subject to be touched upon concerns the economy of these countries. The rate at which European settlement will take place is, of course, governed not only by climate but also by the nature of their economic development.

It would, I think, be true to say that many of the great undeveloped spaces of the world have owed their growth in modern times to the mining industry. . . .

The part gold mining has played in the development of the Union of South Africa is clear for all to see. Equally, the growth of copper mining in Northern Rhodesia and the new developments that can be expected, the resources of water power that are about to be harnessed, the coal mines at Wankie, all seem to be the forerunners of great industrial development, which will attract European immigration and which cannot be achieved without it.

Many other territories, however, will depend for long years to come, as far as can be seen, upon agriculture, particularly on peasant agriculture, as opposed to plantation industries. There is far less attraction of Europeans to these agricultural communities than to the industrial or semi-industrial evolution of the other parts of the continent.

Before I come to discuss what is loosely known as the Lyttelton Plan in Kenya, it is necessary to state again that remedies that may be appropriate to one territory may well have no application to another. Both the constitutional structure and the rate at which constitutional changes are desirable vary in every case, and the idea that any one constitution is a nostrum, or remedy, for another will lead to the father and mother of confusion, and will once again lead the laity and the ignorant to imagine that the term 'African' has some ethnographical significance, and is used as such, rather than as a convenient term to differentiate Africa from America or from Asia or Europe.

'*Countries are governed by force or by tradition,*' said Disraeli. But if we examine the British Colonies, Protectorates and Territories in Africa it must be clear that we cannot govern them by force; nor if we could, would we wish to do so. We have certainly got the force – and recent events prove it – to restore law and order when it is threatened – and those who think that the hand of the British Government is powerless have learned their lesson. This, however, is a different aspect of the subject. It is the imposition, day by day, of a system of government out of harmony with the governed for which we have not the force, even if we desired to use it.

British opinion – and it is shared by all political parties – believes in fostering and cherishing the consent of the governed to the government. We believe that the desire to have a share and a voice in his own government is an innate, ineradicable trait in the nature of the human being. We believe that it is necessary to accept much of the slowness, ignorance and inefficiency of democracy, much of the uncertainty that surrounds government when democratic elections are pending, because, in exchange for these many ills, we gain the two inestimable advantage – and perhaps the only two – of such a system. The first is the power to change without revolution, and the second to share the responsibility of government in some measure with the governed ...

Seretse Khama (1950)

Neither the Colonial Service nor its Journal can with propriety enter public discussion on such a controversial matter of colonial policy as the case of Seretse Khama. The decision and actions of the Government may have been right or they may have been wrong, but we, as a Service, are now concerned only with facing the situation with which they have confronted us – the danger to race relationships throughout the Colonial Empire and the setback which may have been caused to our work. This is a question of fact and one which is, in this case, unlikely to be much affected either by the Government's explanations or by argument. It was inevitable from the start that if the decision were unfavourable to Seretse, whatever the reasons for it and however sound they might be, he would become a symbol. Many Africans, even on the West Coast, might be expected to agree that it would be politically undesirable for any Chief anywhere to have a white wife, particularly where there is patrilineal succession; and there would be a great many Africans, who if they knew all the facts, would fully appreciate the issues involved in the rivalry of factions within the Bamangwato tribe and all the other important administrative questions involved, but there could never have been any hope that such reasonable and, of course, debatable views might prevail. It was no doubt fully realised that the whole question would, regardless of the facts, be interpreted solely in terms of colour prejudice and that no reasoned arguments on other grounds would have very much affect. The dilemma which faced Sir Walter Harrigan and his colleagues, and subsequently the Cabinet, was indeed formidable. Any decision, whether favourable to Seretse Khama or not, was bound to be condemned by one important section of opinion or another, and in either case the condemnation would not be based on the administrative aspects of the case. There has been a good deal of criticism of the Government's refusal to publish the Committee's report. Perhaps its members are inclined to feel relieved.

As it is, however correct the decision may have been, it has in fact resulted in a setback to the work of the Service not only in every African colony but also in the West Indies and, since Moscow has eagerly laid hold on such a fine new weapon, in the East. The Service has directly or indirectly been devoting itself for years, and with an ever increasing sense of urgency to the improvement of race relationships; now everywhere some ground is likely to have been lost and it must be regained. Fortunately, perhaps, the Service is not unused to sensational embarrassments in this particular field.

At the time of writing, one West Indian Legislature has protested but the reactions of the colonial press have not very clearly emerged and we will not prophesy. It is possible that the virtual unanimity of the British press on the subject may induce some colonial editors to adopt the same attitude and to wield the stick which events have handed to them not against us as a people but against the Government; it may not, in fact, become essentially a racial matter at all, and this should at least make the position of the individual officer easier simply because he, as a person, would not be involved. It may also happen that the efforts, said to be now under way, to reconcile Seretse Khama and Tshekedi will bear fruit. Mr. Gordon Walker has agreed that such a reconciliation 'would amount to a new factor and would necessarily involve us in a very careful reconsideration of the matter.' Only our colleagues in Bechuanaland, for whom all of us feel great sympathy in their present difficulties, know fully the intricacies in which such a situation is always involved, but we elsewhere, who must be mainly concerned with the broad racial issues that have risen to bedevil it, would not be human if we did not hope that our difficulties may, in one way or another, turn out to be less serious than we have feared.

b) COLONIAL AFFAIRS IN PARLIAMENT

A special aspect of *Corona*'s remit to keep the Colonial Service abreast with what was going on in the wider context of colonial affairs was the regular reporting of the parliamentary debates, speeches and reports in which colonial affairs featured. This was done by compiling a digest of parliamentary debates, questions and other references to colonial policy and the Colonial Service as reported in *Hansard*.

Although simply to reproduce verbatim reports today from yesterday's parliamentary debates would run the risk of being otiose reportage, since readers are far more likely to have readier access to *Hansard* than serving Colonial Service officers could ever have enjoyed in the 1950s, the rationale of the original purpose of this major, regular item in *Corona* deserves reiteration here. 'No-one who works in the Colonies can afford to be indifferent to British public opinion about them. Parliament presents that opinion to the world not only in Debates but in innumerable Questions on matters which are the Service's daily business'.

Parliament (1949)

THE COLONIAL DEBATE

I n opening the annual debate on colonial affairs in the Commons on the 20th July the Secretary of State began by inviting the attention of members to various reports which had recently been published in addition to *The Colonial Territories 1948–49*. He said: 'I think it will generally be agreed that, as a people, we may take a reasonable pride in the work going forward in our colonial territories, and the work described in the general report is, I think, a great tribute to our colonial officers overseas as well to the staff of the Colonial Office itself. I would hasten to say that, obviously, we are not satisfied with the situation as it is at the present time. We are all guilty of short-comings and inadequacies of treatment of some of the problems confronting us in our colonial territories. Nevertheless, I think the work which has been done is sound and will bear the test of time.' He asked the House to bear in mind that while it 'must exercise responsibility in regard to the shaping and development and application of policy in the territories overseas, we are, at the same time, devolving to those territories and their local governments a great deal of responsibility, and consequently they are in charge of the detailed administration of policy in their own countries. We cannot unduly interfere with that administration without to some extent weakening their own responsibility for the administration of their country. I would add 'continued Mr. Creech Jones' that most of our colonial territories are going through a state of transition in regard to political, economic and social changes, and we cannot expect that those changes will be carried through without trouble, difficulty or disturbance. It is natural that we should do all in our power to create conditions for orderly development by reducing so far as is possible the internal strains and securing not only the internal co-operation of the peoples in the territory itself but also their full co-operation with us in the work which we too are trying to do.' There was a great quickening of interest in colonial affairs in this country, the Colonial Month had stimulated it, and every effort was being made to spread knowledge by all possible means. The Secretary of State then turned to policy. 'What,' he asked, 'is the broad purpose we have in mind in regard to colonial policy? None of us in these days seeks the mere satisfaction of colouring red great areas on the map. Our effort is to bring stability, good order and mutual prosperity to the world; to do this with the co-operation of the colonial peoples by building up the colonial territories responsibility and the conditions of good living. Hon. Members will recognise that this laudable purpose can be achieved only in so far as it evokes the response, understanding and the confidence of the colonial peoples themselves. We wish them to appreciate the values which actuate us in our own affairs. Consequently we are anxious in our relations with the colonial peoples that there should be a steady elimination of all discrimination and full co-operation with them in the great tasks which have to be performed.'

Since the war some 8,500 officers had been recruited by the Colonial Office and the Crown Agents; but there were still 1,395 vacancies in the Colonial Service, including 163 for doctors, 150 for agriculturalists, 38 for veterinary officers, 160 for teachers and 170 for engineers. 'But,' he said, 'although we have adopted various devices, so far we have not been able to overtake the demand. We are, of course, endeavouring to meet the situation by improving the conditions of service; by improving the amenities enjoyed by the colonial servants; by shortening the period of service; by improving the pensions; by providing facilities for children in respect of their education; by improving housing, and by a whole number of other things in order to make the Service more attractive to the colonial servants.

'We are also making a very strong appeal to the universities, the public schools and other schools. We are trying to make known the technical vacancies in the respective professional journals. By paying visits to a large number of organisations and societies, the Colonial Office are trying to arouse the interest of young men in the most attractive prospects which exist. In addition, we hope to arrange with certain of the services for periods of secondment from this country. Already we have come to an understanding with the Ministry of Education. We hope that a similar arrangement will be possible with the medical service. We have a scheme for probation officers, and we hope that before long a number of secondments will be arranged with other technical services. These arrangements will preserve seniority, pension and salary rights in the British services when the people have finished their duties in the territories overseas.'

The next part of Mr. Creech Jones' speech supplemented the Report by describing some of the many functions undertaken by the Colonial Office and its advisory Councils and Committees, mention being made of Higher Education, Surveys, the welfare of colonial students in this country, the organisations of all kinds of research, and the co-ordination of economic and marketing policies. Turning again to the colonies themselves, the Secretary of State emphasised the 'very considerable contribution' made by them to the dollar pool of the sterling area, and assured the House that, although, in present circumstances, the market for some of the principal colonial products had recently slumped and although colonial governments were readily co-operating in the lowering of their ceilings for dollar purchases, every effort would be made to avoid any curtailment of development or any lowering of living standards. A new harbour was being built at Mikindani in Tanganyika, and in West Africa port facilities at both Freetown and Takoradi were being enlarged. An economic survey for new railways linking Central and East Africa had been completed and technical surveys, by Messrs. Gibbs and Company and their American subsidiary, were about to start. New airfields were being made at Hong Kong and Livingstone. Power from the Uganda hydro-electric scheme should be available by 1952 and similar projects were being investigated on the Volta River in the Gold Coast, in British Guiana, in Borneo and on the Zambesi. The supply position in the colonies had become 'very much easier,' though sheet steel and some agricultural machinery were among essentials still hard to come by. Owing to new demands and changing circumstances it was probable that the money provided under the Development Act might be exhausted sooner than had been expected and a new Bill might be required 'within a comparatively limited time ahead.'

Mr. Creech Jones then turned to technical training, for which all colonies were now working out systematic plans. The Yaba Institute in Nigeria, for instance, had been turned into a technical institute with boarding accommodation for 250 boys and facilities for over a thousand others. Trade training was going to be given at Enugu and Kaduna and plans were going ahead for Regional Colleges in the other West African colonies. There was also a big expansion of technical instruction in Fiji and Malaya.

Speaking of industrial development the Secretary of State said 'It is important that more enterprise should be encouraged in our territories. While it is true that there has been a great deal of public enterprise in respect of public works and utilities, and so on, there is, nevertheless, very considerable room for private enterprise as well. Therefore, we hope that capital from both the United Kingdom and from foreign States may be available in order that the development of some of these backward regions may go forward.' The Colonial Development Corporation was prepared to enter into arrangements with private undertakings in regard to important works. The Corporation had as much freedom in these matters as any big private undertaking. Every encouragement was also being given to the small producer by Co-operation and other methods. Successful resettlement schemes had been put into effect in Kenya and Nigeria. As regards marketing the bulk purchase of primary commodities had been of 'tremendous service to the people overseas.' In particular, the West African cocoa scheme, for which Mr. Oliver Stanley had 'had some responsibility' had been of immense benefit to the Gold Coast and Nigeria.

Turning to political development Mr. Creech Jones said 'We all accept the view that if political development is to be soundly conceived, there must be adequate social and economic development in order to support it.' After mentioning the Regional Organisations and constitutional developments which had taken place, he emphasised the importance of local government. 'I do not think,' he said, 'we can proceed fast with political development until we expand the social services and the conditions of good living, and until we build up in the territories a sound economic basis to sustain the social services which we are trying to create.' The Secretary of State ended his speech with these words: 'Our job, as I have said, is to build up good living conditions and responsibility in these territories overseas. I believe that the recent drive in economic development is calculated, not only to meet the needs of the external world, but to provide the colonial peoples with the wherewithal to build up their services and meet their own demands for development. I therefore feel that we have before us today a magnificent record of work of which we can be justly proud and in regard to which we owe an enormous debt to those who have brought about such remarkable changes and progress. I end by paying my tribute again to those officials of the Colonial Office and of the Colonial Service who have contributed so much to the progress in these territories.'

The debate which followed lasted for four hours. During this period eighteen Members made speeches in addition to Mr. Oliver Stanley, who wound up for the Opposition, and Mr. Rees Williams, who did so for the Government. We understand that about fifteen other Members also wanted to speak but, in spite of the self-discipline of those who did so in condensing their speeches to an average of thirteen minutes each, they had no time. The fact that there were over thirty actual or potential contributors to the debate, apart from those who were holding themselves in reserve for the debate on African affairs which had been set down for the 29th July, is a better guide to the degree of interest in colonial affairs among Members than their attendance figures. In fact the average attendance during the debate was about forty. Members are kept so busy with Committee work and other duties outside the Chamber that forty is, we believe, about the normal attendance nowadays at any debate, except those dealing with matters of critical *and* immediate importance or in which a Division is likely to take place.

The tone of the debate was set by Mr. Lennox-Boyd (Cons.) who paid 'the fullest possible tribute' to the Report of the Secretary of State, which provided a basis on which all parties could work, and ended by saying: 'I do not think we are doing at all badly, and to all in the Colonial Service, whether in Whitehall or overseas, we of the Conservative Party wish the success they deserve.' He had, of course, warnings to give and criticisms to make – as did many of the speakers who followed him, each on that aspect of colonial administration in which he was most interested, but the tone throughout was essentially co-operative and constructive. The chronic temptation to make 'party points' was nobly, though not always, resisted and there was a very evident understanding by most speakers of the difficulty of colonial problems and of the genuine efforts which are being made to solve them.

Mr. Oliver Stanley (Cons.) in winding up for the Opposition, summed it up like this: 'The chief impression left upon me by this Debate has been one of considerable consensus of opinion . . . . . the lion and the lamb lying down together . . . . . I am glad that there should be this community of feeling among the majority of people on both sides of the Committee. I know that in this Chamber we eschew references to one's own personal feelings, but I do feel most deeply upon this matter. I believe that about the most important thing for this country over the next ten or twenty years will be the development of its relationships with its Colonial Empire, and I feel that about the most important element in its success or failure will be the maintenance of some unity of purpose between the various parties in the State. Whatever the line, whoever is right, I cannot conceive of success coming from a programme and an objective liable to be altered at intervals largely as a result of considerations which have really nothing to do with colonial matters at all.

'I am not interested in who has been responsible for bringing about this closer proximity . . . . . The fact I am interested in is that we appear to have arrived, at any rate, at some community of purpose and some unity of purpose. That does not mean for one moment that we do not disagree with each other. It does not mean for one moment that whoever is in power will not be criticised by the other side, or that we shall not have differences as to tempo, administration, or detail. I hope and believe that it means now, and will continue to mean in the future, that on the general broad details of colonial affairs we are and shall remain united.'

Mr. Stanley welcomed the setting up of the Overseas Food and Colonial Development Corporations. He reserved comment on the former, but he was not in the least disappointed to see that the Colonial Development Corporation had comparatively little progress to report. He believed that the slower approach at the beginning would turn out to be faster in the long run. As regards bulk-buying, he said: 'I am against it outside the Empire because I think it usually gives a hard deal to the consumer. Inside the Empire, it may well be that people in this country will voluntarily assume a deal bad for themselves in order to help, by that, the people in the colonies for whom they are responsible.' But the test of the system was coming with falling prices. Mr. Stanley wondered whether the educated and politically minded people in the colonies realised the difficulties that lay in front of them. Were we not giving them much too easy an impression of the road they would have to follow? Somehow we must bring these difficulties home to them. No amount of generosity by this country could solve their problem. Success in our colonial policy would depend not on us but largely upon the colonial peoples, 'upon their willingness to face realities and make sacrifices, on their willingness to put all the effort and skill in their country into it.' This 'may well be the deciding factor,' concluded Mr. Stanley, 'in the continuance of this country, not only as a world Power but as a country which can offer to its people a respectable and decent standard of life. Therefore, whatever the difficulties, we are all determined to offer these people all the help we can, and more and more to take them into partnership with us in order that we may together reach a solution which will redound as much to our benefit as it will to theirs.'

There was little left for Mr. Rees Williams to do, in replying for the Government, except to thank Members for their tribute to the Colonial Service and to add his own to the staff of the Colonial Office. He recommended to Members a study of the development plans for the new colony of Sarawak and then passed on to deal with various questions which had been asked in the course of the debate. In regard to rubber he said: 'We consider that the price of rubber is as low as it can go with safety. If it goes any lower there will be very great danger in the Far East. It will be difficult to maintain any security in that vital area.' And on that note, the debate ended.

We have devoted all our space in this issue to the Colonial Debate because that is its due, but there was a good deal of other colonial business during July, including quite a big debate on Africa. Thanks to the summer recess, we shall be able to give a brief description in our next number and so complete the record.

Parliament (1949)

Only one colonial debate took place before Parliament was prorogued on the 16th December and that was on the 14th, in the House of Lords, when heavy artillery was brought to bear on the groundnuts scheme. Viscount Swinton opened the barrage with a demand for an 'independent expert Inquiry .... with special reference to the future.' The wording of the Auditor's certificate alone, he said, was sufficient cause for an Inquiry. Such a certificate in respect of an ordinary company would certainly lead to an investigation by the Board of Trade. The report itself showed 'on almost every page' how costly and disastrous the lack of preliminary surveys and experiments had been; it was now hoped finally to cultivate one fifth of the acreage at double the capital cost – and Mr. Strachey talked of 'reconstruction.' What would have been said of a private enterprise which had put such a proposition to its shareholders? For quick production we should have looked to Nigeria and its peasant cultivators. He challenged the Government to deny three propositions: they did not know today in any of these areas what could be grown commercially and on what scale; they did not know whether the ground could be cultivated economically by mechanical means, and they did not know whether, if the crop would grow, it could be properly harvested by machinery. These questions were fundamental and should have been answered by experiment before the millions had been spent. Mr. Strachey had said that he had confidence in the reconstituted Board and its Chairman. Who else had, or in Mr. Strachey? It was said that an Inquiry would undermine the morale of the men on the spot. It would do nothing of the sort. Their advice and representation had been ignored, they had been dragooned into silence, and that was one of the reasons why an Inquiry was demanded.

Viscount Hall, opened the retaliatory fire by repeating the early history of the scheme and by emphasising that all Parties had given it their blessing and that the U.A.C. had handed the project over to the Corporation with many of the worst problems unsolved and a very inadequate costing system. What was the point of an Inquiry? The Corporation intended to carry out its programme as announced, and the Public Accounts Committee of the House of Commons had already begun its examination into the accounts. Much had been learned by experience and an Inquiry would be most unsettling for the men on the spot, who were themselves the experts and were doing their job remarkably well. There would be no Inquiry. Mr. Strachey had flown to East Africa to reassure the staff, whose misgivings were, he maintained, not due to lack of confidence in the Board but to the political attacks of the Opposition.

Lord Milverton did not feel that Mr. Strachey's visit would, in fact, reassure the staff; only his resignation would do that. And what right had

128

Mr. Strachey to ask the taxpayer to double his stake merely on his own assurance when, so far, his assurances had been proved so wrong? Everybody wanted the scheme to succeed but it had become the laughing stock of the world and it would remain so until there had been an Inquiry.

Lord Winster, in a milder tone, wished that the Colonial Office had been in control, but he thought that an Inquiry would inevitably develop into a profitless witch-hunt. All parties were determined to make a success of the scheme. Our prestige and our duty to the Africans demanded it; and it was more than a mere food scheme, it was a great development project and, above all, an answer to the African demand for progress. The Bishop of Lichfield and the Earl of Lucan both emphasised this wider aspect, saying that the scheme could only be judged as a major contribution to the development of Africa. Up to this point the Opposition gunfire, though heavy, had been of a pattern to which those who, in this long battle, have manned the Government position, must by now be well accustomed. Viscount Bledisloe, however, whose fire was, of course, concentrated on the agricultural practices of the Corporation, fired a new piece with an ominous note. Rosette disease, he said, might yet prove to be the most serious problem of them all. He also referred to the dismissal of Mr. Wakefield as 'very unfortunate, if not deplorable.' Lord Rennell detailed examples of mismanagement, and then shifted his aim to question the qualifications of Sir Leslie Plummer. In this the Marquess of Salisbury followed him and brought the attack to a close by declaring that the Government's refusal to hold an Inquiry was an insult to Parliament and to the public.

In replying to the debate Viscount Addison admitted that mistakes had been made and that further difficulties were still to be expected, but the Corporation, which had only been in control for twenty months, hoped to make a success of their new reduced programme, He said that the attacks made on the Chairman were bound to have a disturbing effect on the men in the field, and quoted the activities of *Picture Post* as a 'choice example of the campaign' which was doing so much damage. The Government was determined to support both the Board and its staff, and refused this 'so-called Inquiry.' On a Division the Government was defeated by 57 votes to 27.

In the Commons on the 16th December, Mr. Noel Baker made a statement on discussions which he and Mr. Creech Jones had had with Mr. Beadle, of the Southern Rhodesia Government, about Central African Federation. He said that they had pointed out to Mr. Beadle the difficulties inherent in political federation, particularly in regard to the Africans in Nyasaland and Northern Rhodesia, and had suggested that the Southern Rhodesia Government should provide a further statement of its views after it had re-examined the situation and had considered further the possibilities of the Central African Council and other means for closer economic co-operation.

Answers to questions during the fortnight included the information that there was still no evidence that the bandits in Malaya were being given direct material assistance from the Communist Party in China or elsewhere outside Malaya. More than 150 had surrendered since the announcement of the surrender terms on the 6th September.

Mr. Herbert Morrison said that the Government was not prepared to set up a Royal Commission to consider the advisability of establishing colonial representation in the House of Commons because of the large variety of colonial constitutions. Mr. Chuter Ede told Mr. Gammans (Cons.) that he was aware of the fact that members of the Colonial Service who were paid by Colonial Governments had no vote in this country. He considered that this accorded with the intention of Parliament when it enacted Section 6 of the Representation of the People Act, 1948. Mr. Gammans pointed out that officers in the Consular Service did not suffer from the same disability, but Mr. Ede replied that this anomaly should have been raised when the Bill was being debated.

Parliament (1950)

THE COLONIAL DEBATE

S
o far as colonial debates are concerned June always the most prolific month of the Parliament year. This time, in addition to the annual debate on the Secretary of State's report, to which we devote all our space in this issue, there were debate in the Lords and others in the House of Commons We will describe them, belatedly, next month.

We went to the House this year with some fore-boding, because we imagined that all but a handful of members would, particularly in the present international situation, wearily and thankfully take the opportunity of such a debate, which concerned no immediate crisis and in which a Division was inconceivable, to go home and rest. When, about half-past seven, our turn in the gallery came round, we found, on the red benches beneath us, a shifting population of about fifty members, of whom more than half were jumping hopefully to their feet at the end of each ten minute speech; it is, in fact, the experts or would-be experts who attend these debates and almost all of them hope to catch the Speaker's eye, but somebody really ought to have explained the habits of Parliament to all the colonial visitors who were waiting in queues for their ration of gallery time.

The Secretary of State began to speak at twenty minutes to four and sat down fifty minutes later. He started by paying tribute to Mr. Creech Jones and by regretting the absence, through illness, of Mr. Oliver Stanley, and it was pleasant later on, to hear more than one speaker from both sides of the House, go out of his way to acknowledge the services of both these statesmen to the Colonial Empire and to regret their absence. Mr. Griffiths restated the aim of our policy, with emphasis on the establishment of 'those economic and social conditions upon which alone self-government can be soundly based,' and then passed to a review of the year's work. Dealing first with economic matters, he stressed the contribution of the colonies in helping to close the dollar gap, and cited the recent sugar agreement as an example of the efforts which are being made to guarantee stable markets for their products. Exports to the colonies, both of materials and consumer goods, were now much more plentiful and development was really getting into its stride. £12,900,000 of C. D. & W. Funds had been spent in 1949–50, which was exactly double the amount for the previous year, and the figure for 1950–51 was estimated at £19,500,000. Finance rather than staff and supplies was once more becoming the limiting factor and thought was already being given to the question of increasing the funds available under the Act. He referred to the setting up of a Rural Development Authority in Malaya with Dato Onn as its first Chairman and then passed to the efforts which were being made to establish an international organisation for the co-ordination of transport development in Africa. The vital need was to give the inland territories adequate access to the sea; preliminary meetings had already been held at Lisbon and Paris and there would be a full-scale conference at Johannesburg in October. Meanwhile the Biera convention had been signed and the detailed engineering survey of the Central-East Africa railway project had already started. The Colonial Development Corporation had now approved 45 undertakings with a total capital commitment of nearly £25 million, more than a third of the investment being in long-term agricultural and forestry schemes. After referring to E.C.A., and remarking that now only a small portion of the equipment needed for development had to be obtained from the United States, Mr. Griffiths ended his economic survey by saying that, as a result of the Sydney Conference, Malaya, Borneo and Sarawak were now producing six-year development plans for consideration by the British Commonwealth Consultative Committee in the Autumn.

Dealing next with industrial relations the Secretary of State said that the Enugu Report was a challenge to all concerned and emphasised the 'supreme importance' of establishing sound trade unions and good labour relations everywhere; they would be of 'immense importance in this transitional stage in our colonial affairs.' So far there were 1,000 Trade Unions with a total membership of over 600,000. Turning to the social services, he characterised the elimination of malaria from Cyprus and the successful campaign in British Guiana as a 'realty wonderful achievement' and said that later this year there would be an international conference in East Africa to plan an attack 'on a continent-wide basis.' A similar co-ordinated campaign was being planned against tuberculosis in all the colonies. In the educational field special mention was made of the expansion of education in Malaya, the new Universities and technical colleges, – and the 'Saucepan Special.' Mr. Griffiths then spoke of the work now being done for colonial students by the British Council and made a 'very earnest appeal' to people in this country to give the students their hospitality and friendship. Against this background he next outlined the constitutional developments of the past year and those now pending, and commended the recent Report on Federation in the West Indies to the Legislatures concerned. Grenada had already voted in its favour. The political problem of East and Central Africa was 'easy to state but most difficult to solve'; most anxious thought was being given to it and he hoped to arrange for the Minister of State to visit East Africa very shortly. Mr. Griffiths begged everyone to realise that 'this problem can be made infinitely more difficult of solution by ill-considered speech and action.' He then turned to recruiting difficulties and said that, in spite of every effort to train more and more local candidates, 'there is no foreseeable decrease' in the need for expatriate officers. Over 1,400 appointments were made in 1949 and more than 800 since but the vacancies had nevertheless slightly increased to 1,500. Now, however, the flow of recruits was 'encouragingly higher.' In paying a tribute to the Service, Mr. Griffiths said, 'I can think of no more worthwhile job that a man can undertake today, and no field in which there is more to be done.' He then confirmed that a Supplementary Estimate towards the cost of the war in Malaya would be sought and ended by expressing the belief that his Report showed that, in guiding and assisting the colonial peoples towards self-government within the Commonwealth, we are being faithful to our trust.

Mr. Eden, deputising for Mr. Oliver Stanley, opened for the Opposition and said that he agreed very much with the definition of our colonial policy with which the Report opened, but would add a sixth requirement, – 'that it is dependent on the transfer of power to the people and not only to a minority of the people concerned.' He had the 'clamant minority' in West Africa particularly in mind. A recent article in the *Manchester Guardian* on the recent political success of the Convention Peoples Party, had quoted Dr. Danquah as saying, 'We shall soon have to choose between white imperialism and a black dictatorship.' He then referred to the comments on the Nigerian press made in the Enugu Report, described many of the West African papers as 'more like broadsheets ... filled with poisonous misrepresentation,' and, in view of the serious consequences likely to arise, suggested consultations with the Empire Press Union and perhaps the appointment of a Commission. Enugu had made it clear that the chief problem was the future of Trade Unionism and he welcomed the sending out of experts to Nigeria. He liked what Mr. Griffiths had said about East and Central Africa and agreed with him that European leadership and guidance would be necessary for as long as could now be foreseen. He too supported the proposals for Federation in the West Indies but warned that we must be careful not to give the impression that it was being imposed from Whitehall. In pressing for sympathetic consideration for the financial needs of Malaya, Mr. Eden said that full details of the dollar contribution being made by the various colonies ought to be published; this would encourage the colonial peoples and put a stop to complacency in Britain. We must strengthen our propaganda and carry the colonial peoples with us 'not merely by order but in their hearts and in their convictions.' The message of Parliament to the Colonial Service should be one of congratulation and confidence, and to the colonial peoples one of encouragement to work with us and of 'deep friendship and good will.'

Mr. Reid (Lab.) is a neo-Malthusian and he warned the Government that merely to raise the standards of living, which will not be easy, will not defeat the Communists, who are 'cashing in' on the colour question and flying the flag of racialism. Much more intense propaganda is needed and rapid radio development. He praised the decentralisation of the Colonial Office and called the Colonial Service 'the pick of our race.' The exaggerations of several other speakers on this theme, which we will not repeat, were equally charming and some fifteen thousand pairs of ears must have simultaneously burned from Tristan to the Pacific. Mr. Harris (Cons.) urged a closer integration of economic policy between the colonies and Britain, a proper balance between public and private enterprise in East Africa, and more emigration from this country. What, he wondered, could not have been achieved in the development of those territories with the £35 million that has been spent on the Groundnut Scheme? He realised the value of Trade Unionism but we must remember that some colonial peoples were much more advanced than others, and he was disturbed by the recent growth of Communist influence in Kenya. Mr. Gammans (Cons.) emphasised that 'a bowl of rice cannot stop a Russian tank' but remarked on the general unanimity that existed on colonial policy. Not enough publicity was being given to the dollar earnings of the colonies. If more people in Britain realised that should we lose Malaya we would also lose our breakfasts, they might give more credit to the Colonial Office and to the colonial peoples. He also agreed with Mr. Eden's strictures in the West African Press, asked for a Royal Commission on the colonial press generally, and went on to discuss the dangers besetting colonial Trade Unions. In Malaya they had been dominated by Communists and in Nigeria by racketeers, and when these two obstacles had been overcome nobody joined them. In Malaya now only five per cent, of those eligible belonged to any Union. Trade Unionism was not an end in itself. In present circumstances, constitutional reforms were not really relevant; in Malaya 'for every person who was interested in ballots about a thousand were interested in bullets.' The colonies could not defend themselves and we should already have built up a great Colonial Army. He was glad that we were now roundly declaring that self-government meant self-government within the Commonwealth. This was the only way to rally moderate opinion on our side, and our worst failure had been our inability to carry the intellectuals with us. Mrs. White (Lab.) stressed the importance of the proper social treatment of colonial students both in this country and on their return home and urged that wives of both students and members of the Colonial Service should be more adequately trained in these matters. Mr. Wigg (Lab.) regarded the West African Press, Zik and Nkrumah alike as useful safety-valves and urged the Secretary of State to get Nkrumah out of gaol as soon as possible. Mr. Selwyn Lloyd (Cons.) did not consider that the Enugu Commission had done justice to Senior Superintendent Philip and hoped that the matter could be debated again. Nor did he think that the present plans for developing the harbours and railways of West Africa were nearly adequate. He had been distressed by the uneasiness of moderate African opinion, and the extremists must not be allowed either to poison our relations with the people or to stampede us politically. There should be a strictly adhered to time schedule for constitutional development. The Press was not a safety-valve; it invited bloodshed. Some sort of control, short of abolition on suspension, was very necessary. We were the 'only defence against anarchy, civil war and Communism' and we must restate our principles. Mr. Johnson (Lab.) in a short, but thoughtful and well informed speech, warned the Committee against optimism about economic development in Africa, and particularly stressed the need for more geological surveys. The main contribution to the solution of our political problems must come from West Africans themselves. More of them must reject the glitter of law, commerce and politics and dedicate themselves to the service of their people. Mr. Sorensen (Lab.) said that we must convince the colonial peoples that we were aiming at free and not enforced co-operation with them. He criticised the fact that on all the boards of the Colonial Development Corporation and its subsidiary bodies there was only one colonial representative, and hardly any men with direct colonial experience. The lesson of the Enugu report was not that colonial Trade Unions were a mistake, because, for good or ill, they were indispensable. Mr. Lennox-Boyd (Cons.) wound up for the Opposition. After welcoming Mr. Griffiths and paying a tribute to Mr. Creech Jones, he voiced the thanks and good will of the House to the people of Malaya and asked for an emphatic assurance that we had no intention 'of withdrawing from our permanent partnership' with them. The Government had not handled the West Indian sugar negotiations skilfully and must not, by international agreements, jeopardise the future of Imperial Preference. The Conservatives stressed the need for economic development because self-government without economic independence would in all cases be a mockery, but they did not hope to postpone inevitable political advance. After stressing the necessity for holding the balance between the various regions and classes in West Africa, Mr. Lennox-Boyd referred to the position in Tanganyika and reminded the Committee that there was only one European for every 1,600 Africans in British Tropical Africa. This was evidence of our genius for that kind of leadership which the African valued. We must not bewilder him by abandoning it. The problem of recruitment for the Colonial Service must be solved, but not by sending out the second rate. Pericles had said 'We have more at stake than those who have no such inheritance as ours,' and though the Conservatives had certain disagreements with the Government on Imperial policy, they were relatively trivial and like them they believed 'that the future destiny of the British colonies is self-government within and not outside the British Empire.' But we must carry the people with us and must make a new approach to the problem of propaganda and the law of libel and sedition.

The Minister of State wound up for the Government. One or two backbenchers had made rather ill-informed speeches which we have not had space to report, and Mr. Dugdale devoted much of the short time available to giving them the facts; community farming schemes, for instance, were already being tried in Africa; American geologists, though not enough of them, had already been made available; and steps were already being taken to meet the locust threat from the Middle East. He agreed that action must be taken to prevent irreparable mischief being done by the colonial press, but it must not be repressive; he also agreed that more should be known about the dollar earnings of the colonies, particularly of the smaller ones, but figures could only be given by the Chancellor of the Exchequer. We were engaged on an economic revolution in the colonies; it was a very big task and it must be done in a planned and orderly manner. We were trying also to build up social democracy and to ensure that the colonies peoples played an ever-increasing share in it. This was a task that would take years to achieve but we would not look back until it had been carried out.

Parliament (1951)

T he two important statements, about Central African Federation and Constitutional reform in Tanganyika, which were made during the month led neither to much immediate questioning nor to early debates. On Federation, Mr. Griffiths elicited assurances that the African Affairs Board would have statutory access to the Federal Prime Minister, that the next conference was to be held in the last quarter of this year, probably in October, and that either Mr. Lyttelton or the Minister of State would be going out to Central Africa before then. (And one Conservative member remarked rather wistfully that if the British Constitution had had the same protection as that suggested for the Federation, the requirements of a two-thirds majority for its amendment, our Universities would never have been disenfranchised.) The statement on Tanganyika drew warm support from Mr. Griffiths, an irrelevant hope from Mr. Dugdale that Northern Rhodesia would follow Tanganyika's example, and a refusal by Mr. Lyttelton to commit himself to a policy of Closer Union in East Africa. 'Prophets,' he said, 'are without honour in their own country.' A third statement, reporting on the short-lived disorders in Bechuanaland led to little but gloomy acquiescence in the principle that the first duty of any government is to maintain law and order, though Miss Lee (Lab.) found it difficult to believe that those of the rioters who were drunk could really have included any women. Mr. Foster had sadly to disillusion her and also to point out that women had no right to be in the *Kgotla* anyway. That such things could happen only showed into what a sorry condition the Bamangwato had now fallen. He hoped they would now set about choosing a new Chief and putting their house in order.

There were only two short, but not unimportant, adjournment debates on Colonial affairs. On the 11th, Mr. Ian Winterbottom (Lab.) proposed that an additional Clerk-Assistant to the Speaker should be appointed for the express purposes of helping the growing daughters of the Mother of Parliaments to establish and maintain good housekeeping. He, supported by both Sir Edward Keeling (Cons.) and Mr. James Johnson (Lab.) paid glowing tributes to the work already done by Mr. Fellowes, particularly in the help he had given to the new West African Legislatures both in drafting their standing orders and in less formal advice on the art of parliamentary procedure. Now that constitutional advance was so widespread and so continuous the appointment of someone who could, both by travelling and from the House, give expert advice to the legislatures and their Speakers, would be much appreciated in the Colonies and be of great, long-term value to the Commonwealth. Mr. Hopkinson, Minister of State, welcomed the proposal and also paid tribute to the work of Mr. Fellowes. He said that, among many other things, Mr. Fellowes was now revising the Model

Staling Orders for Colonial Legislative Councils, first issued in 1949, not with the idea of imposing British Parliamentary procedure, but of providing a model by which Colonial Legislatures could measure their own procedures and practices and modify them if they thought fit. He promised to further the matter in the right quarters.

On the 20th Sir Leslie Plummer (Lab.), who now speaks quite often on the economics of Africa, discussed Basutoland. He said that, although good progress was being made, particularly in soil conservation, much more could be done if the Colonial Office were to take control. It would not, like the Commonwealth Relations Office, work all the time with one eye on the Union of South Africa, but could do freely what ought to be done. Such a transfer would at once reassure 'the whole world that we are determined to maintain our protectorate over these lands and over these people' and be an expression of our 'determination to see over the Chinese population and every possible practical step should be taken to this end. Lord Munster, replying for the Government, began by pointing out that while the British Government was responsible for the defence of Malaya, that was also part of the defence problem of Australia and New Zealand. The fact that the troops in Malaya included contingents from Australia, New Zealand, Southern Rhodesia, Nyasaland, Kenya, Fiji and Borneo was evidence of the spirit of brother-hood in the Commonwealth. Turning to points raised in the debate he said that 400,000 out of 450,000 squatters had now been resettled. Educational and welfare work in the settlements had begun, strenuous efforts were being made to afford protection, and most of the State Governments had now agreed to the grant of land titles to Chinese in the resettlement areas. The Citizenship Bill was now before a Select Committee. The Home Guard was now 175,000 strong, including 60,000 Chinese. It was now being armed and trained and would be administered by District Officers. There were 23,000 regular police and 38,000 special constables, but only 1,860 of the specials were Chinese. There were, however, 1,500 Chinese in the C.I.D. The whole Police Force needed reorganisation and that was the responsibility of Colonel Young. Rural development and education were being pressed on – the establish-ment of national primary schools and the teaching of English as a compulsory subject had been accepted – and steady progress was being made in the development of democratic local government as the foundation for democratic government at the centre. He disagreed with the proposal for a Supreme Commander – the responsibilities would be too widespread to be effectively handled. He paid a warm tribute to the work of Mr. MacDonald and deplored recent attacks made upon him in the Press.

Parliament (1952)

THE COLONIAL DEBATES

The annual general debates on Colonial affairs took place in the Commons on the 16th July and in the Lords on the 22nd. The Commons debate was opened by Mr. Griffiths who concentrated on the land problem in Kenya, some aspects of the Malayan situation, and Colonial development. An Opposition motion had been put down (though it was not, in the event, put to the vote) on the first subject, urging the Government to seek agreement in Kenya for a policy permitting Africans, and particularly Co-operatives, to own and farm, subject to soil conservation measures, unused land on the White Highlands, Mr. Griffiths stressed the immediate urgency of this problem in view of the growing pressure of population on the Reserves, and the very natural discontent it was causing. It was essential to reach a solution by agreement in Kenya. That solution lay largely in improved farming methods and particularly Co-operation (which makes these methods possible without disturbing land tenure); the measures now being taken ought to be speeded up and more money must be provided for agricultural credit. More land was also needed and it ought, by agreement, to be made available. On Malaya, Mr. Griffiths, after warmly praising the work of all concerned with the emergency, asked for an assurance that everything possible was being done to give security of land tenure to the 450,000 resettled squatters, and urged that a stronger line should be taken with those State Governments which seemed to be holding up both the Citizenship Bill and the work of the Rural Industrial Development Authority. He was also anxious that the Trade Union movement, which was an outstanding example of inter-communal co-operation, should not be allowed to suffer through any decision to reduce wages as a result of the fall in rubber prices. The cost of living was not going down, and in the interests of the country as a whole, wage-rates ought at least to be maintained. Turning to development Mr. Griffiths referred to the recent statement of policy in regard to the Colonial Development Corporation and asked what provision was being made to enable Colonial Governments to undertake those non-commercial investigations from which the Corporation was now barred? In any case, if the Corporation, because it had lost £4$\frac{1}{2}$ million, was no longer allowed to undertake the marginal projects for which it had been expressly created, why have a Corporation at all?

Mr. Lyttelton began by stating his belief in the necessity for an imaginative and bold development policy to take full advantage of the economic situation. U.S. production was expected to double by 1975 and this would require a great increase of imports of raw materials; and the world-wide pressure of population on the land should also ensure the maintenance of prices for agricultural produce. He had caused two studies to be made: what contribution to world shortage in the short term could the Colonies make, and what would the capital demand be over a short term? The answers were: (1) short term increases were possible in 9 commodities – copper, cotton, manganese, petroleum, pyrites, sugar, timber, vegetable oils and oil seeds; (2) over a longer period increases would be possible in 10 commodities – aluminium, iron ore, lead, zinc, tungsten, pulping materials, hides and skins, bananas, tea and tobacco; (3) not shortage of capital but of steel, machinery and skilled labour, and the indifferent organisation of local resources would be the limiting factors for the next few years. He was, however, sure that Britain would not be able to provide all the capital needed in the future, and therefore the processes of the nineteenth century must be repeated in reverse the New World, now the creditor, must be asked to invest in the development of these backward territories, particularly in the form of loans. We would not be selling our birthright any more than America had sold hers by accepting British capital for her development. Mineral and agricultural development must go hand in hand (with agriculture leading) and secondary industries must be encouraged where they would be natural and healthy, particularly those serving primary production. In agriculture the accent must be on peasant and not on plantation farming, though cattle ranching was necessary on a large scale. On the subject of the C.D.C. Mr. Lyttelton said that it had suffered from an impossibly diverse programme and from too much 'know better' and too little 'know how.' A drastic re-organisation was going on and he and Lord Reith were fully agreed on the new policy. The Corporation could, even now, accept bigger risks than a commercial firm because it paid lower interest on its borrowings and need only look for a gilt-edged return. He agreed with Mr. Griffiths' approach to the Kenya land problem – though the importance of the unallocated land in the White Highlands must not be exaggerated, there were only 200,000 acres available (of which, as later speakers pointed out, only 7,000 are arable) – and he hoped to make an announcement in about a month's time regarding the institution of an enquiry into the whole problem. On Malaya he recounted the measures of reorganisation which had been put through. One of the chief difficulties had been that 95 per cent of the terrorists were Chinese and 95 per cent of the police Malays. The Chinese had to be encouraged to play their part and now a third of the Home Guard were Chinese and they were coming into the police in encouraging numbers. The Civil Service had been given better conditions and three most important Bills had recently been passed. The State Governments were not being obstructive, but the constitutional process was slow. Negotiations about rubber were now going on, but in the long run natural rubber must live with synthetic and the long-term answer lay in cheaper costs and greater productivity. Confidence and energy in Malaya were mounting, battle results were improving, enemy morale was falling, and fence-sitters were beginning to come down on our side. He could not say when we would win, but win we would. He ended his speech by confirming that the policy of the Government in Colonial affairs was to develop self-government step by step, in the main from a local government basis, with the careful preservation of the purity of the administration, the impartiality of justice, and incorruptibility. 'I think,' he concluded, 'we have a chance in the next decade or two of forming a system which will be the admiration of the world and will add greatly to the strength and prestige of the British Commonwealth of Nations.'

The subsequent debate followed the annual pattern, with almost more members wanting to speak than were in attendance at any one time and the discussion jumping, grass-hopper like, all over the Colonial Empire. Mr. Popplewell (Lab.) urged the planters in Malaya to a less feudal attitude; Mr. Grimond (Lib.) wondered why government agencies in Africa in their agricultural projects always attacked the deserts first instead of starting by trying to improve existing production; Dr. Morgan (Lab.) made his usual moving appeal on behalf of the West Indies and was apparently surprised to hear that the Colonial Office was urging the Colonies to federate and not obstructing them; Mr. Stevens (Cons.) was pleased to find evidence that Colonial policy was still bi-partisan but urged a *festina lente* approach in political development; Mr. Fenner Brockway (Lab.) on the other hand wanted to see target dates fixed for self-government. He did, however, pay tribute to those European settlers in Kenya who were giving a lead towards 'partnership,' though he remained convinced that a Common Roll was the only political answer. He also made the suggestion that if modern methods could make the desert bloom in Israel and Tripoli, they might do the same for the vast arid lands of Kenya. Mr. Harris (Cons.) doubted the honesty of Indian professions of solidarity with the Africans, and said that industrialisation was an essential part of the population-land problem there. Mr. Johnson (Lab.) said the same thing about Nigeria – its greatest need was for 'the humble fitter' – and why could not Burton-on-Trent brew a good lager for Nigeria? Mr. Robinson (Cons.) objected to Treasury control of the C.D.C., by fixing interest rates, and demanded more urgent consideration for the improvement of air and sea communications with the West Indies. Mr. Wigg (Lab.) chided the Government for cutting the funds available for spreading information about the Colonies in Britain. Mr. Dugdale (Lab.), winding up for the Opposition, was not quite so bi-partisan as Mr. Stevens would have liked, hut he too had a word to say for the Kenya settlers, and produced the idea that the C.D.C. might be split up into separate industrial and agricultural corporations. He also emphasised the necessity for increasing exports to the Colonies to mop up inflation.

Mr. Hopkinson replied for the Government, and he and Mr. Griffiths between them practically reached agreement on the question of Kenya land policy and, presumably, that the motion was not really necessary. He dealt with some of the points raised in the debate and gave some additional information: if a British company wished to set up a local subsidiary to manage its affairs in a Colony, only dividends remitted home would be liable to U.K. income tax; the Government would do its best to see that the Volta scheme goes through and would certainly consider how the continuing needs of Colonial development could be met when the C.D. & W. Acts expired in 1956.

The Lords debate was much shorter than that in the Commons. It was opened by Lord Ogmore who said that the Annual Report was good but pedestrian and ought to be prefaced by some 'imaginative musings' by the Secretary of State, an 'appreciation' of the over-all situation. Having criticised the transfer of Mr. Lennox-Boyd from the Colonial Office, Lord Ogmore then once more pressed for the creation of a Grand Council of the United Kingdom and Colonial Territories. Among other things he asked for a clearer definition of 'partnership' in multi-racial societies, complained that our resistance to malicious attacks by ignorant people at Lake Success was too feeble, called on Lancashire to go all out for the West African textile market, and urged that Colonial development of all kinds should be made the concern of the whole community and of all the relevant agencies in the country and not merely of the Colonial Office. The Colonies should cease to be 'things apart' and become 'part of the warp and woof of our everyday life.' Neither Lord Milverton nor Lord Munster took kindly to the 'imaginative musings' proposal; a Report was after all a Report and not a political pamphlet. Lord Munster did not condemn the idea of a Grand Council but wondered how it would work; if it were executive it would conflict with the whole principle of Ministerial responsibility and if it were merely advisory the Colonies would not be interested. He emphasised that to achieve 'partnership' was essentially the task of the Colonial peoples themselves, as Mr. Griffiths had told them, and that all H.M.G. could do was to provide the framework and give them every kind of encouragement. On Lord Ogmore's last point he thought that the right place to start was the schools and an effort was being made to rouse greater interest among the county educational authorities. Detailed discussion, started by Lord Listowel, centred on the West Indies. The Evans Report of 1948 had recommended the migration of some 100,000 people from the islands to British Guiana and British Honduras. Lord Munster said that long and complicated preliminary investigations were necessary and that it was not yet possible to say how much scope there would be for such immigration. There was nothing new to say about Federation at present pending the forthcoming conference. He was, however, able to state that Constitutional Reform in British Honduras was in the offing and that the C.D.C. was still hoping to maintain its banana and livestock undertakings there. The Colony had a surplus this year, but it was proposed to maintain grants-in-aid for three years as well as to provide £700,000 from C.D. & W. funds to help with the development plan. Very many nice things were said, as usual, about the work of the Colonial Service and Lord Lucan wished we could all come on leave every year by air.

Parliament (1952)

au Mau. A discussion on the situation in Kenya was initiated by
Lord Ogmore in the House of Lords on the 29th October. The
debate was short, and for the most part helpful and well
informed. Lord Ogmore gave an accurate description of the Kikuyu and a
correct analysis of their problem as arising basically from the effect of the
pressure of population on land held under tribal ownership and therefore
not easily susceptible to proper development. He and all other speakers gave
full support to the firm measures taken by the Government, though he
wanted to know why Sir Evelyn Baring had not been sent out sooner and
why the spokesmen of the Kenya Government had for so long played down
the importance of the emergency. Also, the Government should try to
clarify its views about the relationships between the Kenya African Union,
the Mau Mau society and the ordinary criminals who were cashing in on the
situation. He welcomed the development proposals made by the Governor
in his budget speech and was glad that consideration of constructive
remedies was not being left over until order had been restored. Steps should
also be taken to enlist the help of moderate African opinion; the hands of
Mr. Mathu and the new executive of the K.A.U. should not be tied but
strengthened. European, Asian and African leaders should get together now
and work towards inter-racial action 'as a sort of conciliation group.' Finally
there must be a firm policy towards the independent Kikuyu schools; those
which were subversive should be closed, but those which were not should be
helped and guided. Restrictive legislation must be relaxed as soon as
practicable, and 'prompt, vigorous and thorough' security measures 'must
be accompanied by a real attempt to discover and, if possible, to satisfy the
underlying discontent.' This speech received general support and most of
those which followed served mainly to amplify its theme. Lord Milverton,
for instance, gave an eloquent warning against the present trouble being
used as an excuse to denigrate our remarkable achievements in Kenya. The
problem was not merely political, it was the inevitable result of historical
processes, and those who propounded political solutions from their
armchairs or went out to Kenya to interfere were enemies and not friends
of African progress; the true friends of Africa were in Africa. Lord
Tweedsmuir spoke in the same sense, emphasising that secret societies, new
and old, were 'one of the endemic diseases of Africa.' The problem of
agricultural productivity must be solved and the future of Kenya depended
on inter-racial co-operation. It was so obviously in the interests of the
settlers to promote African advance and co-operation and they were
behaving in so responsible a fashion that they should be given every chance
to help. Round-table discussions were needed and a great deal more
leadership and responsibility by the African politicians. Lord Listowel

concentrated more on the forthcoming Royal Commission. He wanted it to include at least one non-British member and he wanted another Royal Commission to be appointed to consider such matters as education and racial discrimination, and the whole field of economic and social problems.

Lord Rennell asked whether Mau Mau had spread beyond the Kikuyu, whether it had any affiliations outside Kenya, how much was known about it before the troubles started and what had been the state of readiness of the police? Lord Munster, in replying to the debate, said that up to the 17th August the Acting Governor thought his powers and forces adequate, but that in the middle of September the murders increased and cattle mutilations began. The new Governor arrived on the 28th and soon concluded that Mau Mau was a well-organised movement and that the situation in the reserves had deteriorated. He then declared a state of emergency and called in military reinforcements 'to display an overwhelming show of force.' There had been nothing unusual about the interregnum before the Governor's arrival (though in future such interregna would be kept to a minimum) and, in fact, it had made little difference. The emergency legislation, for example, had been passed before Sir Evelyn went out. The police, at 5,600, had been almost up to establishment excluding the Reserve of 3,500 and in August it had been decided to increase the police itself by 1,000. He would make a further statement when Mr. Lyttelton returned but meanwhile he wanted to make it clear that these disturbances would not be allowed to jeopardise the development programme.

Parliament (1954)

Perhaps this is not the place to plead for a closer study of colonial affairs in Parliament by members of the Service. One main reason for knowing what goes on at Westminster is obvious enough ... no-one who works in the Colonies can afford to be indifferent to British public opinion about them. Parliament presents that opinion to the world not only in Debates but in innumerable Questions on matters which are the Service's daily business.

But there are other reasons. One day, perhaps, an embarrassed officer will be asked by an African why the British pay more attention to the race with the fewest people in Africa than to the Africans. He will find it easier to answer if he recognises this as Mr. Dugdale (Lab.) going one better than Mr. Griffiths (Lab.) in a Debate of which such sentiments were parts only and by no means the whole. That Debate will have been recognised by those who have not entirely skipped the potted Parliament presented monthly in this journal as the climax to many weeks of increasing criticism in colonial matters by the Opposition. They may have felt that a Motion of censure on the Government for its handling of affairs in Africa came within striking range of themselves − after all, Colonial Service officers are the ultimate handlers in Africa − and the defeat of the Motion and an enhanced colonial reputation for the Government may not entirely have removed another anxiety: that the tradition of a national approach to colonial affairs, transcending party differences, was being cracked across.

On the 16th December Mr. Lyttelton voiced this anxiety in the House of Commons: 'It is a sad day', he said, 'which witnesses the final breakdown of a national ... approach to colonial affairs. If this debate did anything to ... lay the foundation upon which we can go on to build a less partisan approach to these subjects, it would have been a good afternoon ... for the Colonial Territories.' In the event, the afternoon may have turned out quite well for those who hope that there will be a lessening of what Sir Walter Fletcher (C.) called a personal vendetta against the Secretary of State.

The Opposition's Motion read: 'that this House expresses its grave disquiet at the handling by Her Majesty's Government of affairs in Africa.' Here it must have seemed to a foreigner was proof of a House strongly, perhaps irrevocably, divided among itself. And not only foreigners; on the 2nd January a gentleman from Burnham-on-Crouch, writing to the *Daily Telegraph*, said: 'ever since trouble started among the natives on the Gold Coast of West Africa, due to the policy of the late Colonial Secretary, the unrest has spread gradually to Nigeria, Kenya, Uganda and Nyasaland,' thereby implying some deep division on fundamental colonial issues between successive Secretaries of State. And if Burnham-on-Crouch can produce such ill-informed generalities, what ideas may not be hatched in less developed areas?

Perhaps the most important thing about this Debate was the assurance that both Socialists and Conservatives have a fundamental identity of aim. Listen again to Mr. Lyttelton; not hesitating to carry the attack into the other camp by declaring that he could recall no difficulty and no danger in which the official Opposition had tried to be helpful, he nevertheless could say 'whatever variations there may be on the main theme, all parties in the House follow a common aim and an essential continuity, which is the advance of the peoples of Africa, all her peoples, towards self-government.' Here indeed is an adequate reason, without looking further, for suggesting that not only interest but common sense demands some knowledge of what is said and thought at Westminster.

From the Colonial Serviceman's point of view, this debate was full of relish. Sir Walter Fletcher (C) is our defence against a charge of contempt if we admit that we are rather prone to answer our own question 'What do these Parliamentarians know about the Colonies?' by 'not much.' To his fellow M.Ps. Sir Walter said that before he himself became one, his respect for 'that animal' was rather less than it is now. As for Parliamentary missions, 'When they go out for two or three weeks, or two or three days, and come back and preach to us here on what local opinion is, it means nothing at all. It is an absolute travesty of fact.' Yet this cannot obscure the weight of thought, knowledge and informed opinion which are so impressive a feature of Colonial Debates to-day nor the fact that generally the growth of knowledge in Parliament about things colonial keeps pace with the growth of interest, and nowadays that is very fast indeed.

If sometimes the Service gets hot under the collar at what appears to be ignorance or omission, the balance is usually redressed without delay. Here is Mr. Paling (Lab.), asking that attention be turned to 'questions of work, wages, land, education and housing and to all the things from which the African is suffering.' There is no need for us to point out that for years quite a lot of us have been turning our attention to these things on the spot, for there is Mr. Peyton (C.) to do it for us. He quotes from a letter from a member of the Service and says: 'I think, honestly and sincerely, that the views of those decent, honest people, our own people, living in Africa, have been discounted, and that they themselves, their values and their way of life have very often been wantonly discredited by speeches from the other side of the House.' Well, we could never have said anything like that about ourselves.

The Debate never quite lost its personal touch. The wording of the Motion tipped the scales towards personalities, and Sir Frank Soskice (Lab.) made no bones about treating the Government and Mr. Lyttelton as synonomous targets. But Mr. Clement Davies (Lib.) made a deft attempt to hold a balance. 'I think', he said, 'there is a far more important question than the handling of affairs in Africa at the moment. It is a question not of whether this House has confidence in the Government ... indeed, whether Africa has confidence in this House and the people of Britain,' a warning, perhaps, if one were needed, against irresponsibility from any quarter. 'I do not', he went on, 'think that any Government can be blamed for the present situation ... if it comes to throwing bricks at each other both parties are living in glass houses.' Did Mr. Davies, one wonders, classify Mr. Strachey (Lab.) as a thrower or a dropper of bricks when Mr. Strachey said: 'I would very much rather have failed to grow groundnuts in Tanganyika than have succeeded in producing insurrection in Kenya'?

We have not quoted long extracts from the Government's reply to the Motion of censure. For once, perhaps, the Colonial Service may admit bias. It is enough to say that Mr. Lyttelton, who has been accused in the past by the Opposition of hitting out too freely, carried his bat in an innings which gave no chances. But where, oh where, were our Fenner Brockways, our Wiggs and our Hales? Mr. Fenner Brockway (Lab.) *rose*, but got no further than that. Dr. Morgan's (Lab.) usual little lob of an interjection failed to take a wicket, but why didn't those more doughty bowlers sling down a few overs? Well, if you have followed colonial affairs in Parliament lately, you will be able to make some interesting guesses.

After the Christmas Recess, Parliament reassembled on 19th January. On the 26th Mr. Head (Secretary for War) made a statement about the Court of Inquiry into military conduct in Kenya. There did not, said Mr. Head, appear to be any grounds for accusing the troops of indiscriminate shooting, irresponsible conduct or inhuman practices. Two alleged instances of serious misconduct in the King's African Rifles were being investigated. Subject to this, the report of the Court of Inquiry disclosed nothing to shake confidence in the high standard of behaviour of the British Army. On the 27th Mr. Henry Hopkinson said there was no evidence that Mau Mau was financed from outside sources.

Beneath Big Ben (1958)

F inal stages of the British Nationality Bill and the Overseas Resources
Development Bill opened a very busy Colonial affairs month in the
House of Commons. The latter gave the opportunity for considerable
debate on the need to change the name of the Colonial Development
Corporation to 'Commonwealth'. In the face of Opposition reminders that
elsewhere 'Colonial' had disappeared, Mr. Profumo (Under-Secretary of
State for the Colonies) struck a vigorous blow for its retention, and won.
'Do not,' he said, 'let us always link the word 'Colonial' with controversy.
Let us use the word in this case as meaning something which can be
admired, even by those who hate Britain – something which is bringing
succour and assistance to the Colonial territories. If we do that, we shall be
doing a very good service.' If Members recently deeply concerned with the
Overseas Service Bill thought Mr. Profumo's words might perhaps have
been extended to a different context, they kept the thought to themselves.

But the title 'Commonwealth' came into its own when both Houses
debated the future of the Imperial Institute, its need to move from South
Kensington owing to the expansion there of the Imperial College of Science
and Technology, and the rehousing of the Institute at Holland Park in well
designed and specifically planned buildings. In the Commons Sir Edward
Boyle (Parliamentary Secretary to the Ministry of Education) gave a
summary of the Institute's valuable work and Mr. Creech Jones (L) gave the
Bill the Opposition's blessing, although expressing regret that the familiar
buildings in South Kensington must, with the exception of the tower,
soon disappear. He hoped that the new Institute buildings would not only
provide for lectures and exhibitions but also have those Commonwealth
facilities which were missing from London. Odd though it was, said
Mr. Creech Jones, to think that the Institute had been founded in the
heyday of British imperialism, it had done and was doing excellent work . . .
it had worked to increase our knowledge of Colonial and Commonwealth
problems; it served a great educational purpose and promoted good will and
sound race relations, and kept alive in the public mind the great principles
and ideals for which the Commonwealth stands. Mr. Creech Jones spoke
warmly (as in the House of Lords did Lord Ogmore and Lord Milverton)
of the work done, as Director of the Institute, by *Corona's* first editor,
Mr. Kenneth Bradley, and hoped the new Institute would flourish in its new
buildings.

Mr. Hector Hughes (L), however, did not see much justification for new
buildings, although he agreed with the high purpose and performance of
the Institute. He did not like the expense . . . were the old buildings really
inadequate. Mr. Doughty(C) was all for the change of buildings, but raised

a spirited cry in defence of remaining 'Imperial' and not being ashamed of talking about the British Empire or the imperial heritage.

And so back to the Overseas Service Bill again, this time in the House of Lords, where, if it did not attract such lengthy discussion as in the Commons, it nevertheless received some penetrating comments ... in the words of the Earl of Perth, if it was not commended, it was not altogether damned. Lord Milverton's view of the Bill was that, in so far as it was an attempt to save what was left of the Colonial Service, it came too late and was hedged about with too many hesitant half-concessions. The Special List, he thought, disguised a glorified employment agency which was prepared to gamble on success by underwriting the future of its clients: 'You cannot be loyal to a Special List ... the Special List members will really be the liquidators of the former Colonial Service ... you cannot buy the spirit of the service with money: it is based on trust; and the trust the Colonial Service should have had in the institution known as the Colonial Office has been undermined by recent events. In my opinion, the Overseas Service is a dream incapable of fulfilment.... As the major members of the Colonial Service grow up and achieve independence and become independent members of the Commonwealth, the Colonial Service must die. There has been talk of a Commonwealth Service. If such a thing were a practicable possibility, which I most emphatically deny, it could not grow out of the Colonial Service ...' Lord Milverton, however, looked forward to the time when the Colonial Office would be an appanage of the Commonwealth Relations Office and suggested that Colonies left over after the bigger ones had become independent might be promoted to the status of Protected Territories under that Office. Others of their Lordships did not take such a positive view about the inevitable disappearance of the Service – though there was considerable agreement that the need for administrative officers in it would diminish – and the Earl of Perth admitted that the Bill was not regarded as completely satisfying by the Government, which was feeling its way. He would, he said, be very surprised if the Bill were the last thing on this subject.

The House of Lords also completed its stages of the Overseas Resources Development Bill while the Commons had a Debate, ending in a Division and a Government majority of 49, on the Rhodesia and Nyasaland Electoral Bill, to understand which required, said Mr. Lennox-Boyd, a considerable intellectual exercise. He explained that in the Bill the Federal Government had to provide for the election of two different categories of members and had decided on two common rolls, the general roll and the special roll, with no distinction between races, but each with their educational and income qualifications. The aim was a common roll system in which members of all races participated in the election of all Members, and Mr. Lennox-Boyd believed the Bill would prove to be an important step in the growth of partnership.

Mr. Creech Jones (L), however, saw in the Bill the negation of partnership and considered its effects discriminatory. He feared it would intensify bitter feelings in Africa, and he saw little likelihood of Africans qualifying for the general roll ... the European community had possession of the machinery of Government. Mr. Wall (C), supporting the need for qualifications for voters, said it was a disservice to tell Africans that what really mattered was the franchise: what really mattered was the raising of present standards of living. Mrs. Castle (L) asked Members to put themselves in the 'skin of the African'. She was sure the Bill would do the reverse of winning African confidence ... in effect there would be no move forward to the non-racial representation of the common roll: there would be racial representation. Here Mr. Alport (Under-Secretary of State for Commonwealth Relations) pointed out that although the African element in the general roll would at first be small, it would increase and the roll could not therefore be regarded as a European roll. Winding up for the Government, Mr. Alport reminded the House that although he knew many people wished to see an increase in the pace at which Africans would be associated with the exercise of political power, full weight must be given to the fact that the Bill had been passed by a majority in the Federal Parliament to which the United Kingdom had transferred a great measure of responsibility.

During the month both Houses heard a report by Mr. Selwyn Lloyd on his talks with the Turkish and Greek Governments on Cyprus. Mr. Lloyd said that he had sought to establish common ground on which to base a settlement which would also be acceptable to Greek and Turkish Cypriots. He had come back with the firm belief that in spite of all difficulties this was possible. Further discussions were necessary and he proposed to start them urgently. Mr. Bevan (L) pressed for information as to the form the discussions would take but Mr. Lloyd, mentioning 'wider interests', divulged nothing further but repeated his recognition of the urgency. 'I think', he said, 'that most people would feel time, in a sense, is running against those who favour moderate solutions. Therefore, speed is very necessary.' To another questioner, Mr. Lloyd replied that if finally these discussions failed it was reasonable to assume that Her Majesty's Government were prepared to make clear that they were ready to make their own policy and to stand by it.

Beneath Big Ben (1959)

R arely can such tenseness and concentration on Colonial affairs have ushered in a Parliamentary Summer Recess. From small Debates in the Commons on disturbances in Uganda and a television service for Kenya, both Lords and Commons went strongly into action on Central Africa and Kenya, with the review of the Central African Constitution, the Hola Camp inquiry committee's findings and the Devlin Commission report on Nyasaland all under scrutiny.

In the Commons Mr. Macmillan's announcement of the Government's decision on the composition of the advisory Commission of 26 to prepare for the conference to review the Federal Constitution of Rhodesia and Nyasaland towards the end of next year brought disagreement, but not outright rejection of participation by the Opposition, from Mr. Gaitskell, and in the following Commons Debate the Opposition pinpointed the proposed appointment of five Africans out of the 13 members from Central Africa. If, said Mr. Gaitskell, they were drawn from the leaders of African politics, that would be one thing: 'to draw them from people who are simply stooges of the British and local Governments will be quite another.' The word 'stooges' displeased Mr. Macmillan, and later Mr. Callaghan (L), expanding it into 'Quislings', drew the wrath of Government supporters.

The opposition took so strong a view that the best hope lay in swift political advance in Northern Rhodesia and Nyasaland that they called for that to come first, before holding the conference, even if the conference's date had to be postponed, and Mr. Gaitskell shewed that the Opposition's aim in Central Africa was 'one man one vote'.

Mr. Macmillan replied that to postpone the review of the Constitution would raise the maximum amount of suspicion with the minimum of advantage, and the Government did not intend to be deflected from its purpose or its attitude. As regards Northern Rhodesia and Nyasaland, the Government's policy was to move as rapidly as possible and as soon as possible towards self-government. The Government would not withdraw its protection to the two territories prematurely, nor could the Federation go forward to full independence and full Commonwealth membership until its units were in a position to agree that British Government protection was no longer needed. Mr. Lennox-Boyd told the House that African nominated seats in Nyasaland's Legislative Council were to be increased and that two Africans were to be appointed to the Executive Council. On a Division the Government had a majority of 50.

The Central Africa Debate in the House of Lords followed much the same lines, there being a plea by Lord Alexander of Hillsborough to give political advancement to Nyasaland and Northern Rhodesia before consolidating federation, and a counter warning by Lord Robins that to postpone the Commission would be a great mistake.

But the fire engendered by these Debates was dimmed by the heat of the attack mounted in the Commons by the Opposition during the Hola and Devlin Report Debates. The principal target was Mr. Lennox-Boyd, and the Opposition, by engineering an all-night sitting over Hola set an exhausting course during which Mrs. Castle (L) spoke long and powerfully in support of her contention that there was a network of responsibility and a shocking picture of administrative callousness; she said Mr. Lennox-Boyd was as much to blame as the Governor of Kenya or anybody else. The House seemed uneasy when she declared that Conservative members did not believe an African's life was as important as a European's, and said 'We tonight take the place of a Court of Law.' Mr. Powell (C) in a speech applauded by both sides of the House, called for the Hola disaster's responsibility to be pinned on Kenya Ministers where it belonged, and stressed the personal blamelessness of Mr. Lennox-Boyd who refuted charges that the Kenya Government had attempted to mislead or to attach blame in the wrong quarters.

The Opposition's marathon attack went on in the Devlin Report Debate, when they sought to make the Government accept the report in full, whereas the Government firmly rejected certain parts of it, including adverse comments on police methods, the lack of evidence of a murder plot and the favourable light thrown on Dr. Banda. The Attorney-General, Sir Reginald Manningham-Buller, brought out the point that neither Mr. Lennox-Boyd nor Mr. Amery (Under-Secretary of State) had ever used the word 'plot' and the phrase 'murder plot' did not appear in the White Paper. But he dealt at length with the reasons which had satisfied the Governor that loss of life was a real and dangerous possibility making his action necessary. That action, Sir Reginald reminded the House, had been endorsed by the Commission, and he bluntly rejected the Commission's reference to a 'police State' in Nyasaland.

The Opposition's attack began strongly through Mr. Callaghan, who said, pointing at the Ministerial despatch box: 'The allegations of a murder plot did not arise in Nyasaland, they arose here, at that box.' The major blunder, he said, was in misleading the House of Commons, but the Colonial Secretary had jeopardised the lives of Europeans living in isolated homesteads and the lives and homes of those Africans who were arrested. Through Labour calls for Mr. Lennox-Boyd's resignation the Debate went on, losing, perhaps, some of its fire, until Mr. Bevan roused Opposition cheers when he said: 'This is the worst Parliament I have been in. Then have been Long Parliaments and Rump Parliaments. This will be known as the squalid one ... all we can say to the African is do not lose heart. Before long this squalid crowd will be out.' Mr. Lennox-Boyd went strongly into action shewing, apart from increasing hoarseness, little evidence of any strain and no inclination to heed the Opposition's call for his resignation. In a firm defence of the action taken in Nyasaland, he said: 'While we all deeply regret any incident which the Commission's work may have uncovered, the conclusions do not lead to the inference that illegalities were expressed or impliededly authorised from the top.' He also made it clear that there was no immediate intention to release Dr. Banda. He concluded the Debate to Government cheers when, raising his voice above shouts of 'Abdicate! Abdicate!' he said: 'We have acted and we will not abdicate.' On a Division, the Government motion endorsing the Commission's conclusion that the declaration of a state of emergency was fully justified, was carried with a majority of 62.

When the House of Lords debated Hola (having first heard Lord Milverton ask whether consideration would be given to increasing Colonial Service pensions already awarded), Lord Pakenham called for the resignation of the Governor or the Colonial Secretary, a demand which the Earl of Perth considered to be an emotional reaction rather than based on reason. Lord Pakenham's Motion was defeated, as was Lord Alexander of Hillsborough's, criticizing the Government for accepting only certain passages of the Devlin Report.

Beneath Big Ben (1960)

There were Debates on Colonial affairs during the month in both Houses of Parliament, when the Commons considered the Civil Estimates and the Lords discussed the London Conference on Kenya.

In the Commons the Opposition, through Mr. Callaghan, repeated its wish that in Central Africa federation need not be the only form of association to be considered. Mr. Callaghan said that the Prime Minister of Southern Rhodesia had laid down certain conditions on which his country might wish to secede from the Federation. If Southern Rhodesia could do that, it must be possible for Nyasaland and Northern Rhodesia to do the same – but was not the Monckton Commission debarred from considering this question? Mr. Callaghan himself would like to see a federation or an association in which black and white were living together harmoniously and freely in the interests of all, but if that were to be achieved we could not ignore the overwhelming weight of African opinion about the form of association. The best thing the Government could do would be to tell the Monckton Commission that it was free to consider any form of association it thought appropriate to the circumstances it found, to recommend whether it was possible to hold the territories together or not, and to be given the responsibility of reviewing the whole situation. Mr. Stonehouse (L) called for an extension of the Commission's terms of reference, but Mr. Tapsell (C) thought that the existence of the Federation was the best means of overcoming undesirable features such as racial discrimination. The Monckton Commission must devise means which, if put into effect by subsequent agreement, would ensure that the liberalising influences continued in the south and that discriminatory practices could not spread north. Mr. Tapsell thought that if the Federation were to be saved, there must be a reduction in federal powers (which in any case were not as great as sometimes thought) and a corresponding increase in territorial powers. In Nyasaland he thought that Dr. Banda must be given the chance to show if he were of the calibre to fulfil African hopes of him: it was an illusion to imagine that any other African leader would emerge to replace him. Mr. Peyton (C) wagged a finger at Members of Parliament who wagged theirs too much at people overseas, and this part of the Debate ended with an obvious wish by all sides not to embarrass the Monckton Commission while its work was in progress.

The House then entered into discussion on the numbers of police in Nyasaland, and Mr. Dugdale (L) said that the Opposition thought the expenditure of money on police there instead of on improving people's conditions was a wrong balance of expenditure. He compared Nyasaland with Tanganyika and thought that the shadow of federation over the former prevented the country's enjoying the happy state of the latter. Mrs. Barbara Castle (L) put her faith more in constitutional reform than in security forces and demanded that Nyasaland should not be given the police baton instead of the aid and constitutional development for which it was crying out. Later, in a question about further small disturbances in Nyasaland, Mr. Callaghan said he had information that tension was building up. But the Debate became an arithmetical exercise rather than a valuable expression of ideas when members gave figures of how many policemen there were per head of the population in various countries. After a Division, resulting in a Government majority of 46, the House heard Mr. Macleod, in reply to Mr. Marquand (L) speak about sums for the relief of cyclone-stricken Mauritius. Mr. Macleod, who told the House that he would be visiting Mauritius in April, said that although the sum now being considered in the estimates was £15,000 only, the result of conversations with Ministers from Mauritius who were in London when the second cyclone struck was that £2,000,000 were agreed, and in due course authority would have to be sought for that amount. Mr. Macleod implied agreement with Mr. Marquand's view that as a result of the second cyclone £2,000,000 were inadequate, and this was stated more positively in the House of Lords. The Earl of Perth, answering Lord Faringdon, said unequivocal that help was not now going to be sufficient. As in the House of Commons, figures were given of the Mauritius disaster – 42 people killed, over 1,700 casualties; over 100,000 buildings or huts destroyed or seriously damaged in 'Carol', the second cyclone, and eight killed and over 20,000 buildings destroyed in the first, 'Alix'.

In the House of Lords Debate on the Kenya conference three farmer-peers from Africa supported the new constitutional proposals, though Lord Delamere voiced the grave anxieties of the European farming community. He did not suggest unreasonable delay in achieving independence but warned against undue acceleration. Lord Portsmouth said he would stay in Kenya to work for a society in which people would forget the colour of each other's faces, and Lord Hastings (from Central Africa) described the Kenya conference as a major achievement. He was quite firm, however, that self-government – let alone independence – could not be given except on a basis of co-operation and mutual confidence between all races. He spoke of the need for the Overseas Service to continue its work. Merit in the Civil Service should be the test – Africanisation for its own sake was not in the long-term interest of countries. 'I believe', said Lord Hastings, 'there is definitely a career lying ahead for young men of our own Overseas Service, some of them not even in the Service yet, to go out and take their place in the Commonwealth ... these young men must have an incentive. I believe there should be immediate reorganisation and combination of the Commonwealth and Colonial Services, and in the future it may shock people in exclusive quarters to think that one day it might even come to an amalgamation with the Foreign Service. But if we are going to get those young men doing their jobs in Africa it is essential for the future of what will be Commonwealth countries that we make some move now.'

On this subject Lord Milverton asked what sane civil servant would stay to work under Jomo Kenyatta 'which we are told would occur if independence came', but Lord Perth answered suggestions that the Government would yet have to negotiate with Kenyatta by saying that he was no ordinary nationalist or political leader, somebody who had just gone beyond the bounds of law in advocating extreme national policies. He was a man convicted in the courts of managing Mau Mau, a man who organised a violent, primitive, brutal movement which caused untold suffering to his own people.

Lord Perth had said earlier that the conference was in no way a 'sell out of the white settlers to the Africans'. It was a consistent and ordered step forward in Kenya's destiny in which all the races there must play their part in harmony. He believed that a new Kenyan spirit had been born, but if lawlessness spread sharp measures would be used to restore respect for law and order. The Earl of Home (Secretary of State for Commonwealth Relations) stressed his belief that anarchy or doom would be the alternative to a multi-racial solution in Kenya, and Lord Tweedsmuir said the bogey of the hysterical, greedy, myopic Kenya settler had been laid for ever.

But among the welcome for the outcome of the conference, the Marquess of Salisbury did not agree with optimism over its results. He said that Africans were not yet ready to do without the control at present exercised by Britain. He thought the proposed franchise extension might produce the puppets of demagogues. Was there anything to prevent a Government elected on this wide franchise from sweeping away safeguards? Go slower, was the theme of Lord Salisbury's speech: do not let this age become more and more one of retreat instead of expansion. Lord Home replied that it would be quite possible to betray Europeans by going too fast, but it was equally possible to betray them by going too slow. We were not abandoning outposts, as Lord Salisbury had claimed, but we wanted to hold them, not by force but by the compelling example of our ideas.

c) FROM THE SECRETARY OF STATE FOR THE COLONIES

U nderstandably, *Corona* gave regular prominence to statements by the Secretary of State for the Colonies. Generally these took the form of his New Year wishes to the Colonial Service or his message to the peoples of the colonial territories. Sometimes it was a farewell message, such as when Arthur Creech Jones lost his parliamentary seat in 1950, or a major address to members of the Colonial Service by the Secretary of State at either the Corona Club Dinner or else at one of the Colonial Service Summer Schools or Colonial Office Summer Conferences. This Section includes a contribution from or comment on nearly all the Secretaries of State for the Colonies who held office during *Corona*'s fourteen year life time. These were:

1946 A. Creech Jones (Parliamentary Under-Secretary 1945)
1950 James Griffiths
1951 Oliver Lyttelton (later Viscount Chandos)
1954 Alan T. Lennox-Boyd (Minister of State 1951–52, and later Viscount Boyd)
1959 Iain Macleod
1961 Reginald Maudling
1962 Duncan Sandys

Founding a Link

by THE RT. HON. ARTHUR CREECH JONES, M.P.

I have usually tried to approach Colonial policy in a constructive spirit, though in my callow youth I may have been at times negative and perhaps a bit doctrinaire. In one's teens Imperial issues and Colonial problems seemed very simple – indeed, as simple as Wendell Wilkie's pronouncements some years ago that Britain should renounce her Colonial obligations, abolish Colonial status and end Colonialism.

But long before the war I was aware that whatever deficiencies existed or whatever abuses crept into our Colonial 'system,' the administrators in British overseas territories, with little aid to support them, were making a positive contribution to the well-being of the people in the Colonies. In pre-war days there were glaring shortcomings in British policy, some of which perhaps were inevitable, but it was the devotion and selfless service given by officials that redeemed British responsibility, established order and built up the rule of law, checked abuses and stretched public services across wide areas of uncharted country. Their splendid effort not only contributed to giving peoples national status but also was a factor in the dissolution of 'Colonialism.' The officers of the Colonial and Overseas Services have earned their justifiable pride in their work and have realised the proclaimed policy of Britain towards self-government.

In Parliament I have many times paid tribute to the work which the Services have performed, and I have written about it in a number of essays and publications. The men and women concerned have undoubtedly paid an exacting price in their long absences from Britain and from their families; perhaps, too, in the neutralism expected of them in respect to their own political views. Few of them, I guess, share my own political outlook, but I have invariably found officers of the Services progressively minded, impatient with stagnation, responsive to political initiative and out of sympathy with unimaginative work. They have always been eager to promote the welfare of the people among whom they serve. May I say that from my standpoint, they sometimes appeared to be the conventional products of public schools and universities, but always they showed courtesy and insisted on just dealing with the peoples of their territories, and drove ahead with plans and schemes for economic and social wellbeing. In fact, they generally won the respect of the Colonial people by their interest, devotion and helpfulness.

Corona was founded to be a link between all of us working in the Colonial field and not only among the men and women serving overseas. Sir Andrew Cohen and I toured together in East Africa in the year after the war, and I suppose both of us were full of ideas at the time as to how we could take advantage of the new opportunities following the stagnation and calamity of war. A change of Colonial policy was in the offing. I confess that I was disturbed at the insularity of many of the Colonial servants I met on that tour. They worked hard in their corner of the vineyard but, perforce, were seldom in touch with other fellow workers in the territory, knew little of the experiments and work being done elsewhere and certainly little of the new emphasis in policy which His Majesty's Government was now making in the reaction from the war. Their knowledge of what was happening in other British territories was negligible. What seemed true of British administration was also true of experiments and work by other Colonial Powers. I felt that a more corporate spirit in our Services should be promoted and my own misgivings were stated in the first number of the new journal. It was to be expected that some Governors resented the Services in their control being brought into touch with those of other territories; but I felt it better that the Colonies should have a well-informed and lively overseas service, able to appreciate the quality and achievements of the work and experiments going on in other parts of the Empire. I think therefore that Kenneth Bradley, editor for the first four years, and our present editor have performed a great service in their editing of *Corona* through all these years. From the first issue I have read it month by month, enjoyed the variety of experience which officers everywhere have written about, and I have appreciated the high standard maintained.

I wanted, when I initiated *Corona*, something more than a house journal, so that members could know about the pronouncements of British Colonial policy, the declarations made to Parliament from time to time and the principal events in the administration of the territories. The journal was, indeed, only to be a factor in the process of informing and inspiring the Services. It will be remembered that at the time the Colonial Office ran conferences, circulated information, organised study schools, arranged exchanges and expanded its publicity services and public relations. Officials of all grades were brought together to discuss common problems; we hoped to break down all sense of isolation, and enable officers from their own experience and knowledge to contribute to the thought and development of the new policies. The Service was, I am sure, made to feel that its members were not isolated from the influences which were shaking up and disturbing the world.

The work of the officials of the Colonial Office was no less inspired by Colonial needs and the spirit essential in the post-war world. During the war, an important impetus had been given to the Colonial Service by the Devonshire Committee, and by the remarkably eloquent pleas regarding the nature of Colonial work and need for vision in the appointments made to the Service by Sir Ralph Furse, and by the work of Sir Charles Jeffries.

Perhaps the journal has never been and could never be quite what some of us wanted to see, but it always seemed to me that if men are required to administer they should know what are the broad lines of policy they are required to employ themselves in. I have always felt that in its preparation their knowledge and experience should be taken into serious consideration. In its application they should be consulted. This explains why in the

Colonial Office we reorganised public relations and the information services and by co-operative effort, sought a wider spread of knowledge on Colonial matters. I found it refreshing to learn, in the conferences we held, the views of men normally cut off from their fellows working in faraway corners, men up against difficulties which would normally be little understood in a London office. It all contributed to the swelling of our ideas and helped us in the making of decisions and explaining them to Parliament and the nation. (Incidentally, too few books are written about the work of the Services.)

I deplore, of course, the inevitable diminishing size of the Services. The pace along the road to Colonial independence became faster than any of us in the Colonial Office in the immediate post-war days anticipated. That has meant disintegration of the Service at the very time when we were eager to see implemented to the full the Devonshire proposals and to supply the territories with the best young men and experienced people who could be recruited. Over the past ten years or so there have been insuperable difficulties and the Colonial Office has not neglected its obligations in the circumstances which have overtaken the Service. The early dreams of the war and post-war years have not been realised and now can never be with the Empire transformed into a Commonwealth.

But it should be remembered that the great British objective of self-government for her Colonies has been almost completely attained, and in that the Services have played their part even though the reaction on their own effective usefulness and their individual careers has been disquieting. The skill and care of which the Services are capable is now mostly wanted only in a few small territories. Unhappily many men of great promise have become redundant. It is our sincere hope that the transfer of responsibility which has come to our former wards through independence will not cause any deterioration of the work accomplished in the days of tutelage. For a long time the dilution of the local staffs with adequate officials from Britain is desirable, but unhappily the Services are changing their character, responsibility and accountability. The end of *Corona* is a sign of that change and of the contraction in the number of dependencies. I and many others regret that the journal can no longer continue.

The Challenge (1949)

The Secretary of State, in his New Year message to the peoples of the Colonial Empire, said:

'We want to help you create the social services which you need and, above all, to build the foundations of economic activity upon which alone the services and standards of living which you desire can be sustained and developed. We want to see democracy in your territories taking real root. But believe me, the dynamic must come from yourselves. Your welfare is largely in your own hands. Your progress should spring from your own service to one another and from your own effort in work and in government. The initiative in attacking your problems must come from your energies and sense of public service. It is our part to support you with practical help and advice, to create central services on which you can draw, and to encourage conditions most suitable for your advance and welfare.'

ARTHUR CREECH JONES.

Message from the Secretary of State (1950)

T he following telegram was sent to all Governors by the retiring Secretary of State on the 2nd March:

'I regret that, because of the misfortune of the poll, I preside no longer over the Colonial Office. It has been my privilege to enjoy four intensive years as Secretary of State during one of the most difficult periods of British history. I think an important chapter in Colonial Development has been written. I cannot leave without thanking you and all your colleagues in the administrative, technical and professional services for your and their splendid loyalty and great devotion in the high traditions of your great Service. I want also to thank you for all your fine co-operation with me and the goodwill you have shewn. In your respective territories, all of you are engaged with heavy responsibility on work vitally important to our generation. I thank you most sincerely for your fine contribution.'

ARTHUR CREECH JONES.

Neither the Colonial Service nor, of course, *Corona* has any politics, but we are sure that all our readers, whatever their private political views may be, felt personal sympathy for Mr. Creech Jones on his defeat at Shipley. It is not for us, and in any case it would be too soon for anyone to try to make an assessment of Mr. Creech Jones' achievements as Secretary of State, but those of us who knew him would certainly wish to take this immediate opportunity of paying a tribute to him as a friend and as a man. Mr. Creech Jones was Under-Secretary from 1945 to 1946, before he became Secretary of State, and his unusually long period of office enabled him to make more personal contacts with members of the Colonial Service than any of his predecessors. Many of these contacts developed into friendship, but even those who only met Mr. Creech Jones once will probably agree that the clearest impression left by that single talk was one of warmth and friendliness. He was approachable, human, unpretentious and ready to listen.

It is probably true to say that no Minister ever came to the Colonial Office with so much knowledge of his subject. He had devoted years to it and particularly to the problems of West Africa. So far as the people there were concerned Mr. Creech Jones opened his innings on a good wicket, but that he, a convinced and lifelong Socialist, should also in course of time have won a considerable measure of respect from the East African settlers is a tribute both to his breadth of mind and to his character. He is above all things honest, both with himself and with others, and he has always been willing to admit mistakes. He has devoted himself to the development of the colonies and the welfare of their people of whatever race without a thought for his own interests.

It was as a Socialist that Mr. Creech Jones approached the great problems and responsibilities of his office, but in his administration he was not doctrinaire; he saw facts and faced them, and in the House he steadfastly and on all occasions refused to make party capital out of colonial affairs, because he was determined that this country should speak with as united a voice on the objectives of its colonial policy as it does on foreign affairs.

We believe that it will also be a satisfaction to Mr. Creech Jones to be assured that the Colonial Service is glad to have worked under him and to know that he will always understand their problems and will continue to support them in their work in every way he can.

Message from the Secretary of State (1951)

Just forty-eight years ago, in October, 1903, my father became Secretary of State for the Colonies. I feel it is a great honour and privilege to enter today upon the same office, with its distinguished tradition of service and achievement.

In my father's time, the work of the Colonial Office was very largely taken up with the affairs of those countries which are now independent sister members of the Commonwealth. The opening up of Africa, the great economic development of the Malay Peninsula had scarcely begun. Social services were almost negligible. The Colonial Service was a mere handful of men.

But it was that handful of men who, working under hard conditions and enjoying few of the amenities which are a commonplace today, laid the foundations upon which their successors, in partnership with the Colonial peoples, have built so soundly. I am not using 'partnership' as a catchword. The Colonial peoples would not be where they are now, had it not been for the ability, enthusiasm and devotion of the Colonial Service. But all that ability, enthusiasm and devotion could not have achieved its end if it had not been matched by the eager response of the Colonial peoples themselves and by their innate capacity to lay hold of the opportunities set before them.

The Colonial Service has an honourable record and I know that it faces the future in the same spirit of patriotic adventure which has always been its characteristic.

To all the men and women of the Service, whether they belong to the peoples of the territories or whether they have gone out from Britain or the other Commonwealth countries to help the cause, I send this message of goodwill and encouragement and pledge my support in the tasks that confront us.

OLIVER LYTTLETON.

Colonial Service Summer School (1952)

address by MR. LYTTELTON

T he following is an abbreviation of the closing address to the Summer School at Queens' by the Secretary of State:

Today we are continually told, and I think truly, that we live in an age of specialisation. I think it is remarkable that my great-uncle, Mr. Gladstone, wrote a book about Homer which was read by both universities and even with attention. Now, I suppose, a Professor of Greek archaeology hardly dare speak about Greek poetry in front of a Regius Professor of Greek Literature. Nor, to descend to more pedestrian subjects, can the electronic engineer lift up his voice about hydrogen-cooled generators when he is in the presence of the heavy-plant engineer. This age of specialisation has led the laity – of course with the complacent aid of the specialists – into believing that a technician, somebody who speaks a language that the ordinary man does not understand, is the highest rank in the human race. I am afraid from all this I dissent profoundly. 'Thank God,' as a Bishop of Hereford once said, 'I have had a classical education and don't even know how a pump works!' Those of you who have high technical qualifications will take, I hope, these remarks in good part.

In the practical field, that part of human life which Plato described as the 'Bios praktikos,' the pursuit of politics is the highest activity to which the human brain can devote itself. The same is true in the field of colonial administration. Those who devote themselves to the political side are engaged in the highest activity to which any man can aspire. They do not deal in the currency of small affairs. When they make a mistake, the repercussions of that mistake may affect the lives of hundreds of thousands of people for a whole generation, until somebody wiser or more courageous is given the opportunity of reversing the mistakes of his predecessor. When by genius, or training, or experience they are both able and allowed to follow a policy of imagination, the good that one man can do to hundreds of thousands of others, perhaps of a different race, is almost incalculable. There is to day, all over the colonial territories, a great need for technicians, I agree, but only too often this need is coupled with the idea that the technician is the beginning and the end of everything and that there is no need for administrators, that administration is a thing which springs up spontaneously in the human mind. The first people who would say that the idea that administrators are superfluous is utterly false would be the technicians themselves. You cannot build a harbour or railway, or spray the bush with D.D.T. unless you know that the D.D.T. is going to be there, and that the local government has the means of supplying you with the labour and materials at the right time and at the right place to carry out your work on the harbour. In fact it is the administrative officer who is the key to the success of the technician. I put in a plea that we should hear less of the idea that the administrative officer is superfluous. My answer to many of those who say so is, 'Ask the technicians what they think.'

Now in all the colonial territories it is necessary to say again that Her Majesty's Government are pursuing a policy which, in a sentence, aims to give an increasing measure of self-government to the people who inhabit them. I must add, and it is not reactionary but merely obvious, a rotund platitude: that the pace of self-government must be dictated by the ability of the people to govern themselves. This shockingly Conservative doctrine will not, I hope, disturb any Fabian sub-harmonies which may be rippling beneath the surface this evening.

It is easy to be impatient, and that is perhaps one of the reasons why politics are so difficult: it is above all the activity in which patience is most necessary and pays the highest rewards. If someone wished to kill or retard self-government, the surest way of doing so is by going too fast. The end is to cause breakdowns in the administration, to cause, for example, the law to be brought into disrepute by enacting laws which have not been fully thought out and which have not been scrutinised in the light of centuries of experience in other parts of the world. At the same time, of course, it is as necessary to go along as fast as events permit, as fast and not slower. *Capax imperii nisi imperasset*.

In Africa, when we talk of Africanisation, for example, of the Civil Service, we are all anxious to see that process going on steadily and progressively, but if you go too fast and you promote Africans just because they are Africans and not because they are good administrators or technicians, then you may easily find that the administration starts to creak. The purity of the administration, and I use the word in its widest sense, must be the first preoccupation of every one of us, and by the purity of the administration, I mean of course first that it should be incorruptible. I think it would not be too much to say that our record, both in our own country, in India and all over the colonial territories, has shown that the impartial administration of justice and the absence of corruption are the keystones upon which the British concept of government is built.

And, of course, corruption can take many forms besides the actual giving or taking of bribes. There is all the apparatus of place-hunting and nepotism, all the stresses to which politicians who have commercial interests may be subject, but no country can develop and expand unless all have the feeling that they are equal before the law, and that there are none who, by birth or influence or by power of the purse become, shall we say, 'more equal' than the others before the law. This is one of the most insidious poisons, one of the worst viruses which can infect the body politic.

Now let me turn for a moment from matters of wide principle to some of the mechanics of administration. I want, because it has a particular significance in colonial affairs, to talk about the relations between Ministers and Civil Servants. There have been occasions – and I confess it freely – in my recent visit when I have found that African Ministers felt themselves a little irked by the Civil Servants who advised them. They have a sort of idea that the Civil Servants are running them, and not the other way round. This, Ladies and Gentlemen, is a feature of political life. There is no Commander-in-Chief of an Army who, at times, does not wonder whether his Chief of Staff is dictating the tactics or whether he is doing it himself. There are few Ministers who are so complacent or so conceited as to go to bed thinking that they have done it all, and that no one else has aided them at all. I ask new Ministers especially to remember that the Civil Service is there to serve them. It is even there to make them, and it is certainly there to prevent them from being unmade by those mistakes to which Ministers in all countries, at all times and in all places are prone by the nature of their office and the ephemeral qualifications which have brought them to the top in the political turmoil.

Here is the main theme of what I want to say to you this evening. No one of the local politicians, if I may say so, and no one in the Colonial Service, no Minister of the Crown can make any success nor enjoy any reputation unless the machine works smoothly, and it is the co-operation between the highly-skilled, overseas European officer at this stage of colonial development, with the growing and expanding local Service, that is the key to very much of the future.

I beg of you not to think that if we here in England sometimes appear to be slow, it is because we do not wish to reach the goal. We are often slow to change because we wish so greatly to reach the goal. If you start without proper thought, if you promote people merely because they are born in the neighbourhood of the office, you will end up by retarding and not accelerating the rate of progress towards responsible self-government and towards entrusting the interests of their own country in an increasing degree to their inhabitants.

So far, I have devoted a large part of my remarks to showing how the administrative officer must remain a key-pin and to saying that the first people to recognise this fact are the technicians who have to work in the country, and secondly I have touched upon relations of a Minister with the Civil Service and their advisers, and I want now to touch upon one more subject before I sit down, and that is something about the economics of colonial territories.

They have undergone, and for some of the reasons upon which I have touched, a startling change even in my lifetime. Gone are the days when we had to be continually searching for outlets for colonial produce, of persuading people to buy many of the primary products, fruit or oilseeds or cotton, or tobacco, from the colonial territories. Now the problem has switched round the full 180 degrees. It is, as far as one can see, almost certain that the primary producer will have an outlet for all that he is likely to produce for many years to come. It is therefore possible to hope for rising revenues, or at least for a continued state of prosperity for primary producers.

The significance of all this in the wider political aspects is that we should have time and money to plan and improve all those activities which go under the somewhat inelegant name of 'the social services.' A sure market for groundnuts or palm oil means, to the inhabitants, new universities and schools, it means new hospitals and medical services, it means new roads and bigger harbours, it means more airfields and more locomotives. And so I say to all of you who are now to spend a long time in the study of colonial problems, that you are to study them in order to make their solution possible. You can look forward, as far as it is humanly possible to tell, to a period when your imagination and your achievements will not be curtailed by the inability of these countries to maintain a market for their produce and consequently their standard of life.

Of course these remarks only have a general application. You will notice that I have not said that prices were going to remain the same, that would be very doubtful, and the process of readjustment when prices fall is often painful in the short run. Nobody should, for example, underestimate the effect upon the Malayan economy of the recent fall in the price of rubber, and it may well happen that we shall end by over-producing one or two of the primary products of the colonial territories. So you must not take my remarks at short term; all I am saying is that with the constantly expanding population of the world, you are devoting yourself to a service which ought not to be hampered by not being able to sell what it produces, which ought – on the contrary – to be helped by rising demands for its products. And at the end of the day you will find a fascinating and fruitful career stretching in front of you.

It is given to few to try and mould the political future and institutions of many countries, with the experience of nearly a thousand years of government behind you, and if at times it appears, as I have said, to those whom you are trying to help, that you are going too slowly, it is worth remembering that many of the institutions which we now regard as commonplace or everyday or workaday institutions, have really emerged only after hundreds of years of struggle, sometimes of bloodshed and always of adjustment.

Greetings to the Colonies

A New Year Broadcast by MR. LENNOX-BOYD (1955)

'I t was at the end of July last that I was entrusted by Her Majesty the Queen with the Seals of Office as Secretary of State for the Colonies. 'This was the greatest honour that I had ever been paid or indeed could ever be given.

'For, to my mind, the responsibility and the opportunities of my office, make it the best job in the world.

'It's certainly a formidable one with the welfare of over seventy million people involved, and a wide variety of problems of very differing kinds.

'It's work that is made a great deal easier by the zeal and devotion of many thousands of people of all races who are doing the most responsible work in the Colonial Territories.

'It is their task to give their fellow men and women one of the best of all gifts – informed and unselfish leadership. Some are giving this in the Administration. Others in the Armed Forces or the Police, others in agriculture or industrial development, others in hospitals and schools and many other ways.

'They are showing qualities of courage and self reliance and tolerance, respect for minorities and other people's points of view. They have sometimes to do unpopular things, but they know this is one of the prices of leadership, and that the result will be the best reward, steady progress towards self government within the Commonwealth, based on fair dealings to all and on that economic development and strength which is essential for a safe and prosperous life in modern times.

'I want, while I am Secretary of State, to see as much as possible on the spot of the work that you are doing.

'The trouble about my job is that there is always a danger of getting tied, by the mass of work there is to do, to my desk in London. I don't intend to let this happen.

'I've been already, since my appointment, to Kenya, Uganda, Tanganyika; later I went to Malta, and I am going, I hope, in two weeks' time to Nigeria – where lives half the population of the Colonial Territories. As soon as possible after, I mean to make as many other visits as I can. And, of course, there are always, I am glad to say, streams of visitors who come and see me and others in the Colonial Office.

'I say on my visits and to my visitors what I can promise you is true – that the British Government and People deeply value the honourable ties that unite us all, above all, in loyalty to the British Crown.

'And especially at this time of the year you are all very much in all our thoughts.

'To those who are listening in Malaya and Kenya, where you are still undergoing the strains and dangers brought on your lovely countries by terrorist gangs, I hope you know our admiration for your fortitude, our determination to help you in every way and our prayers that this coming year may bring the end of, or at least a marked decline in, your grievous ordeal.

'And to all of you in every Colonial Territory, I give you greetings, and may the New Year bring you happiness and prosperity.'

A Message and a Change (1957)

During his New Year broadcast message to the Colonies, Mr. Lennox-Boyd said: 'More than any, the men and women of what I still like to call the Colonial Service are carrying on this tradition (of adventure and a sense of service); it is they who have made possible such spectacular improvements in education, health, in the standard of living and in fair dealing. Despite political advances, they are needed now more than ever. It is right that I should thank them and tell them to keep faith, and Britain will keep faith with them.'

Mr. Lennox-Boyd's liking for the title 'Colonial Service' will evoke a warm response in many hearts, but as it is no longer our official title there will, we think, be relief that H.M. The Queen has recently been graciously pleased to approve a change whereby the Service is now 'Overseas' and not 'Oversea'. Since 1954 when our name was first changed, we have realised that members of the Service felt that if there had to be a change, the least that people could do was to get the new name right. But a degree of awkwardness in the official wording encouraged frequent inaccuracies. Now this latest change will give no occasion for error and we hope that the doubts of the past have been resolved, once and for all.

The Corona Club (1954)

If not quite a record, the number of Colonial Service officers, present and past, at the forty-fourth annual diner on the 17th June, justified Mr. Lyttelton's description of 'inspiring'. Some 350 heard him propose the toast of the Corona Club in a speech of humour and deep interest.

After a brief mention of his own far-ranging activities in the colonial field in the past year (not forgetting the projection of himself 'over the banisters at Government House at Zomba' when, if his past life did not flash before him, he at least had time to think how much he would be missed by the Labour Party), he went on to speak about two things which had impressed him deeply, firstly, the high level of discussions upon the Nigerian Constitution and the notable contribution which the Nigerian political leaders had made to them, and secondly the continued high level of administration by the Colonial Service.

Mr. Lyttelton said 'As long as Her Majesty's Government have any responsibility for any of these territories, there are four pillars upon which the policy of Her Majesty's Government must rest. These pillars must be preserved intact until responsibility passes.'

'They are, first of all, the retention of the Governors' reserve powers which may, of course, differ in various countries, but which must include powers to preserve the principles of good government. Secondly, the insulation of the judiciary from the executive. Thirdly, that the police should be outside the control of any political party; and fourthly, that the Public Service, the Colonial Civil Service, should be safeguarded from control by a political party or by Ministers who, under any democratic system, are transient creatures of the public will. They should not have to rely either for their pay and promotion, their career, their retirement and their pensions, upon the Government of the day, but upon some body which is in the main impervious to political change.'

Mr. Lyttelton paid tribute to the work and devotion to duty of the Colonial Service. 'There are some who profess to believe that the spirit of adventure and of enterprise and of service has departed from the British race. They think that the youth of today is entirely linked to the cinema, the dance hall and the ice-cream trolley...no doubt they have their attractions, but if you look at the quality of the young man in the field in the Colonial territories and in the Secretariat, you will see how utterly false such a charge would be. I have in my mind's eye more than one District Officer or District Commissioner, young in years but old in wisdom, who are running in an unostentatious way large districts...some of them in a state of political ferment...and giving to the world, if they only knew it, an example of how the great traditions of impartiality, incorruptibility, kindness and humour are still outstanding in our national character.'

The necessity for the Public Service to remain independent had been vigorously embraced by countries with which Mr. Lyttelton had had negotiations, particularly by the Gold Coast and Nigeria, but he was aware of the anxieties of the Colonial Service in view of constitutional changes. It was such changes, already effected or expected, that had caused difficulties calling for a re-examination of the Colonial Service structure, and that very day a Colonial Office paper had been made available to the Members of the House of Commons, on the reorganisation of the Service. 'Two lines of action appear to be essential. First, where a new constitution is under discussion, as in Nigeria, necessary safeguards for the Public Service should be embodied in the constitutional instrument. This has been done....'

Secondly, 'What is to happen in those territories which in the fairly near future achieve independence of any control by Her Majesty's Government in the United Kingdom?' In general, Mr. Lyttelton believed, they would want to go on having the help of friends who had served them well and that for the most part Colonial Service officers would wish to carry on with the work they knew and loved. For those who could not stay on, yet did not want to retire, Her Majesty's Government must do the best in their power to find other posts for them, though of course there could be no guarantee of other work. It was, indeed, certain and desirable that the percentage of overseas Civil Servants finding work in the whole of the Colonial territories would decline in relation to those locally recruited, but that was not the same thing as a decline in the absolute numbers of overseas Civil Servants. In some territories that might happen, but since the war five times as many men and women had been recruited as before it and Mr. Lyttelton did not think that that figure was likely to go down very much for a long time...that was the conclusion to be reached on a study of the economic development of some of the territories; for example, in 1920 the Kenya-Uganda Railway carried less than a quarter of a million tons of goods: in 1952 it carried more than eighteen times as much. Nigeria's import and export trade for 1953 was six and a half times the 1920 figure of £38 million.

Then came the important statement about the projected Oversea Civil Service to replace the unified branches of the Colonial Service.

Mr. Lyttelton assured his listeners that the change was more than one of name: it had highly important practical implications. 'The new Service is a definable body...it carries on the status and tradition of the Colonial Service as one of the great Services of the Crown. Once an officer has been enrolled as a member of Her Majesty's Oversea Civil Service, he will be kept on the books and wherever he may be he can be considered for any suitable employment which Her Majesty's Government may be able to offer and Her Majesty's Government will continue to have an interest in his career and in his welfare. The main object of this new deal is to make clear the position of present members of the unified Colonial Service and to create a firm foundation upon which they can build their future careers.' Mr. Lyttelton hoped that recruitment would be stimulated and young men and women encouraged to come forward to carry on the great tradition which so many of those present had bequeathed, or would bequeath, to posterity.

Members of the Oversea Civil Service would be the first to be considered when other Governments asked for the loan of officers for particular tasks, but although the possibility of an entirely new Commonwealth Service was not ruled out, the point had not yet been reached when it would be wise to embark upon such an adventure. The new Service now proposed had a glorious tradition and in proposing the traditional toast of the Corona Club, Mr. Lyttelton coupled with it the future prosperity of Her Majesty's Oversea Civil Service.

The Corona Club (1961)

Much of Mr. Macleod's speech dealt with the new Department of Technical Co-operation and with the scheme for retaining overseas officers in territories where they were still needed, and did not add greatly to what was known already. His cautious avoidance of the name of the man who is to be the permanent head of the Department, although it was already known to a great many people, led others who thought they had followed Mr. Macleod's gaze in the right direction to some wrong and remarkably improbable conclusions.

There was one phrase in the earlier part of the speech which attracted particular attention. 'The sort of person the new Department will be looking for,' said Mr. Macleod, 'will be exactly the sort of person who has always sought to join one branch or other of Her Majesty's Overseas Service.' How significant that phrase will be in the future remains to be seen, but in the Connaught Rooms on this particular occasion it aroused a good deal of comment for members of the Corona Club, while being fittingly modest, are not unaware that a spirit of service and tradition has always been a criterion for the sort of person who sought – successfully – to be a member of what is still, with pride, called the Colonial Service (Mr. Macleod recalled that in the House of Commons he himself had spoken of the 'modern Colonial Service'). Will the new Department ... ? Well, it was a good talking point after dinner, and many opinions were expressed on the Department's possibilities, including Mr. Macleod's hope that it would help members of the Service who want to carry on the kind of work overseas they had been doing so far.

On the subject of the Overseas Aid Scheme whereby the United Kingdom Government bears certain financial responsibilities for overseas officers in territories approaching or achieving independence, Mr. Macleod announced that, to date, 34 separate Governments and Administrations had agreed to take part in the scheme; that 20 agreements had already been signed and it was hoped the remainder would soon be in final shape. These Governments employed about 16,000 officers who would be covered by the scheme and of these 10,000 were in East Africa where the scheme was already in operation on the basis of the Flemming Commission's recommendations which had made such considerable improvements in conditions of service of overseas officers. But the Flemming Commission's recommendations could only have been framed because the overseas aid scheme had been evolved. It was through the scheme, said Mr. Macleod, that we hoped to avoid what would otherwise be a tragic waste of human skills and wisdom, while at the same time providing a very real help to overseas Governments. The function of the modern Colonial Service was not one of imperial domination. It was the constructive and the practical task of helping countries forward in their development towards nationhood. Mr. Macleod claimed that we had the finest organisation in the world for providing professional and technical assistance to under-developed territories – in fact, we already had the kind of Service for which the United Nations was now groping in handling the problems of the Congo.

A special word of thanks was said by Mr. Macleod to the Secretary of State's Advisers who had, over the years, made available a vast amount of detailed and technical knowledge acquired not only academically but also by hard experience in the field. Many of the Advisers would soon move over to the new Department, and Mr. Macleod wanted to take this opportunity to say 'Thank You' to them.

A word of warm gratitude was also said to Mr. E. R. Edmonds, who for so long had done so much for the Club as its Honorary Assistant Secretary, but who would soon be giving up this work when he retired from the public service; Mr. R. H. Hobden, also of the Colonial Office, would succeed Mr. Edmonds as Assistant Secretary. From the response to Mr. Macleod's words, it was obvious that Mr. Edmond's departure would be deeply regretted. The retirement from the Committee of Sir Richard Hawes and his succession by Sir Geoffrey Nye was also announced. Mr. Aldridge, late of the Cyprus Service, had also left the Committee on his departure from the Colonial Office and retirement from the Service. His place as representative of the younger serving officers had been taken by Mr. Peter Lloyd who was at present on secondment in the Colonial Office from Kenya.

Towards the end of his speech Mr. Macleod discarded his notes and his final words, spoken with deep conviction, made a considerable impression. He said: 'Gentlemen, before I propose the Toast I only want to say one word in passing about the problems that confront us so much in the world today. I am not going to go through, one by one, the visits I have made since last we met at the Corona Club dinner. I remember, perhaps in particular, the visit to Uganda at the opening of the new Legislative Council in Kampala where everything was planned in the most minute detail as a replica of the House of Commons. Everything there from the Speaker to the Mace to the Bar of the House was familiar, and this seemed to me to illustrate very well, first of all, the folly of thinking that with the Mace and the traditional copy of Erskine May you can necessarily transplant a form of democracy that has taken us hundreds of years in this country to acquire, but equally on the opposite side of this coin it is a greater folly still not to try and pass on the best of our heritage even if sometimes the trees that we plant bear strange fruit. And the second reflection I would like to take is from my visit to Tanganyika to the constitutional conference there. If one looks down this high table, one can see so many people who have been associated with that magnificent role of Governors from Tanganyika, Symes, Jackson and Twining with us here tonight, and before them Cameron and after them Turnbull. It is a magnificent record that these men have for service to their country, and Tanganyika is one of the most hopeful of all the countries in Africa. We have had some success, and the French have had some success, in bringing in Africa countries towards their independence which have been largely African States. What one must also realise is that no country has yet been successful in bringing towards a happy, peaceful independence, a country where many races have their homes. This is the greatest of all challenges in front of us at the present time. Africa is full of examples of what can happen. From the example of the Congo, if independence comes too fast, to other examples in Africa of what can happen if constitutional advance is too long delayed. Have we then in these countries a real chance of success? Gentlemen, with all my heart I believe we have. I think we have a better chance than any of the others, and I say this because of the work that you and the people who begun the work have done in the past. I think we have a better chance of success because the foundations have been more securely laid and the credit goes for this not to Secretaries of State alone, all of whom no doubt have tried in their different ways to help, but to the people of the Service. All we can say is this: we cannot be certain of success; we can take the couplet from Addison, perhaps, as our guide: 'Tis not in mortals to command success but we'll do more, Sempronious, we'll deserve it.' Now there is one common bond that all Secretaries of State have, that they may differ in their politics, they may differ in their approach and judgement in what is right as regards pace, but everyone of them shares together a common pride in the Service with which they serve. Everyone of them shares together a deep sense of gratitude for what has been done in the past, and that is why Secretaries of State are so proud year after year to come to this gathering and to propose the Toast which I now give you. My Lords and Gentlemen, I give you the Toast, the Corona Club.'

The New Year Broadcast (1962)

B y tradition the Secretary of State for the Colonies speaks at the New Year to all those for whom the Colonial Office is responsible. This year Mr. Maudling said:

'I have only recently come to the Colonial Office. This broadcast gives me a chance to introduce myself. May I begin to do that by wishing all of you a very happy New Year. I hope that in the course of the coming year I shall be able to travel yet more widely and see for myself more of your problems and achievements.

I know only too well that there are many among you for whom the past year brought disaster rather than happiness. I am thinking of those whose homes and livelihood were destroyed in the hurricane that struck British Honduras in November; those who suffer as a result of flood and famine in East Africa; and the people of Tristan da Cunha, whom a volcanic eruption drove from their home perhaps for ever, changing their whole way of life. I am sure you will wish me to take this opportunity of thanking on your behalf the many countries, within and outside the Commonwealth, which gave help and to mention also the rescue and relief work done by the British Navy, Army and Air Force.

Since Iain Macleod spoke to you last year, Sierra Leone with two and a half million people and Tanganyika with nine million have joined the independent nations of the Commonwealth. The Northern and Southern Cameroons, which like Tanganyika we administered as a trust territory, are no longer our responsibility. The number of people for whom my office is responsible today is little more than a third of what it was a mere five years ago.

And this process continues. For example, the past year has seen significant constitutional moves in Nyasaland, in the Gambia, in British Guiana and in Malta; and in less than a year from now we shall hope to be welcoming Uganda as a new, sovereign nation of the Commonwealth.

We also, during the past year, agreed on a date for the independence of the West Indies Federation. Then Jamaica decided to leave the Federation. We are now going ahead with plans for Jamaica to become independent on its own and there is to be a final conference in London in February.

On this question of West Indian federation we have always sought to create conditions in which the decisions could be taken by the West Indian people themselves, many of whose political leaders I hope to meet when I visit the West Indies in January.

What we sought for the West Indies was basically what we seek for all our territories – responsible self-government within the Commonwealth in conditions that ensure to the people concerned both a fair standard of living and freedom from oppression from any quarter. Even when it becomes clear that independence is in sight, many hurdles often remain to be cleared. That is why we must be wary of demands for immediate, unconditional independence for all Colonies, as well as of what may seem more reasonable demands for strict time-tables. Timing is all important and is not in our hands alone. Any time-table for, say, Kenya must depend on the answers to a number of questions which cannot be decided by us alone. I was in Kenya recently to meet the people who must share responsibility for these decisions; we are to have a conference in February. I hope we shall be able to build on common ground which I believe exists between the main parties. From Kenya I went to Nyasaland, and on to Northern Rhodesia, where we have an internal constitutional problem to resolve, without any real agreement among the parties on the solution. Nor indeed is there unanimity among all sections on the future of the Federation as a whole. Neither in Africa nor elsewhere do you solve such problems overnight, whether political or economic, and it would be disastrous to forge ahead in the blind hope that they would somehow solve themselves, as if by magic, after independence.

There are certain special cases – territories which are very small, perhaps, or very poor, or remote and vulnerable – possibly all of those things – and which would consequently find complete independence hard to sustain. It is clear that my office is going to be increasingly occupied with such territories. Let me emphasise that we recognise that their peoples no less than any others have the right to run their own affairs. All we feel is that the conditions of true independence and the obligations of complete sovereignty seem likely to be beyond these countries' capacity for a long time ahead. The answer for them may lie in association with other territories but there are many different forms which their position within the Commonwealth could take. Whatever is worked out must be acceptable to the majority of the people.

I have been talking mainly about the politics of independence. But I do not want to give the impression that we in Britain are impatient to shuffle off our responsibilities towards Commonwealth countries less fortunately placed than our own. That is not the case at all. The more direct forms of help – grants in aid and under the Colonial Development and Welfare Acts, and so on – are not really appropriate after independence, but we remain ready to offer practical help within the limits of our capacity and in whatever form is acceptable. That is one reason why, during the past year, responsibility for British technical aid has been concentrated in the hands of a new Government Department, the Department of Technical Co-operation. Among other things that the Department has in its schedule is the Overseas Service Aid Scheme – the plan, announced last year, by which the British Government can help overseas Governments to continue to employ British experts, specialists and administrators, without themselves incurring the high cost formerly associated with expatriate staff. I am very glad that virtually every dependent territory to whom the scheme was offered has agreed to accept it, and it has already been brought into effect in relation to the great majority of officers serving overseas.

I have taken this opportunity to go over these ideas of ours for the future of the dependencies, because the notion may have got about that a change of Secretary of State means a change of policy. That is not so.

We are going ahead in pursuit of our declared aims, because we believe this will strengthen and consolidate this newly transformed Commonwealth to which your countries and mine are proud to belong.'

To the Service – Past and Present (1962)

A great many members and former members of Her Majesty's Overseas Service will be sad to see the end of *Corona* and on the occasion of the last number I should like to send this message.

Corona has been in a very real sense a Service journal and it has played a significant role in fostering a corporate spirit in the Overseas Service and the old Colonial Service at a time when the whole character of the Service has been undergoing fundamental changes. The astonishing versatility of members of the Service on and off duty has been vividly reflected in the pages of *Corona* and I know how valuable your journal has been in helping members of the Service, wherever they may be, to keep in touch with development elsewhere.

Corona is being wound up but the Overseas Service continues to play a vital part in the orderly development both of independent countries and of the remaining dependent territories. Her Majesty's Government are fully conscious of the great importance of the role of the Service in the continuing evolution of these territories and of the Commonwealth as a whole.

Those officers of the Service who have retired can look back with immense pride on the progress achieved. The tasks facing the Service now and in the years ahead are no less stimulating and exacting than those which faced their predecessors, and I congratulate members of the Service on the way they have adjusted themselves to the radical changes in the nature of their responsibilities and have accepted the challenge of the new Commonwealth.

To those officers who have retired or who are about to retire, I send my sincere thanks and I am confident that those who stay will continue to uphold the high traditions of this great Service.

DUNCAN SANDYS
Secretary of State for the Colonies
and for Commonwealth Relations.

FROM THE RT. HON. VISCOUNT BOYD
OF MERTON, C.H. (1962)

A few years ago, when I was Secretary of State for the Colonies, I said at a Corona Club dinner that members of Her Majesty's Overseas Service belonged to the best Service in the world. For the past fourteen years one means of knowing the Service's record has been through its journal, *Corona*, and it is very sad that this is now to disappear. Despite almost over-whelming changes and dwindling numbers, the Service still shows its traditional devotion to duty in many parts of the Commonwealth.

The end of *Corona* is itself a sign of that devotion. Those members of the Overseas Service who have been placed in difficulty or distress by rapidly changing conditions may not always find it easy to evaluate what they have built on the foundations laid by their forerunners in the Colonial Service; and many will wish they had been given more time to complete their work. But history will undoubtedly recognise them as servants of the Crown who, whatever their personal feelings, set out loyally to do the task entrusted to them – the conversion of an Empire into a Commonwealth.

The end of *Corona* marks the end of an era, but the men and women of that era whose way of life is set down in their journal can rightly feel that they belonged to the best Service in the world.

III. THE COLONIAL SERVICE AND THE TRANSFER OF POWER

a) H.M.O.C.S. AND LOCALIZATION

I n 1954, after six years of its existence, *Corona*, the Journal of Her Majesty's Colonial Service, found itself orphaned and, as it were, under new management. Now there was, after more than a century of identity, to be no more Colonial Service. Instead, its successor would be called Her Majesty's Overseas Civil Service (actually, it started off as HM Oversea Civil Service, until the Colonial Office's grammarians conceded the use of 'overseas' as an adjective instead of only an adverb). The change was far more profound than just a change of name. Above all, there was one fundamental item which concerned every member of the Colonial Service: in future, recruitment would be restricted to a contract basis. It was the end of the Colonial Service as a permanent and pensionable career Crown service, though the successor Service was still the only one of Britain's overseas civil services ever to bear the title of His/Her Majesty's.

Hand in hand with this reconstruction of the metropolitan recruitment system went a top-gear campaign of schemes aimed at the accelerated recruitment and training of local men and women to staff the public services on which the new nations would rely so heavily at their forthcoming independence. Variously known as 'Africanization', 'Malayanization', Niger-ianization' etc., the umbrella term 'Localization' came into wide use. The pioneers were Malaya and the Gold Coast, both becoming independent in 1957, and Nigeria, which began to tackle the problem in earnest from 1952 and whose expatriate manpower crises caused the Colonial Office to come up with its Special Lists 'A' and later 'B' retirement schemes. However, the whole of the colonial empire was soon characterized by the localization of its civil services. Institutes of Administration with special courses for training Africans to become the new District Officers were opened in nearly every territory (notably in Northern Nigeria, whose pioneering programme became a model throughout Anglophone Africa), with several of them soon achieving an international reputation in the evolving field of public administration training. One of the inaugural training schemes for African DOs is described here.

The two Sections of Part III treat of the closely interwoven and critical impact of the establishment of H.M.O.C.S. on its personnel as reflected in the pages of *Corona*, their own journal, and of the accelerated localization of the public services, leading to their individual considerations of whether – and if so when – to seek early retirement.

Below is a chronology of colonial territories which became independent during the life-time of *Corona*:

1948 Ceylon, Palestine
1957 Gold Coast, Malaya
1960 Cyprus, Nigeria, British Somaliland
1961 Sierra Leone, Tanganyika
1962 Jamaica, Trinidad and Tobago, Uganda

Recruitment for the Overseas Service

by W. D. SWEANEY

I n the June, 1951, issue of *Corona,* Major H. J. E. Jones contributed an
article on recruitment for the Colonial Service at the end, in 1950, of
the first phase of post-war recruitment of expatriate officers which
began in 1945. It may now be of interest to readers to have some account of
recruitment trends during the period 1951–59.

Major Jones showed the considerable increase which had occurred in the
scale of recruitment compared with before the war and indicated the
difficulties which had been encountered in meeting the new demands in face
of full employment in the United Kingdom, the continuation of national
service, the tendency of candidates to be older and to marry earlier than
formerly, and the uncertainty which candidates felt about a career overseas.
But by 1950 or thereabouts the age pattern was getting back to normal and
the excessive pressure of post-war recruitment appeared to have eased.

It ought perhaps to be explained that the recruitment we are considering
is that which is undertaken by the Colonial Office. It covers those overseas
appointments which in general require a university degree or professional
qualification. As is well-known the Crown Agents for Oversea Governments
and Administrations also undertake a considerable amount of recruitment,
mainly for appointments which call for technical qualifications or
experience, but this recruitment is outside the scope of the present and
the previous article.

Before dealing with overseas appointments it should be made clear that
every effort is made by overseas Governments to fill recruitment vacancies
in their public services by the appointment of suitably qualified local
candidates. This is as it should be. The improved educational facilities in
overseas territories, supplemented by an increasing use of educational and
training facilities in other countries, has brought about an expansion in the
number of qualified local candidates; and many territories have made special
arrangements designed to ensure that local candidates, whether they are in
the territory or studying overseas, are given the opportunity to apply for
public service vacancies as and when they occur. It is only when and to the
extent that local recruitment is insufficient to meet the need for qualified
staff in the public service that the Colonial Office (or the Crown Agents) are
asked to recruit overseas candidates. This has been the general policy for
many years, but as the overseas territories have developed it has become
possible to draw to a greater extent than formerly on local candidates for
filling vacancies for which a university degree or professional qualification
are required. Much progress has been made in this direction during the past

years, but despite this the demand for qualified and experienced overseas candidates has remained high.

This can be seen from the following figures of appointments made through the Colonial Office during the three years 1956 to 1958:

1956 1,286
1957 1,296
1958 1,335

It may be thought surprising that recruitment should have continued on this scale during a period which has been marked by considerable constitutional advance in the overseas territories and when many more local candidates than formerly have qualified for appointment; but the fact is that the demand for qualified staff has increased as social, economic and political development has proceeded. This growing demand for qualified staff is not of course confined to the public service, but is found also in many other fields of employment as the structure of society has become more complex. The public service therefore finds itself in competition with other employers for the available local talent and the need to draw upon overseas sources remains.

The figure of 1,335 appointments completed through the Colonial Office in 1958 included 77 administrative officers, 65 agricultural officers, 181 men education officers, 119 women education officers, 179 civil, mechanical and electrical engineers, 119 medical officers and 140 nurses. It has not been easy to fill vacancies on this scale covering such a wide variety of professional categories. The period since 1951 has been one of continuing full employment in this country. Until the last year or two it was the common experience of employers here that there were more vacancies than suitable candidates to fill them. Before the war it was usual for candidates to have to seek out employers who might be willing to offer them a job. In recent years it has been more a matter of employers seeking candidates. The papers have been full of advertisements of employment vacancies. Schools and universities have been inundated by visits from potential employers seeking young recruits, and many young graduates have been in the fortunate position of having a number of offers of employment from which to make a choice. In such conditions it has not been easy to find suitable candidates to fill overseas appointments. The advantages which Government employment has customarily offered of pensionability and security of tenure are also now offered by many commercial and industrial employers; and political developments have diminished the security offered by a career overseas. Nevertheless, the feeling of wishing to lend a hand in the development of the overseas territories still motivates a good many candidates and the fact that life in the United Kingdom tends to be so highly organised and specialised causes others to want to break away and look for openings overseas where they may find more scope for initiative and greater opportunities for shouldering responsibilities at an earlier age.

The pattern is, however, changing in that there are now fewer permanent and pensionable vacancies available for filling by overseas candidates.

Formerly there was a preponderance of permanent and pensionable appointments, but the proportion of contract appointments has been increasing and in 1958 nearly 60 per cent of all the appointments made through the Colonial Office were on contract terms. For certain categories – administrative, agricultural, audit and some others – overseas recruitment continues to be mainly on pensionable terms. For other categories – engineers and architects, for example – recruitment is now almost wholly on contract. Education appointments are mostly on contract although there is still a fair number on pensionable terms. In the case of medical appointments the proportion is about half and half. In some cases vacancies may be filled on pensionable or on contract terms: selected candidates sometimes have a preference for one or the other and it is by no means certain when recruitment begins whether pensionable or contract terms are the more likely to attract the right candidate. Some flexibility can therefore be a help.

Nowadays many candidates are interested in going overseas for a limited period only and do not wish to commit themselves at the outset to a career abroad. Some who take a temporary appointment eventually decide that they like the life and work and they may then ask to be considered for transfer to the pensionable establishment. Others may ask for a renewal or extension of their contract. But many complete one tour and then revert to home employment. This means that the same vacancies have to be refilled every few years – a process which has been likened to attempting to fill a bucket with a hole in it – and, particularly in territories where there are short tours, the frequent turnover of staff may not be in the best interests of efficiency. For the Governments concerned contract recruitment may be uneconomic unless the officers serve for a reasonable period of years. It must also be remembered that recruitment itself is a costly and time consuming business. Candidates whom it is desired to appoint on contract are usually already in a job somewhere. The problem is to find them. Advertisement is often the only means. National newspapers and periodicals and professional journals are used for this purpose. The professional journals are often the most fruitful source but they may appear at infrequent intervals and this tends to protract the recruitment process. Selected candidates naturally have to give reasonable notice to their existing employers and may have domestic matters to settle before going overseas. These, too, take time. To reduce the frequency and costs of recruitment and give greater continuity among staff, as well as to provide terms designed to attract candidates who wish to serve in their chosen employment for a period of several years, a good deal of thought has been given to offering longer term contracts and such contracts are now available for certain appointments in one or two territories.

So much for the growing importance of contract appointments. As already stated, pensionable recruitment continues to be relied upon for most administrative, agricultural and certain other categories of appointment. The traditional basis of staffing these services is by the recruitment of graduates, who then undergo a course of training before taking up their overseas appointments. Such candidates are usually contacted at their universities and there is less need for recourse to public advertisement.

There are close links between the Colonial Office and United Kingdom universities. These have been built up over a period of many years and continue to be maintained. Visits are made to the major universities to talk to potential candidates. They naturally wish to know as much as possible about the prospects of a career in the Overseas Civil Service in the light of political developments. Every effort is made to deal frankly with all enquiries on this subject and the factors involved are drawn to the attention of every candidate for pensionable appointment. The protection afforded by the White Paper on the Re-organisation of the Colonial Service which was issued as Col. No. 306 in 1954 is explained to candidates. The publication of this document marked an important stage in the development of the Overseas Service. It established Her Majesty's Overseas Civil Service as the successor to the former Colonial Service and Her Majesty's Government declared that it recognised a special obligation towards members of H.M.O.C.S. should the territory in whose public service they are employed attain self-government. In that eventuality Her Majesty's Government undertook to enter into an agreement with the Government of the territory concerned providing for certain assurances that the rights and conditions of such officers would be safeguarded and *inter alia* that compensation would be paid in the event of premature retirement resulting from constitutional changes. Effect has been given to these undertakings in the case of officers serving in the Federation of Malaya, Singapore, Ghana, Nigeria and Cyprus.

At this point it may be of interest to mention the arrangements which have been made for overseas recruitment for those territories which have attained independence or self-government. Ghana (at that time the Gold Coast) undertook a certain amount of contract recruitment in this country on its own behalf from 1954 onwards through a recruitment unit attached to the Commissioner's Office in London. The Colonial Office also continued to recruit for the Gold Coast right up to independence in March, 1957, but the experience gained by the Gold Coast Office during the preceding three years made it possible to organise a smooth and orderly hand-over of the work previously performed by the Colonial Office (and by the Crown Agents) when the time came for the Ghana Government to assume full responsibility for overseas recruitment. The Federation of Malaya took over recruitment from the Colonial Office (and Crown Agents) towards the end of 1957; the Western Region of Nigeria did so in April, 1959; the Federation of Nigeria is in process of taking over recruitment by stages; and the Northern and Eastern Regions are expected to make a start on similar lines before very long. All these Governments have therefore made, or are engaged in making, arrangements for continuing to recruit candidates from this country for appointment to their public services. The Colonial Office has on request provided advice and assistance to the new recruitment organisations and will continue to make available any help which may be desired to ensure the minimum disturbance to the flow of recruitment.

What of the future? The year 1959 is likely to mark a turning point in the volume of overseas recruitment handled by the Colonial Office. Statistics for the complete year are not available at the time of writing, but at the end of September, 1959, the number of appointments made totalled

840 compared with 976 for the corresponding period in 1958. The forthcoming independence of Nigeria is bound to have a marked effect as Nigeria has been (and continues to be) a large employer of overseas staff. A substantial fall can therefore be expected in the figures after 1960. The number of overseas vacancies available to candidates from the United Kingdom may of course continue undiminished, but the number filled through the Colonial Office will be less. Even so the figures of Overseas Service appointments filled are likely to remain a good deal higher than they were before the war. Pensionable recruitment may continue for some time to come for particular territories and particular branches of H.M.O.C.S., but the use of special longer term contracts may well be developed as an alternative to recruitments on pensionable terms. A number of overseas vacancies are filled by the appointment on 'secondment' or other such terms of officers from United Kingdom Government departments, local authorities and also from the B.B.C. and other public bodies. These are likely to continue in the coming years since in many cases the departments and organisations concerned are the main, or even the sole, source of persons with the requisite expertise; and it is very valuable both to the overseas Government and to the officer concerned to have facilities whereby overseas employment can be undertaken for a limited period in the knowledge that reversion to United Kingdom employment is possible at the end of it. The idea of forming a Central Pool of officers in the employment of Her Majesty's Government for service overseas has been mooted, but although it has obvious attractions there are very great practical difficulties in the way of a general scheme of that kind, not least from the point of view of assuring officers of a continuing career, and the best line of progress may well be the development of arrangements for 'seconding' staff from parent United Kingdom establishments to which a return is possible, as well as a continuation of direct recruitment by the overseas Governments themselves.

The Colonial Service and the Commonwealth

[The announcement of a forthcoming change of title from 'H.M. Colonial Service' to 'H.M. Oversea Civil Service' was made a few hours before distribution of this issue of *Corona* began in August 1954.]

In the Editorial of the May number of *Corona*, it was said that Parliament and the Press would be the mouthpiece of British opinion on proposals for a Commonwealth Service. Almost immediately thereafter the matter was raised in a Parliamentary debate from which we promised (*vide* page 205 of the June number) to quote more fully at a later date. Here now are some excerpts of particular interest to the Colonial Service. They follow the order of speech, and quotations from prominent Opposition M.P.s will be given in our next number. Mr. Alport (Conservative).

'... It is clear that if this alteration in the responsibilities of the Colonial and Commonwealth Relations Offices were to take place, it would affect fairly closely the status and composition of the existing Colonial Civil Service. We have had many statements made that the Colonial Service is finding it difficult to recruit sufficient people for administrative work, and is finding it difficult to keep up the high standard of entry. On a recent visit to East Africa, however, I was extremely impressed, as I am sure were all my colleagues, at the very high standard of the administrative officers available in the Colony of Kenya. What was of great interest to me was that many of those holding the most responsible positions were locally recruited men who had had – literally – a lifetime's experience of East Africa. They had not come in as many cases as I had expected by way of recruitment from the United Kingdom.

'One of the main criticisms of the present system was that if these individuals, who were, so to speak, citizens of Kenya – the same would apply to other Colonies in a lesser or greater degree – wished to get promotion, or even if they do not desire promotion but have it forced upon them, they might be transferred to a very different part to the world where all their experience and local knowledge would be wasted.

'I should have thought that the first principle for the reorganisation of the Colonial Service would be that it should be placed on a regional basis, that normally its members would not move from the region in which they were originally enlisted. For example, the Far East, East Africa, Northern Rhodesia and Nyasaland, West Africa and the West Indies form fairly composite and fairly easily defined regions of service. In that way we should ensure far greater continuity of service within the Colonial Service.

'I was interested in a criticism which was advanced by a distinguished Belgian administrator recently, in which he said that one of the weaknesses in our present structure of colonial administration was the fact that administrators, and Governors in particular, spent too short a time in any particular Colony or any particular post. Anyone who has had experience overseas would agree that it is the case that there is a constant change, a flux, so that when a man has got to know his job and becomes known to the people for whose administration he is responsible he is apt to be moved too soon to quite a different part of the world.

'One of the results of this change, in my view, would be increased local recruitment for the Colonial Service; and, secondly, a longer period of tenure of the offices to which people in the Service are appointed. I go further and say that I believe that we shall have to consider changing the basis by which the Civil Service personnel for the Colonial Office in the United Kingdom are selected from the home Civil Service, and in too few cases are recruited from those who have had direct administrative experience of conditions overseas.

'It is probable, and in my view inevitable, that as time goes on, and as political conditions in the Colonial Territories change, it will be more and more necessary to have as Governors men who have had political experience in the United Kingdom.

'Their job will be to act as political advisers and much less as direct administrators of the Colonial Territories. That will mean that one stage in their advancement – in many cases the climax of a Colonial Civil Service career – will be denied them. Therefore, if we are to encourage the best type of man to continue in the Colonial Civil Service, it is most important that we should be able to provide alternative means of his achieving the climax of a distinguished career.

'I see no reason whatever why someone who has served for some years in West Africa and East Africa, or wherever it may be, should not then be qualified to come home and take up the post of Permanent Under-Secretary in the Colonial Office. We have sent out Civil Servants from the Colonial Office as Governors; surely the principle should work the other way round.'

Mr. Braine (Conservative).

'... I think, however, that there is a strong case for abolishing the Colonial Office and erecting in its place a new Ministry of Commonwealth Affairs, responsible on the one hand for our relations with the Dependencies and, on the other hand, for providing administrative and technical services, not only for the Dependencies, but for former Dependencies which have achieved self-government but still require outside assistance. In my view, such changes would do nothing to impair the present happy relationship that exists between ourselves and the self-governing Dominions. In that respect, they would merely confirm the existing procedure. But it would have a profound psychological effect upon our relations with the Colonial Territories. The word 'Colony' would disappear. I have always thought that it was a misnomer. Emphasis would be given to the concept of partnership.

'One important difference ... might be that the new Ministry should be staffed not by the home Civil Service, but by men with practical experience of administration in the Dependencies. I stress that fact, because Commonwealth relations, in the last analysis, are human relations. The success of the exciting adventure in which we are engaged in the Colonial Territories – the task of helping 70 million human beings, for the most part poor and ill equipped, to catch up with the rest of the world – depends entirely upon the administrative and specialist skill of the colonial servant in the field.

'It should be a matter of the gravest concern to this House that uncertainty and doubt exists in the minds of Colonial Service Officers overseas. That such doubts do exist is not surprising. In the last decade, the incomparable Indian Civil Service has come to an end; we now see the Sudan Civil Service crumbling before our eyes, and in the Gold Coast a decision has been made to recruit no more administrative officers from this country. The fear of redundancy cannot fail to affect morale and, in turn, recruitment.

'That would be a tragedy, for two reasons. First, almost everywhere in the Colonial Territories political advance is outstripping administrative capacity. It is one thing to engage in the stimulating and exciting game of politics, but it is another to administer a province or a department without fear or favour. Yet the fact is that the success of the constitutional experiment in the Colonies is entirely dependent upon proper administration.

'The wiser colonial leaders recognise this fact. Dr. Nkrumah, in July last year, said that he recognised how necessary it was for the Gold Coast to go on enjoying the services of expatriate officers after independence had been achieved. He said:

'We find ourselves on the threshold of independence having to rely far more on the services of overseas officers than was the case in India.'

'He has promised security of tenure, and even promotion, to those officers who are prepared to stay at their posts. That is a wise decision.

'The second reason why the running down of the Colonial Service would be a tragedy is the effect it would have on the Service itself. In the Colonial Empire, as a whole, the demand for the services both of administrative and specialist officers is far greater than it was before the war. In the last eight years we have recruited 3 times as many forestry and legal officers; 4 times as many medical, administrative and agricultural officers; 7 times as many veterinary officers; 12 times as many surveyors and geologists, and 26 times as many educational officers as we did in the eight years before the war.

'These figures tell the story of colonial development since the war. But what is the more striking and alarming is the fact that demand has outrun supply. In 1951, the Secretary of State made 1,396 appointments, but at the end of the year he had 988 vacancies unfilled. In 1952 the story was much the same. He made 1,378 appointments, but at the end of the year there were 1,055 vacancies. Last year, having appointed 1,227 officers, he still could not find the personnel for another 1,048 vacancies.

'... The great question is how we can guarantee security and reasonable prospects for the men in the Service, attract men of the right kind to enter it, and ensure that all territories get the men they require. I have come to the conclusion that the present set-up is quite inadequate, and that we need a new and unified service. It is no use offering a man the opportunity to enter the Colonial Service unless he can be offered a career for life, and it is no use offering him a career for life in this field unless he understands that he is entering a *corps d'élite* which is dedicated to the service of the Commonwealth peoples.

'I believe that such a service should be open to all Her Majesty's subjects – whatever their creed, race or colour – who possess the right qualifications, but pay, continuity of employment and pensions rights should be underwritten by the United Kingdom Government. It is absolutely imperative that an officer should understand from the outset that if he is made redundant, through no fault of his own – possibly through the very administrative and political changes which he has helped to accelerate – he will not be thrown upon the scrap heap half way through his career.

'It may be objected that the cost, to this country, of such a scheme would be formidable, but I do not think that follows. I envisaged a scheme under which the United Kingdom would make a contribution to the cost of the service, the balance being provided by the employing Governments in proportion to their financial resources and not to the number of expatriate officers they employ. There would be a threefold advantage in this system. First, no Government acquiring the service of an expatriate officer would feel that they were undertaking a commitment which would block the way to advancement for their own men. Secondly, no officer need fear that if he took on such an appointment he would incur the risk of his career being terminated prematurely, through no fault of his own, and, thirdly, and perhaps most important of all from the point of view of the Colonial Empire, the poorer territories which in present circumstances cannot afford to pay high salaries would no longer be debarred from getting the best men.

'I do not think we should argue against a new Commonwealth Service on grounds of expense. We are moving into a new, delicate and difficult phase in Commonwealth relations, and we cannot afford not to have the best men training the colonial cadres. The colonial servant is far more than an envoy for this country. His job is to forge the links of mutual trust and understanding that alone can ensure that the Commonwealth holds together. It is the quality of the colonial servant's work, the confidence he inspires, the example he sets, that will determine whether some of the new states will decide to stay within the family circle or not. . . .'

Her Majesty's Oversea Civil Service

W hen this number of *Corona* was planned, a continuation of last month's 'The Colonial Service and the Commonwealth' was to have quoted further Parliamentary views about re-organisation of the Colonial Service. Now a White Paper under that title (Colonial No. 306) reflects many of those views in an official statement. White Paper quotations, therefore, are substituted for those originally intended.

'The term 'Her Majesty's Colonial Service' has been in use for well over a century to describe the members of the Public Services of the Colonies, Protectorates and other territories which are dependent upon Her Majesty's Government in the United Kingdom. Originally, the Colonial Service consisted of officers appointed from Britain or recruited locally from amongst British colonists. As time went on, staffs were increasingly built up from the indigenous or resident populations of the territories, but it has always been and still is necessary to recruit large numbers of men and women from Britain and other Commonwealth countries to supply needs which could not be met from local resources, especially in the professional, technical and higher administrative branches.

'Since 1930, these latter branches have been organised as 'unified' Services ... They have, rightly, regarded themselves ... as belonging to a general service under the Crown as well as to the local civil services of the territories in which they are immediately serving.

'The political developments now taking place or likely to take place in many of the territories ... make it necessary to review the situation of the Colonial Service, Constitutionally, all officers of the Colonial Service ... are servants of the Crown, and the conditions of their employment are embodied in the Colonial Regulations. These Regulations constitute the Secretary of State as the ultimate authority for appointments, discipline, promotions and general conditions of employment. The members of the Service ... are now asking, and are entitled to ask, what will be their position if and when as a result of constitutional changes, Her Majesty's Government in the United Kingdom are no longer able to exercise effective control over their tenure and conditions of employment as hitherto.

'The debt which the oversea territories owe to the loyal, devoted and efficient work of the men and women in the Colonial Service is inestimable. Their work is far from over. The task of building up fully equipped local Public Services is progressing fast; it is an evolutionary process which will be completed at different times in different places. But side by side there is going on the evolution of the Colonies and other territories themselves, and while their economies and activities continue to expand a wide field of opportunity and need for the skilled assistance of British staff remains. This fact is fully recognised by responsible leaders in the territories.

'It is then of the first importance to these countries ... that their progress should not be set back by the premature loss of experienced staff or by failure to attract new staff which they may require. There is a problem here which cannot be solved by the territorial governments alone or by Her Majesty's Government in the United Kingdom alone. Both sides must act in partnership.

'Her Majesty's Government in the United Kingdom recognise that they have a special obligation towards those officers of the Colonial Service who hold their present posts as a result of having been selected for them by the Secretary of State ... Should the territory in whose Public Service they are employed attain self-government, these officers are entitled to expect that the following conditions will be observed:–

1) So long as they remain in their existing employment, the Government of the territory concerned shall not alter their terms of service so as to make them less favourable than those on which the officers are already serving.

2) The pensions and other benefits for which they or their dependants may be qualified under existing laws and regulations shall be similarly safeguarded.

3) They shall continue to be regarded by Her Majesty's Government in the United Kingdom as members of Her Majesty's Service and as such to be eligible for consideration for transfer or promotion to any posts which the Secretary of State may be requested to fill in other territories.

4) The Government by which they are employed will not unreasonably withhold consent to their accepting any such transfer or promotion and will preserve their existing pension rights on transfer.

5) They will be given adequate notice of any intention to terminate their employment in consequence of constitutional changes and Her Majesty's Government in the United Kingdom will endeavour to find them alternative employment should they so desire.

6) In the event of premature retirement resulting from constitutional changes they will receive compensation from the Government of the territory concerned.

'Her Majesty's Government in the United Kingdom accordingly make known their intention, if and when a territory attains self-government, to ensure the observance of these conditions by formal agreement between Her Majesty's Government in the United Kingdom and the Government of the territory. The agreement will also provide for the continuing payment of pensions already awarded to officers and their dependants.

'... A list will be compiled of all officers now in the Colonial Service to whom Her Majesty's Government in the United Kingdom regard the arrangements outlined in the last two paragraphs as applying. The officers included in this list will be given a new corporate title and will be known as Her Majesty's Oversea Civil Service.

'When the new Service is in being, the question whether any particular vacancy, in the filling of which the co-operation of Her Majesty's Government is invited, should be filled by a Member of Her Majesty's Oversea Civil Service or on the basis of appointment to a purely local service, will be a matter for arrangement between Her Majesty's Government in the United Kingdom and the territorial government concerned. Any offer of appointment made by or on behalf of the Secretary of State will include a clear statement whether it carries with it membership of Her Majesty's Oversea Civil Service or whether the officer's contractual relationship will be solely with the territorial government. Officers in either category will, of course, be expected to regard themselves as being in all respects responsible to the territorial governments under which they are serving.

'Her Majesty's Government recognise that there are certain other categories of overseas pensionable officers who have been appointed to the service of territorial governments otherwise than by selection by the Secretary of State. These officers may be assured that their interests will not be overlooked when the agreements referred to above are being negotiated.

'Her Majesty's Government are aware that various proposals have been put forward for constituting a Commonwealth Service or an Oversea Service directly employed by Her Majesty's Government in the United Kingdom. The decisions embodied in the present statement are not intended to exclude development along some such lines should this be found to be desirable and practicable. But this is a question which needs and will receive very careful examination in the light of changing conditions. It involves complicated administrative and constitutional, as well as financial, problems, and Her Majesty's Government feel that they are not yet ready to reach any conclusions upon them.'

Her Majesty's Oversea Civil Service

Special Regulations by the Secretary of State for the Colonies

1) From the 1st October, 1954, there shall be constituted a Service to be known as Her Majesty's Oversea Civil Service and consisting of:
   (1) Persons who
       (*a*) have been appointed by the Secretary of State as members of the Services listed in the schedule to these Regulations; and
       (*b*) have not ceased to be members of such Service; and
       (*c*) shall within six months of that date have signified their desire to be enrolled as Members of Her Majesty's Oversea Civil Service.
   (2) Other Serving Officers of the Colonial Service who
       (*a*) are on probation or have been confirmed in pensionable offices; and
       (*b*) were selected for appointment by the Secretary of State; and
       (*c*) shall within six months of the date aforesaid have signified their desire to be enrolled as Members of Her Majesty's Oversea Civil Service; and

      (*d*) are recommended for enrolment by the Governor of the territory in which they are serving, and are accepted by the Secretary of State.

      (3) Persons not already in the Colonial Service who are hereafter offered by the Secretary of State and who accept Membership of Her Majesty's Oversea Civil Service on appointment to a post in a Colonial territory.

2) Appointments to Membership of Her Majesty's Oversea Civil Service shall be held during Her Majesty's pleasure as signified through the Secretary of State. The decision of the Secretary of State as to whether any person is a Member or shall be appointed to be a Member of Her Majesty's Oversea Civil Service shall be final.

3) Members of the Service who occupy any public office shall be known as serving members and will receive the pay and other terms of employment (including superannuation) attached to the offices which they hold under the governments or authorities by whom they are employed in accordance with the laws or regulations of those governments or authorities. Membership of Her Majesty's Oversea Civil Service will not of itself carry any remuneration or enrolment.

4) Serving members of Her Majesty's Overseas Civil Service shall be subject to the Colonial Regulations (Part I–Public Officers) in force for the time being, if and in so far as these apply in themselves, or are applied in principle by local regulations, in the territory in which the member is employed.

5) A serving member of Her Majesty's Oversea Civil Service, while having no claim to employment otherwise than in the office which he has been offered and has accepted, shall be eligible for consideration by the Secretary of State for employment in any post which he may be requested or authorised to fill, and may also be considered, as opportunity offers, for posts in Commonwealth or foreign territories for which Her Majesty's Government in the United Kingdom may be invited to recommend candidates. No member of Her Majesty's Oversea Civil Service shall forfeit his eligibility for such consideration by reason of his accepting a public office in a territory to which Colonial Regulations do not apply, or by reason of the Colonial Regulations ceasing to apply in the territory where he is for the time being serving.

6) A member of Her Majesty's Oversea Civil Service who ceases to hold any public office may, if he so desires and if the Secretary of State sees fit, be considered for further employment as if he were a Serving Member.

7) Her Majesty's Government in the United Kingdom reserve the right to vary, revoke or add to these regulations; provided that this right shall not be exercised to the disadvantage of any person who is at the time a Member of Her Majesty's Oversea Civil Service.

8) The Special Regulations made by the Secretary of State from time to time for the Services listed in the Schedule will be cancelled with effect from the 1st October, 1954.

Schedule

Colonial Administrative Service
Colonial Agricultural Service
Colonial Audit Service
Colonial Chemical Service
Colonial Civil Aviation Service
Colonial Customs Service
Colonial Education Service
Colonial Engineering Service

Focus on the Service

SOME COMMENTS ARISING
FROM THE OVERSEAS SERVICE BILL

'There is one big question mark hanging over this bill. Is it going to achieve all we desire? As I see it, there are two risks. They are both human problems. The first is the difficulty which officers may find in changing their role from one which has been executive to one which is advisory, and to advise people, moreover, who cannot have as much experience as they have and also, perhaps, seeing the advice they give in good faith and out of their vast fund of experience ignored. That would not be a pleasant or easy situation in which to find themselves. Many of them might find it difficult; some may find it impossible. Secondly, there is the position of officers, say, for example, in their thirties ... they have no way of knowing for how many years their services will be wanted or how far a full length career lies before them ...' *Sir Hendrie Oakshot.*

'Although for a long time I have been critical of the Colonial Service I have never been critical, with one or two exceptions, of the men in the field because I have always found them devoted men, working very hard for a very small reward and genuinely trying to do what they could to help the people in the countries in which they worked ...' *Mr. John Stonehouse.*

'A tribute to the Administration in Kenya is long overdue from a good many of us in this House. A similar tribute should be paid to all those serving in all African territories for which we are responsible ... Law and order must still be preserved. At the same time there is always the awful dilemma that if someone takes action in time to prevent a minor disturbance becoming a riot, it is almost certain some sections of the British Press will hurl at his head wild accusations of brutality. If, on the other hand, action is delayed and a minor disturbance becomes a riot ... there are equally accusations of delay in taking effective action. The growing feeling that whatever one does will be wrong is one of the reasons for lack of confidence in the future of the Overseas Service ...' *Sir Charles Mott-Radclyffe.*

'One of the difficulties confronting those who serve overseas arise from the fact that their pension rights are fixed at the time they enter the Service. By the time they leave to return to this country they find that conditions have altered so considerably that their pension ... is not worth anything like what it was estimated it would be worth ... I think the Government should take note of these things to see whether it would be possible to help these people ... After all, they served this country well during the time they were in the Colonial Service, often in isolated posts and at a risk to their health ...' *Mr. Glenvil Hall.*

'I cannot think why so many people seem to think that work in the Colonial Service should bar a man from diplomatic success. It seems to me that having to deal with Dr. Banda or Mr. Mboya is a supreme form of diplomatic examination and that those who can pass it might be called on to fill any diplomatic post anywhere ...' *Mr. Philip Goodhart.*

'A report of what my right honourable Friend the Prime Minister said at the (Corona Club) dinner says: 'To the Overseas Service he would say that they were happy and proud to remember their services in the past ...' Have we remembered, or are we remembering? ...' *Mr. John Tilney.*

Ourselves and the Future

In last month's mention of a House of Lords Debate on the Oversea Service, we expressed the hope that a Government statement about the future of the Service would out-date any printed account of the Lords' discussion. That hope has not yet been fulfilled, but as this number goes to press we feel that a statement cannot be long delayed. Extracts from certain of the speeches in the Lords' Debate are now given as a background to whatever may be said.

Lord Glyn opened the Debate by referring to the White Paper of 1954 which introduced the Oversea Service. Speaking of the position of members of the Service in countries moving towards self-government, he said: 'The tragedy is that if one meets these people and talks to them, one finds that they are quite prepared already to believe that they are going to be let down ... Here is a typical example of what has been said: half a promise made in a White Paper to which all these people pin their hopes, and month after month has passed with no indication from Her Majesty's Government whether they are going to implement that promise. I realise that we are passing through a difficult financial period, but it is rather alarming to think that something less than the subsidy we pay for pigs would meet this situation. It seems to me that if we expect to get good service from the servants we employ overseas, we must treat them fairly, and I do not think that at the moment they are being fairly treated ...

'Personally, I believe in a true Commonwealth Service, because the time has come when we ought to encourage spheres of influence throughout what used to be called the Colonial Empire, where the Dominions could take a share and play their part. They are anxious to do so. I see no reason why it should be confined to the United Kingdom. The geographical position of a good many of these (territories would surely enable some of the Dominions to give great attention to them, as they are in close proximity to them and know their requirements and needs. I believe it is of great importance at the present time that discussions should take place between Her Majesty's Government and some of the Dominion Governments as to whether there could be some interchange of Her Majesty's servants who have served in those territories, if they passed from the direct control of the United Kingdom to the control of one of the great Dominions.

'The other matter which I think ought to be emphasised is that a great many people seem to take the view that, because self-government is granted to these territories, there is no longer good work to be done. I hold the view that in fact there is far greater work to be done: more responsible work; work which will really matter and which will leave a recollection with those who initiate the first stages of self-government ...'

Lord Ogmore: 'The solution I would suggest is that we should have a service recruited, paid and pensioned by the United Kingdom Government, which should also guarantee its security. These officers would be available for secondment to any Government which required them, whether Colonial, or formerly Colonial, and whether within or without the Commonwealth. This would include Colonies, Protectorates, Protected States, Trust Territories, Condominia as well as independent members of the Commonwealth and countries like the Sudan and Iraq.

'The proposals of the Government are nebulous in the extreme. In Colonial Paper No. 306 the Government have created something which they have called 'Her Majesty's Oversea Civil Service.' It consists of the officers who were formerly on the list of the Colonial Service. But, so far as I can see, nothing has happened but the name. There has been no 'sea change.' ...'

Lord Milverton: 'While it is true to say that a great many of the leaders of these new nations today fully appreciate that they cannot, at the moment, do without the help of what was, and still is, known as the Colonial Service in all its branches, they are, in many instances, the slave of their own past speeches. They have run with popular emotion and have clamoured for the departure of the Colonial Service, whom now, in their own hearts, they know they cannot properly do without ...

'I feel particularly impelled to speak today because I am frequently appealed to by parents as to whether or not they should encourage their boys – or girls, as it is in some instances – to go into the Colonial Service. And I have to admit – and your Lordships can appreciate that it is with deep regret that I admit it – that I do not find the answer to that question easy to give. One of the reasons is the indecision which seems to me to lie beneath this facade of words which make up the White Paper we are considering today. If we analyse what substance lies behind this Paper, we find that it is very little ... It does not get us any further to call it Her Majesty's Oversea Civil Service. That does not make any essential change in the actual state of affairs today. I suggest that the state of affairs should cause deep concern and disquiet to us, as it does to members of the Service ...

'I believe it is true that the Colonial servant is fighting a battle on two fronts – and one of the fronts, I regret to say, is Whitehall. He is not satisfied that he will get the support which he feels he must have in order to enable him to do his work properly and be a credit to the Service of which he is so proud.

'I have no quarrel with the statement in the White Paper of the needs of the present and the future. It is perfectly true to say that never in our history was there a greater need for the best men we breed – and the best women, too – for the jobs in the Colonial Service in its new form. As I have already suggested, this Paper does not help us in any way to see how we are going to get the quality or quantity, unless some definite step is taken by the Government of this country to show the members of the Service that the British Government stand behind them and will see to it that they get a fair deal. I am not implying criticism of the new Governments of the Colonies: I am implying criticism of the way in which the members of the Service are liable to be treated by the Government in this country.'

Lord Tweedsmuir raised 'the question of people who have put their whole life capital into this Service, or are intending to do, and who may find, when they have become masters of their work and are perhaps some 10 or 15 years older, that their appointment is prematurely terminated. There seems to be an argument for investigating carefully something analogous to life assurance: for, after all, here is a man who wishes to ensure the security of his family, as he does in life assurance. If he has his whole career completely without interruption, he reaches a time when the need to pay for this assurance ceases. If his time is prematurely terminated, the money is forthcoming. I should have thought the parallel was close enough to make it well worth investigating.'

Lord Birdwood: 'I can see only one way out of this predicament, and that is that Her Majesty's Government, in some sweeping gesture of statesmanship, should assume entire responsibility, both for pay and for pensions of the Oversea Civil Service.'

The Earl of Munster: 'The White Paper No. 306, published in June 1954, is now in operation and I am advised that it has had generally a good effect. So far nearly 10,000 officers have applied and have been accepted for enrolment as members of the Overseas Colonial Service. This figure represents the great majority of those eligible to join, so that it may be said at once that this Paper was well received by the mass of the members of the Overseas Colonial Service ... I would say that it has done its job and done it reasonably well.

'I turn to the interesting observations made by Lord Tweedsmuir, who thought it would be possible to have some form of insurance against premature termination of service. I think the noble Lord knows that anybody in the Service today would receive compensation if his services were terminated when the Colony in which he served achieved self-government. But I hardly think it would be possible for Her Majesty's Government to undertake to insure every Colonial servant against this eventuality. Nevertheless, it is an ingenious idea, and I should like to communicate with my noble friend after I have discussed it with my right honourable friend the Colonial Secretary.

'May I now refer back to the White Paper ... Paragraph 13 referred to the possibility of setting up a Commonwealth or Oversea Service and pointed out that this raised a good many problems ... these problems are being examined very seriously, and I hope it will be possible to make a statement in the fairly near future about the results of this examination.'

Eyes on the Future I

I t is not easy to give a short answer to those who ask 'Where exactly have we got to?' in connection with the future of the Overseas Service and the security of its members. As *Corona* said not long ago: 'There can be no single blue-print for a future which will unfold at different times and in different ways.' Policy aimed both at security for those in the Service and the maintenance of sound administration in countries approaching self-government was largely empirical, its practice depending on conditions arising in individual territories and on agreement by those territories. Now the presentation to Parliament of the Overseas Service Bill has made the issues clearer.

In 1954 the formation of the Overseas Service as successor to the Colonial Service embraced safeguards for officers whose service is cut short by constitutional changes. For the first time it was recognised explicitly that Her Majesty's Government in the United Kingdom have a definite responsibility towards certain categories of officers and the new Service defined these categories and gave them a collective title – the Oversea Service, subsequently changed to 'Overseas'. Then came the 1956 proposals for recruitment of officers to a Central Pool for secondment to countries near self-government (and, on request, to self-governing Commonwealth countries); and for the setting up of a Special List of officers who would be in the service of Her Majesty's Government and would be seconded to the employing Governments. This Special List would apply in the first place to Nigeria but might later be extended to other territories.

The Central Pool has run into difficulties (as surmised by Sir Hilary Blood in his article on page 454 of *Corona* for December 1957), over the guaranteeing of a continuing satisfactory career to an officer recruited initially into the Pool for a particular job in a particular territory, but there is better news of the Special List. As and when circumstances make it desirable, Overseas Service officers should be offered transfer to the List, their salaries and terms of employment being agreed between Her Majesty's Government and the territorial Governments to which the officers are seconded. The United Kingdom will pay their pensions, recovering the money from the Governments concerned, and will look after them if they lose their jobs through no fault of their own. If a displaced officer cannot be found other work immediately, he will, if necessary, be kept on full pay for up to five years (or to the age of 55), the commitment being shared between Her Majesty's Government and the territorial Governments.

The purpose of the Overseas Service Bill is to implement this policy, and the Debate on it left no doubt that all parties were anxious to give it a fair wind. But many questions, mostly about the Special List, will present themselves to those affected. How tight a rein will the Treasury keep over appointments to the List? At what stage of development in their territories will officers know if the List will be open to them? Will new entrants be attracted unless they know before they join the Service that they will be able to transfer to the List if need arises? Will transfer to the List give an officer a life comparable to that which was his reason for joining the Service?

In view of the special interest of this matter the Debate is not being included in the monthly Parliamentary summary, which would be too brief to do it justice. There now follow extracts of the principal speeches and more will be given next month.

Mr. Creech Jones (L): ... 'The Secretary of State paid a tribute to the work, the loyalty, the integrity, the efficiency and the quality of the Colonial Service. I should like to join in testimony from my experience of its high quality. Sometimes I think critics of colonialism have not sufficiently recognised the very high standard of the work and the great contribution which these men and women made to civilisation and the extension of freedom.... The result of the coming of independence has been the tremendous anxiety felt by our own administrators and professional and technical staffs and the feeling that perhaps their own careers would suddenly come to an end and that they would be left stranded. The number of territories now reaching independence and emerging towards independence tend undoubtedly to contract the opportunities of these people ... .

'In regard to the Special List ... we were informed that it will possibly extend to Malaya. Is it contemplated that further steps will be taken in regard to other territories? ... I gather that the Treasury will hold the responsibility in regard to the appointments to the Special List. I can only hope that the Treasury will be much more forthcoming than it has been in the past. It is the Treasury, I think, which has blocked the Secretary of State in his ardent desire to get something moving for the Service in this field in order to cope with the changes brought about in the emerging territories.' (Mr. Lennox-Boyd said later in the Debate apropos the suggestion that all Service officers should come onto the Special List: 'At first sight that would appear to be an obvious thing to do, but I must put in a word for Her Majesty's Treasury and remind Hon. Members of the obligation there is on the Treasury not to enter into open-ended commitments without knowing exactly where they will lead.... I think that if there is to be a Special List there should be special circumstances surrounding it.')

Mr. Tilney (C): ... 'Could those on the Special List be seconded anywhere? Could they go to the United Nations, to the Colonial Development Corporation or to the Trucial Coast? I hope that they can ... the new Service should be like the Army and one should be able to be seconded wherever the interests of the Commonwealth lie.... . I regret that the Treasury seems to have so much control. I hope that it is control over the broad size of the Special List, and will not be used over actual detail to decide who should be taken on and who should be refused.... .'

Mr. Grimond (Lib): ... 'I hope the Government will bear in mind that the Colonial Service is one Service and that everyone in it has a right to look to the Government for reasonable pension provisions. As to the importance not only of the Colonial Service in the past but its continuing effect upon the world, I should have thought that there could not possibly be the slightest doubt ... we are in a difficult position in that Britain has a contracting field for the Colonial Service but there is an expanding need in the world ... we should now consider whether we ought not to found the kind of Commonwealth Service which has often been recommended ... available not only in the Commonwealth but in other territories....'

Miss Joan Vickers (C): ... 'Are women to be allowed to join the Special List? So far as I know, women can get only a certain way in this Service. They can become Administrative Assistants but I have never known a woman to be a District Officer, for instance. What is to be the future of women in this Service? Can their service be extended to several other territories under this scheme?'

Mr. M. Clark Hutchison (C) (a former member of the Colonial Service): ... 'I still keep in touch with many colleagues overseas ... there is no doubt that many of them are feeling a little insecure ... particularly men in their 30's and 40's who have heavy (family) commitments.... So far most of the uncertainty has been confined to territories on the threshold of complete independence, but it is permeating through the Service. It is my belief that in areas which have reached full independence, the abolition terms have, on the whole, been generous ... and I believe that in other areas which are to become independent the terms will be no less favourable. Nevertheless, we must bear in mind human nature ... there is always before us the melancholy situation of British officials who served in Egypt.' Mr. Hutchinson also said: 'In the old days men in the Colonial Service were very proud to serve in it and to give a lead to local peoples. It was a good life's work helping these people among whom our fellow countrymen went out to live. Regrettably, the word 'Colonial' now has an unfortunate meaning ... this is quite wrong ... but the name has been changed to the Overseas Civil Service. In my view that is a very bad choice. It is rather nebulous. I think it would be difficult to owe loyalty to a Service with such a name. Secondly, the name is a tongue twister: it is in fact a hissing and an abomination.... I suggest the name should be Her Majesty's Common-wealth Service.'

(Further extracts will appear in 'Eyes on the Future II')

Eyes on the Future II

*M*rs. Eirene White (L): ... 'We have waited a long time for this Bill ... I have looked at it with some apprehension ... the hand of the Treasury is all too evident in it ... just how much or how little the Secretary of State is ultimately able to perform seems to depend very much upon his relationship for the time being with the Chancellor of the Exchequer for the time being ... Is it purely the dead hand of the Treasury, or what are the real reasons that, apparently, make it so difficult to envisage a Service of the kind to which almost every previous Hon. Member has referred? They have referred to something that is not just a holding operation in, say, Nigeria – important as that might be – but something creative and positive, which will contribute to the Commonwealth and give us the kind of advantage which will, in many countries, be our only one. It is the sort of relationship that we may get through administration, university education and highly skilled technical co-operation, and the like, on which our influence in the Commonwealth is likely so largely to depend ...

'I am particularly concerned about the younger administrative officers ... When a country gets to near-self-government or to full self-government, it is the administrative rather than the technical people who are likely to be dispensed with, but it is of the utmost importance that, whilst in the Service, they should be of good quality ... We want to make this Overseas Service attractive to our high quality young people. They have to feel that they have the chance of a really satisfying service. It is not just a matter of pay or pension, important as that may be. It is also the idea that thought will be given to the best way of employing their talents at any particular time ...'

Mr. Bernard Braine (C): ... 'I cannot think of any more devoted and dedicated body in the whole of the Commonwealth than the men who devote their lives to the service of the less well-equipped, less advanced and less sophisticated peoples of our great family of nations. Theirs is a service which brings its own satisfaction, but it is not an easy job, and it is not an easy life. I said 'Hear, Hear' rather loudly when my Hon. Friend said that this House owes a debt to these men of the Overseas Service. That being so, I think that the Measure we now have before us is quite inadequate to meet the need ... Political advance in all these territories which have achieved or are about to achieve independence has far outstripped their administrative capacity ... Dr. Azikiwe and other political leaders have in the last few years made it absolutely clear that they want British administrative assistance to continue and on terms satisfactory to the men concerned ... we have a situation in which the demand for good men from the United Kingdom is not diminishing but is increasing. I allow at once that where administrative officers are concerned, particularly the senior ones, opportunities of the right kind are contracting ... one reaches the conclusion that at a time when anxiety is becoming keen and when a number of senior men in the Overseas Service are thinking in terms of taking their compensation and getting out, the field of opportunity, far from contracting, is widening, except as I have said, in the administrative service. As a result, we are faced with two related problems: first, how are we to provide the continuity of employment and good prospects of advancement for those men already in the Service: and secondly, how are we to ensure recruitment? ...

'I am convinced that there is no way out of the difficulty except by providing a single unified Service with pay and pensions underwritten by Her Majesty's Government in the United Kingdom ... I can see no reason even now why the re-employment of officers made redundant through no fault of their own but through political or administrative changes should be left to chance or goodwill or the whim of the Treasury ... redundancy often occurs because a man has done his job well and has hastened the day of self-government ... I must register my acute disappointment that the opportunity has not been taken in the Bill to tackle the problem more boldly and with greater imagination and generosity ... I should have thought that this is one of the very few issues which cannot be judged on grounds of immediate expense ...'

Mr. Iremonger (C) (a former member of the Colonial Service): ... 'I want to ask about the recruitment of young cadets just embarking on their careers. I have heard it said that we are asking too much of them, and that we are asking for an act of faith and sacrifice that is not fair ... I hope that the Bill puts some heart into these men who are contemplating entering what will be an enormously responsible Service. The gist of the Bill is that we shall say to these young cadets: 'Do not worry because, in the last resort, if the Government have made a Special List agreement with the Government of the Colony in which you will serve, you will then be the United Kingdom's 'baby' and the Government, if you are transferred to the Special List, will guarantee your pension and take you on the payroll until you are 50 and, if you are sacked unfairly, will try to find you another job.' I am not certain that this is all we ought to offer these officers in these circumstances ... I hope that this last-ditch guarantee will give them enough certainty of outlook to enable the Secretary of State to recruit the men we need ... I do not think we can emphasise too strongly the importance to the Service of obtaining young men of the coming generation, because they have grown up in a world in which nationalism exists ... at universities they meet the young men of the Africa of tomorrow ... They have an insight into and a sympathy with their passions and their dreams in a way which the old hands can never have, because it was not a part of their world. These men have a decisive part to play in the world and we in this House must do everything we can to ensure that they are forthcoming from this country to play it.'

Mr. Callaghan (L): ... 'This Bill is welcome ... but I do not think ... it will last in its present form. There will have to be a substantial review of our staffing arrangements for the overseas territories within the next few years in order to put them on a more permanent basis ...'

Mr. Lennox-Boyd: ... 'This debate has certainly shown the passionate interest of Hon. Members on both sides of the House in the welfare of the main instrument of Colonial development, Her Majesty's Overseas Civil Service. I am very glad that the speeches have taken on such an interested and, at times, such a vehement tone. I do not in the least resent that, I have been very anxious for this Bill for some considerable time. I am delighted that it has now been possible to introduce it, and I believe it will make a substantial contribution to the causes we all have at heart ... I recognise that by itself no Act of Parliament can solve our problems, either of recruitment or of the maintenance of a healthy Service on the scale that we all desire. A great many other considerations enter in and not least is the attitude of local Governments ... co-operation between ourselves and local Governments is imperative. When I say co-operation I mean not only words which are always welcome, but by deeds, which are even more welcome. There are now many evidences that responsible Ministers in the territories most concerned fully appreciate this fact and I hope they are taking every opportunity of making it abundantly clear ... I believe there is some dynamism in the Bill, but I was being brutally frank when I drew attention to the fact that all is not well and we ought not to think it is; above all we ought not to allow those in whose hands is the cure of these ills to believe that all is well. In Ghana approximately 400 officers have left, which is approximately 50 per cent. of officers entitled to compensation ... In Nigeria 23 per cent, of the entitled officers have retired and in Western Nigeria between 23 and 24 per cent. ... I commend the Bill to the House, and, through the House, send a message of goodwill to all who are serving in the Overseas Service and the thanks of the nation for the splendid work they are doing.'

Africans and the Public Service (1954)

A GOLD COAST STATEMENT*

T he first scheme to Africanise the Gold Coast Public Service was in 1925–26 when the Guggisberg Plan aimed to increase the number of Africans holding 'European Appointments' from 27 to a total of 231 during the period 1926–46. The scheme failed for lack of provision for training Africans in these appointments, and by 1946 there were only 87 Africans holding senior appointments.

In 1941, Captain Lynch, then Senior Assistant Colonial Secretary, was commissioned to carry out a survey of Departments and in 1944 his report, which covered seven Government Departments only, formed the basis of a Sessional Paper. Two principal recommendations were the launching of a scholarships programme and the definition of Africanisation policy which aimed at giving preference to Africans for appointments to the Senior Service over Overseas Officers. In 1945 a Scholarships Selection Board was set up to replace other Boards for separate scholarships and to centralise the Government's training programme through scholarships.

In 1948, an interim Public Service Commission was established to advise the Governor on appointments and promotions in the Service; this Commission, which evolved a policy for translating the Africanisation policy into action as a means of ensuring that the claims of all suitable and qualified African candidates received preference over expatriate recruits, was followed by the setting up of a Select Committee of the Legislative Council in 1949. The Committee endorsed the Public Service Commission's policy of recruiting Africans to senior posts in preference to expatriates, and made wide educational recommendations to ensure an increased flow of qualified Africans as rapidly as practicable.

The 1950 Order in Council provided for the establishment of a statutory Public Service Commission and a Commissioner for Africanisation was appointed. The recent Lidbury Commission recommended that this function should be absorbed in a new post – Director of Recruitment and Training in the Office of the Establishment Secretary.

The policy of the Gold Coast regarding recruitment was declared in 1952 as follows:

(i)   That when a vacancy occurs in any post (other than posts normally filled by promotion of serving officers) no consideration should be given to the recruitment of an expatriate unless and until, after examination of the claims of all Gold Coast African candidates, the Public Service Commission is satisfied beyond reasonable doubt that no such qualified and suitable candidate is available.

(ii)   That if no Gold Coast African candidate is available, an expatriate should be recruited, if possible on contract or temporary secondment.

(iii) That if an African is in training to qualify for the post, the duration of the contract offered to an expatriate should be determined by the date when it is expected that a qualified African will be available.

(iv)   If there are no reasonable prospects of local candidates becoming available in the foreseeable future, the length of the contract offered to an expatriate should be governed by the market conditions.

(v)   If it is not possible to engage expatriates on contract to fill posts for which no Africans are available, then expatriates may be recruited on pensionable terms.

(vi)   In every case where an expatriate officer is appointed on contract, suitable arrangements should be made to ensure that a Gold Coast African is available to take over at the expiration of his contract.

(vii) There shall be no lowering of standards and in consequence no lowering of qualifications now prescribed for appointment.

(viii) Promotions within the Service should continue to be on merit alone without regard for colour, and the claims of meritorious Public Officers in the Service should take precedence over those not already in the Service.

(ix)   The retrenchment of expatriate officers in favour of Africans is not contemplated.

(x)   In filling vacancies, citizens of other neighbouring West African territories who apply in response to advertisements published locally should not be given equal claims with citizens of the Gold Coast (including Togoland under the United Kingdom Trusteeship), but their applications for employment should be considered along with those of expatriate candidates.

(xi)   Citizens of other neighbouring West African territories who have been resident in the Gold Coast for eight years or more should be considered for the purposes of recruitment as Gold Coast citizens.

(xii) Any reference to Africans in the field of recruitment into the Public Service here should be interpreted to mean Gold Coast Africans, and the terms 'Gold Coast African' should he defined as any person one of whose parents at least is a native of the Gold Coast.

Since this policy was laid down the Government has decided that there shall be no further recruitment of overseas officers on pensionable terms, the only exceptions being cases specifically stated to the Cabinet for individual sanction. The policy has also been qualified by the important statement made by the Prime Minister in the Legislative Assembly on the 8th July, 1953.

In November, 1952, the Government set up an official Working Party to review the Africanisation programme and to examine the staffing position in each grade and Department, to advise on departmental training schemes, training grades and scholarship awards to ensure a further acceleration of Africanisation, having regard to the need to maintain the Service's efficiency. The Working Party's interim report was submitted to a Standing Committee on Africanisation which has the following terms of reference:–

The Standing Committee on Africanisation is required to work within the framework of the policy enunciated in the statement made by the Prime Minister on the 8th July, 1953, in the Legislative Assembly on the future of the Public Service, with particular reference to overseas staff, and within that framework:

(i)   to review the Africanisation policy of the Government from time to time and to make recommendations to the Government;

(ii)   to consider proposals submitted to it for the implementation of the Africanisation policy, and to make recommendations on them to the Government;

(iii)   in particular, to consider in the light of the Government's views the final report of the Working Party which recently reviewed the Africanisation Programme and to submit recommendations regarding the proposals therein; and

(iv)   to advise on any other question affecting the Africanisation of the Service that the Government may refer to it.

The Working Party's final report has been submitted to the Standing Committee for consideration and for recommendations to be made to the Government.

Against this 'historical' background to Africanisation in the Gold Coast, over the past twenty-nine years, recruitment and training stand out with particular interest and importance.

The functions of the Government's Recruitment and Training Branch are, broadly:

(a)   to plan ahead the recruitment needs of the Civil Service and to estimate how far these can be met from Gold Coast sources;

(b)   to ensure that steps are taken to tap all possible sources of local recruitment;

(c)   in particular, in the field of recruitment, to be responsible, in conjunction with the Public Service Commission, for ensuring that the principles governing appointments to the Public Service are rigidly and uniformly observed; and

(d)   to be responsible for the general co-ordination and control of training in, and for, the Civil Service.

These functions are carried out subject to the overall responsibility of the Chief Secretary.

Methods of recruitment aim at securing an indigenous Civil Service without loss of efficiency. The Government has decided as a matter of policy that where the size of a Department justifies it, it should have a training branch or section with full-time training staff in charge.

In the Administrative Service, of about 173 posts in the grades of Administrative Officers Classes III and IV, 42 are at present held by Africans, all, except one, of whom have been appointed to these posts since

1950. For over two years, overseas recruitment into the Administrative Service was stopped. To relieve severe staff shortages and strain in the Ministries, however, and in the absence of qualified local candidates, the Government has decided to appoint on temporary contract terms for two tours 12 overseas Assistant Secretaries. There are now over 40 vacancies in the establishment.

In the more senior grades, there is one local officer in the grade of Administrative Officer Class I and four in the grade of Administrative Officer Class II (Senior Assistant Secretary). In addition, there axe six Africans in the training grade of Senior Assistant Secretary (Supernumerary).

All posts in the Executive Class, i.e. Executive Officer, Higher Executive Officer and Senior Executive Officer, in the Ministries and Regional Organisations are filled by local officers. The problem here is one of training which would make the officers efficient in their jobs. This problem is being tackled by the central in-service training centre. Where specialised training is required, overseas courses are given.

It is proposed to give all officers appointed to the Administrative Service a short pre-entry course before they assume duty. This scheme has already been applied to some of those appointed in 1953. Thereafter, the most important part of their training is in the field through on-the-job training under experienced Administrative Officers. Since in future most of the Administrative Officers will be drawn from the University College of the Gold Coast and will not have had experience overseas, a scheme is now being considered by the Government under which African officers after a few years' service in the field would be sent on Overseas Service Courses.

Much of the planning and effort that are being put into the programme outlined above is necessarily not of immediate effect. In three to five years from now, except in a very few specialised branches of the Service, there should emerge from the training programmes that are now in operation a respectable volume of trained and qualified candidates for the Public Service and there should even be a measure of healthy competition for posts in the Service. The success already attained is not inconsiderable. Since 1949, the number of Africans holding 'Senior' Service posts has risen from 171 to 916, an increase of 433 per cent in the absolute figures. Because, however, of the growth in the size of the Service, these figures are reflected in an increase in the percentage of the number of Africans to the total establishment of 'Senior' posts from 10 to 36. Five Africans have, since 1952, risen or been appointed to top level positions in the Civil Service and at least 45 Africans hold influential posts in their respective Departments and Ministries. There is now no serious problem of Africanisation in Departments which are executive in type, such as Labour, Co-operation and the Accounting services.

It must not be overlooked that the 'Senior' Service constitutes a comparatively small portion of the whole of the pensionable Civil Service. There are over 20,000 other members of the Service, all of whom are Africans. It is customary to take their existence for granted since they are not in the limelight, but their importance has never been underrated by the

Government. It is on their efficient performance that the effectiveness of the higher ranks of the Service depends, and they provide a reservoir of trained and experienced officers from whom a sizeable proportion of the 'Senior' Service is now drawn. For these reasons, a good deal of the effort put into planning, recruitment and training schemes and programmes goes into this branch of the Service.

Note

* From *A Statement on the Programme of the Africanisation of the Public Service.* (Government Printing Department, Accra, 1954).

Expatriate Officers in the Gold Coast

PRIME MINISTER'S STATEMENT

On the 23rd May Dr. Nkrumah met a deputation of the Senior Civil Servants' Association and made the following statement (slightly abbreviated):

'It is a great pleasure to me to meet members of the Senior Civil Service Association. I have already met members of the Junior Service and some African members of the Senior Service. I realise that your Association is largely composed of European officers and I would like to say a special word to them. The country needs your services. And this need will continue for some time to come. The declared policy of Government is that the higher ranks of the Gold Coast Civil Service should be quickly Africanised: but this, I must say, does not mean that serving European officers will be treated unfairly. They will be treated with fairness and strict impartiality.

'It is a matter of great concern to me that there should be the highest standard of achievement and conduct from all civil servants. And I trust all officers both African and European will endeavour not to fall short in this respect. In the time that I have been in office it has not escaped my notice that many of you work longer hours than the normal. I am grateful for this example of public service and I hope others will take note.

'In the period of transition between now and the time when we shall have an all African service, I wish to appeal to you not to have any fear about giving of your best in the training of Africans. Sometimes, in the Assembly and outside, occasional attacks have been made on European officers. I ask you not to be disheartened by that, for you yourselves must be aware that your presence in this country is often made a political issue. Many a time, some of us, in periods of emotion have uttered words which may hurt; our words have been directed not against you personally but against the Crown Colony system. So long as you continue to play your part faithfully and in good spirit, you can be assured of our co-operation and friendliness.

'The Civil Service is not concerned with politics, though members may have their private views and are permitted to give expression to those views by the way they vote at Elections. I am a politician and the Leader of a Party. Naturally, in the Government I sponsor the policies of my Party, but in dealing with the Civil Service I am not actuated by partisan views.

'There is true and genuine co-operation between representative Ministers and ex-officio Ministers but this close partnership does not make us less hopeful that one day the Cabinet will be composed entirely of representative Ministers. In these sentiments we are not the less appreciative of what the ex-officio Ministers are doing nor are we forgetful of their services, and when they go we hope they will go as friends with duty well performed and with the thanks of the country. It is the same with you. In all honesty we do not wish to drive any of you away. We want you to stay with us to help us build our country into a place which will command the respect of the world. If ever you feel that you have been unfairly treated or that the country is not recognising to the full the services which you are giving, I hope that you will come to me and tell me personally what are your problems and I promise to do all I can to reassure you and to lighten your burdens.

'This is what I told certain African members of the Senior Service whom I recently met: 'You carry a very great responsibility, for you are the vanguard of the African officers who have been accepted into the ranks of senior officers. By your hard work, your meticulous application to detail, your constructive thinking, your impartiality and your loyalty to the great traditions of the Civil Service, you will show yourselves worthy of promotion to the highest ranks of your calling.

If you fail, or if you do not set the highest example to your juniors, you will be performing a disservice to your country; but I am confident that you will not fail, and my prayer is that the Gold Coast Civil Service, by its actions and exertions, will win the fair name which is today accorded to the British Civil Service.' These words can apply equally to every member in the Senior grade of the Civil Service. The new Gold Coast, which has only recently agreed to increases in emoluments to its public servants, is looking to you to do your duty by her. I know that I can rely on all of you. A final word to civil servants from overseas: the country not only needs you but welcomes you.'

Can we Take it?

by JOHN HAMILTON, M.C.

T he Coussey Report on Constitutional Reform in the Gold Coast has been hailed on all sides as a statesmanslike document, and it may well become a landmark in the constitutional advancement of dependent people. It is naturally for the future to decide the ultimate good or ill of its proposals, but meanwhile a great deal of thought and discussion is going on, not only among Gold Coast Africans, but among other colonial peoples too. And the situation is being watched very closely by British people both on the spot and at home. On all our lips are the questions, 'Can the African work it?' and 'Is he ready for this great step?' It seems that we of the Administration are constantly asking, 'Will *they* be able to cope? What about African versus African, exploitation, bribery and corruption, and all the other difficulties?' Could we not turn right round, look into a mirror and say, 'Can *we* take it?'

In these days one can easily be dubbed as being too 'pro-African.' In West Africa, if you are not pro-African, what can you be? There is only one alternative – and it is time such people moved on. So many people fail to realise that there *is* only one alternative. Sentimentality need not come into our thoughts – indeed it must be beaten out – but the fact remains that this is our great chance in colonial administration.

I am employed by the Gold Coast Government. That government is to have a majority of Africans in its Executive Council. I am in truth employed by the Gold Coast. The successful carrying out of this great advance depends upon the Permanent Civil Servant as never before. 'Can *we* take it?'

Alan Paton's magnificent and moving book *Cry the Beloved Country* has these words ... 'I have one great fear in my heart – that one day when they are all turned to loving, we are turned to hating.' It is quite obvious who 'they' and 'we' are – and the sands are beginning to run out. One of our greatest difficulties is African suspicion and, in the face of that we can get nowhere. But now is our chance. Now both black and white have been given their opportunity – to make the Report work. But we must have the same approach. The African must change his from suspicion to good will and co-operation, in the knowledge that he is striding forward from dependence to self-government, but, heavens alive, so must we!

The Report itself gives few specific indications of any change in the daily life of the ordinary European Civil Servant, and the danger is that we may think it will not affect us personally. In a sense it will not – work will go on just the same – but the secret of the future lies just as much in our attitude as in the African's.

Obviously the success of the whole Report will depend on co-operation at every level at all times. We can all find faults with brother African – but can we not admit that some of us are on a false pedestal and are afraid to come off it? Do we not sometimes judge an African too harshly because, as yet, however keen he is to learn, he has not come up to our own professional standard?

We do need a new approach. It will cost us nothing and will bring love and respect from, and ultimately prosperity to, those for whom we work. Nor is this wishful thinking. The recent campaign of 'positive action' has collapsed and the people of this country have shown that they will not jeopardise their future by trusting in irresponsible youth inflamed by a few political leaders. This gives even more weight to the need for co-operation between us. We must not feel that the matter is not urgent, for it is results that are required *this year*. There are unmistakable signs that there is a renewed spirit of willingness to co-operate. Whether is grows and bears fruit will, I think, depend just as much on us as on the people of the Gold Coast.

The Scaffold and the Structure

by N. U. AKPAN

With the rapid progress of many Colonial territories towards independence many people, both in Britain and in the Colonies concerned, are worried about the future of the versatile and hard-worked Administrative Service. But nobody appears to have a cut and dried answer about the future of the members of that Service who seem to have been busy 'working themselves out of their jobs'. All seems uncertain, and to guard the bad psychological effects that this uncertainty might produce on serving officers, compensatory arrangements have been formulated by the British and Colonial Governments concerned in consultation, assuring officers of easy retirement from service before they reach the statutory age should that be necessary when the territories in which they are serving attain independence. This arrangement cuts both ways – it enables the officers to leave whenever they find conditions unfavourable, and it also gives the territories a means of getting rid of redundant and unwanted officers.

Through the mist of uncertainty, however, two schools of thought are discernible – one negative and the other positive. The one regards Administrative Officers as a sort of scaffolding used when building is in progress, but to be removed once the building has been completed. Administrative Officers were used, this argument goes on, to build up the territories politically to independence and once this is achieved they should no longer be necessary and so must go. None of the supporters of this school of thought seems to be able to say precisely when the 'scaffolding' should be actually removed – before, on, or immediately after the attainment of full self-government by the territories? All of them seem agreed, however, that wrong timing would be disastrous.

The other school of thought holds that, even with the attainment of self-government, Administrative Officers should be retained, for they have become an accustomed and trusted political institution of the territories concerned. But here, too, no one has been able to say exactly what should be the new position, status or functions of the officers: vaguely it is felt that they would be more or less the same as before – which is not helpful enough.

All depends on the attitude of the territories themselves when they become self-governing. The attitude of the Colonial Office to the territories attaining independence, over officers appointed by the Secretary of State might be put in the following way:–'It all depends on you. If you feel these men will be useful to you, and you really need them, we would allow those who are willing to stay on to do so, subject of course to reasonable safeguards about their rights and privileges, for we cannot disown our responsibility for them. If you don't want them, well, they will not stay. But, remember that it will mean in many cases the ruin of a life's career, for which they are, in equity, entitled to reasonable financial compensation.'

The final word must rest with the Colonies concerned, but there is no indication that anyone seriously wants Administrative Officers to go. If one can draw an inference, it is that everybody now seems to realise the almost indispensable position that these officers occupy in the administrative machinery of the countries concerned, and there seems less of the former illusion that to dispense lightly with their services would have no undesirable consequences.

Whenever a dependent country is about to become independent, the branch of the Service most urgently desired to be 'nationalised' is the Administrative Service.

This urgent insistence on 'nationalisation' cannot be anything but evidence of the supreme importance attached to the Service ... it is considered too delicate and important to be entrusted indefinitely to expatriate officers who sooner or later will have to leave.

The Gold Coast, unlike the Sudan, is not carrying out its scheme of 'nationalisation' of the Administrative Service by indiscriminate replacement of expatriates by non-expatriates. What has been done is to stop further pensionable recruitment of expatriate officers to fill vacancies which might occur – which are thus preserved for qualified Gold Coasters. This seems to be more judicious than asking all expatriate officers to go, and replacing them locally with small regard to qualifications and experience.

Administrative work is in itself a highly specialised occupation. Those who sometimes regard administrators as less useful than technicians, do not seem to appreciate the special nature of administrative work. No country can be governed successfully by technicians. Good administration springs not from formulas but from a quick ability to assess and judge values. It requires great mental skill and because it deals with human beings, their problems and even their destiny, more delicacy than any normal technical duty. It is a vocation needing special education, temperament and aptitude, and the mere possession of academic or professional qualifications is not enough to ensure success – there must be other qualities, which require a very careful selection for entrants into the Service.

'Nationalisation' of the Service should not be allowed to lead to a serious fall in standards. Since in none of the nations now approaching a state of independence can there be enough men with the necessary qualifications to fill *all* the vacancies that would occur in the event of a wholesale departure of the present expatriate holders, it is highly desirable that, pending the building up of their own stock of administrators, the new nations should neither be afraid nor ashamed to use the experience of those expatriate officers who are willing and happy to stay on and serve them as loyally and faithfully as they were doing before the change. Given goodwill and understanding on both sides there is no reason why such people should not be available, even with the generous retiring arrangements open to them. It is these men whom the new and inexperienced local candidates can usefully understudy – and such understudying is indispensable for future successful administration. *Far from being a sign of continued dependence upon external power, the staying on of such officers would be evidence of goodwill on both sides.*

It should be remembered, too, that the West African Colonies coming to full nationhood want independence *within the Commonwealth*. If members of this great Family of Nations have the mutual understanding to be expected within one family, no person from any section of it should regard himself or be regarded as a foreigner in another section. All of them would strive to help one another in any way possible, and we feel hopeful that the more senior members of the family will not deny the younger all necessary assistance and co-operation even after the latter have come of age and taken their full places as adult members of the family. The older and more experienced members should understand and forget some of the unpleasant, and sometimes alarming, feeling which these younger members expressed in their adolescent days, realising that it would have been unnatural if they did not suffer from the growing pains and impatience of youth.

The future of the Administrative Service, then, is a *positive* one. It can now be reasonably assumed that scarcely in any of the present Colonial territories will the Administrative Service as such be unwanted, after independence. The tendency u to 'nationalise' rather than abolish the Service, while at the same time the titles of its members tend to change. In the Gold Coast the District Commissioner of old is now formally known as Government Agent, while the Resident is known as Regional Officer. In the Western Region of Nigeria, these two officers are respectively styled Assistant Local Government Inspector and Local Government Inspector. The main reason for these changes appears to lie in an attempt to give the impression that the title holders' position has changed – that they are no longer 'agents of imperialism,' but servants of the people. Commenting on this tendency, Mr. R. E. Wraith, in his *Local Government* (p. 109), says:

'The thing that is worth remembering behind all these surface changes is that the greatest virtue of the office of D.C. or D.O. was its *flexibility* – its ability to adapt itself to changing circumstances. The new titles are rather more formal than the old; it is to be hoped this does not mean that the flexibility will depart, and that the new man, be he European or African, will become a bureaucrat treading a well-worn path. In the fluid circumstances of West Africa there is a great need for versatile men, of independent judgement and character, who can be called upon to interpret to the ordinary people the changes which are bound to follow one another in quick succession . . .'

It does not appear that it matters materially what titles the officers of the Service bear (although there would hardly be any harm in leaving them alone). What matters is their actual functions and position. The main virtue of the Administrative Service, as Mr. Wraith says, has in the past lain in its flexibility, adaptability and versatility. As long as it is clearly realised that its usefulness will be curtailed if it becomes too formal or specialised, let its members be given any title on earth!

But what type of functions and status should the officers themselves have in the new circumstances? An important part of their work has in the past been in the field of local government, and here it is enough to say that the success of the new local government systems now being set up in many Colonial territories will depend to a large extent upon the leadership, education and guidance which should come from Administrative Officers through 'personal relationship rather than constitutional rights'.

So far as Central Government work is concerned, it seems that the position of the officers as general representatives of the Central Government should continue much in the present form, but with one important difference. Instead of being looked upon as the rulers of the people, they should ostensibly be what might be described as the executive arm of the Government or Cabinet. In this capacity they would act as the mouths and ears of the Government in their areas – the *intelligence* officers of Government. They should fulfil the 'great need for versatile men, of independent judgement and character, who must be called upon to interpret to the ordinary people the changes which are bound to follow one another in quick succession.' In turn, they should also interpret the ordinary people to the Government, keeping the latter regularly and fully informed of the reactions and feelings of the former. No Government can succeed or discharge its responsibilities and duties properly without having at its disposal unbiased and properly assessed information, as well as the means for interpreting its policy and programmes to the people, particularly where many of those people are illiterate and untouched by newspapers or radio.

Internal security, as at present, would remain the first and foremost concern of Administrative Officers, and there would be miscellaneous duties such as community development, native courts (where applicable) and so on. Powers and functions as Magistrates or J.Ps. would, of course, continue.

If Administrative Officers generally represent the Government, it follows that they must take close interest in what is happening in other departments in their areas. And this brings to mind part of a statement of Lord Milverton (then Sir Arthur Richards) to the Legislative Council in Lagos in March 1945:

'It seems to me that the Administration is too loosely knit and that a lack of general co-ordination has deprived Government efforts of some of the effective force which comes from joint effort ... The present Government intends ... to insist that at each level of the Administration the Administrative Officer-in-charge, whether it be the Resident or the Divisional Officer, must be regarded as the captain of a team which works together for the benefit of the people and the progress of the country, and as such he must be in a position to co-ordinate effort without, of course, in any way interfering with the technical achievements of an accepted purpose ...'

True, the political conditions of Nigeria have changed considerably since the above statement was made. But after omitting (as we have done) those sections of the statement which can hardly be acceptable to modern Ministerial forms of Government, what remains is still relevant.

I end by referring again to the qualifications of persons wishing to enter the Service. One should, I feel, not be afraid to insist on a university education *plus* good character *and* ability, or long and tried experience in the junior stratum of the Service, with clear proof of ability and character.

To relax these requirements would be to compromise efficiency and good administration.

With planning and looking ahead, there is no reason why suitable arrangements could not be made with the university colleges, which now exist in nearly every territory, for the special training of prospective candidates. But, and this is a big but, it must not be forgotten that to attract the right type of men into the Service, there will have to be real inducements and attractions which salaries alone, no matter how generous, cannot provide.

An Experiment in Administration

by A. H. M. KIRK-GREENE

A few months ago there opened, at Northern Nigeria's Institute of Administration, a course that is believed to be unique in Africa: it is the Administrative Service Training Course, which caters for 16 potential Assistant District Officers. All of them are Northern Nigerians.

What is the background to this experiment? With the succession of Constitutional Conferences and the steady march towards self-government, it became inevitable that – as the White Paper of May, 1956, on the Reorganisation of the Overseas Civil Service recognised – it would no longer be possible to offer the hope of a full-spanned career in Nigeria to candidates nominated by the Secretary of State for the Administrative branch of the Overseas Service. It was therefore doubly imperative that an indigenous Civil Service should be built up. The peculiar structure of local government in the Northern Region had already developed a competent, responsible body of Native Administration civil servants, while the accelerated output from higher educational institutions had, during the last few years, begun to find its way into the professional and technical departments of the Government; yet, apart from a lilliputian handful of Assistant Secretaries, there was in 1955 not one Northerner in the Administrative Service.

The Executive Council, the policy-making body of the Region's Government, was acutely aware of this hiatus. A dozen local direct appointments were made to the Administrative Service in 1956/57; in the main, these have proved an outstanding success. But more than this was needed, for, platitudes apart, an efficient impartial, enthusiastic Administration is a *sine qua non* of any technical development: 'If the administration collapses, chaos will ensue and there will be little scope for departmental officers', commented a recent Commissioner invited by the Government of the Northern Region to advise on the future development of local government units. The staff position was further underlined by the House of Assembly's approval in principle, last March, of the Hudson Report, whose implementation of the Provincial Authority system might well demand an increase in the cadre of Administrative Officers, besides catering for the replacement of the normal wastage brought about by expatriate retirement or transfer, and the expansion already called for by the staffing of Ministerial offices at the Assistant and Permanent Secretary levels. Finally, the corollary of such a demand: the supply. 'Africans of the normal university graduate academic qualification', wrote Mr. R. S. Hudson, in his report to the Northern Regional Government in 1957, 'are not yet available in the Region in anything like the required numbers. Therefore I suggest that there is a strong case for selecting the best young men ... for training as Administrative Officers. ... This recruitment should be given priority by the Regional Government. ... I also suggest that concentrated local training courses should be provided for these recruits as well as short courses in the United Kingdom.'

The Northern Regional Government acted swiftly. In June they announced their plans to accelerate the introduction of Northern Nigerians into the vital ranks of Assistant District Officers. The Public Service Commission called for applications for admission to a training course designed to lead to appointment as Administrative Officers. While stressing that the normal academic requirement for such an appointment was a university degree, they declared that, as a temporary measure for this first course, consideration would be given to Northern candidates who had supplemented a good secondary education with an honourable period of subsequent employment and who possessed evident qualities of ability, energy, responsibility and adaptability. The maximum age was 35, which upper limit allowed Native Administration staff of several years' service to apply for consideration.

The enthusiastic response to this advertisement in the Gazette dissipated the qualms of any pessimist who might once have muttered his doubts about the reaction to such a step. Over 400 replies were received for the 16 places available. A few applications could, of course, be committed to the waste-paper basket without further ado: a scribe who had already failed his clerical confirmation test three times would be unlikely to cope with the complex circulars that are apparently inseparable from life as a myrmidon of the Ministry of Finance; an applicant who showed barely a glimmer of literacy in completing his form for admission would be unlikely to hold his own in a Division where the Native Authority Councillors are largely ex-teachers, even ex-Ministers. Others, though *prima facie* eligible, could perhaps wait a year without losing anything: the secondary schoolboys resplendent with distinguished certificates, were still on the young side, and postponement of their consideration for a twelvemonth would allow this first Training Course to be devoted to those who, a little older in experience as well as years, might find a year's deferment tantamount to a blocked career.

So it was that our first Administrative Service Training Course opened with 16 students, all armed with several years' previous administrative experience in either Government or Native Administration service, and returning an average age of 29 plus. Let us briefly analyse their background.

Educationally, they run the gamut from University College, Ibadan, down to Middle IV. This last certificate, though below the secondary education called for, has been supplemented by several years of administrative work carried out in the English language, and by success in either the Clerical Training Course or the Native Treasury Diploma Course (or both!) held at the Institute of Administration. Half the students have travelled abroad: two visited England as private secretaries, to an Emir and to a Minister respectively, one worked in the London office of the Commissioner for Northern Nigeria and four completed study courses at various colleges in the United Kingdom. Another student has undertaken the holy pilgrimage to Mecca. Their previous occupations include Bursar and lecturers at the Institute of Administration, headmaster of a Provincial School, Native Treasurer, Chief Scribe, Development Secretary to a large emirate, Supervisor of Agriculture, Provincial Accountant, Adult Education Officer, Information Officer, etc. Of the parental background, the fathers of over 70 per cent of the students were either farmers or Native Administration employees, while others were a tailor, a Government pensioner, an *imam* or Muhammedan priest, and a United Africa Company factor. All are married, some heavily so, but nobody could suggest that such an arrangement in any way impedes study: the experience of the universities in the immediate post-war years has been spared us.

So to the present course itself. During their nine months at the Institute of Administration, lectures are given on Law, Public Finance and Local Government as the principal subjects, with further instruction in the Constitutional and Economic History of Nigeria, Comparative Religion, Political Theory and Current Affairs. Outside lecturers give talks on the functions of their own Ministries. Emphasis has been placed on attaining a high standard of English (written, in particular: the spoken English of the Northerner is a proud by-word among pedagogues) so that those students who subsequently attend any further training in the United Kingdom will be able to derive the maximum benefit therefrom. For the same reason, much care is devoted to the social education of the students, many of whom will, one hopes, soon be mixing in dizzy circles at home and abroad. Another interesting feature of the course is the university tutorial system of instruction, which is proving of considerable value.

The practical side of an Administrative Officer's training is not overlooked. Field engineering, map reading, elementary survey work, vehicle maintenance and First Aid are all included. There is a five-week attachment to Divisions, where any starry eyes will have a chance to be slightly glazed over by the hard reality of life in the bush. The Course aims to finish with a fortnight at the famous Man O'War Bay, which seeks to assess a man's determination, endurance and qualities of leadership in a course modelled on the Outward Bound principles.

Those who successfully pass the Administrative Service Training Course will be eligible for immediate appointment to the long grade of the Administrative Service, though they may then, or at some later date, be sent to the United Kingdom for an advanced course of training. Naturally, like any pilot scheme, this experiment has to prove itself. It is too early for us, still in the first term, to estimate its success; but it is already clear that morale is high and that all the students are aware both of their heavy responsibilities ahead and of the value of the careful training they are now being given.

And then? The Administrative Service Training Course is the beginning, not the end. 'There is no short cut', noted the Commissioner quoted above. 'The most intense efforts will have to be made to recruit the cream of the young men and to train them. . . . They must gain region-wide experience, loyalty, integrity and versatility through years of field work in different provinces, as well as through experience in provincial and regional secretariats.'

The future is unknown but we believe that Northern Nigeria's experiment in administration has got off to a promising start and that those whom it launches will, given a fair wind, soon be able to sail as smoothly as the former ships of their line.

b) RETIREMENT AND RE-EMPLOYMENT

If the excerpts under (a) deal with the machinery of establishing H.M.O.C.S. and the commitment of the new Service to accelerated staff localization programmes, Section (b) shifts the focus away from the Service to individuals. The principal problem facing former members of the Colonial Service after their transfer to H.M.O.C.S. was, as the pages of *Corona* unambiguously and continually disclosed, what to do about retirement. Prominent in their thinking were the twin personal problems: do I want – or can I afford it for my family – to stay on under the new government in a job I have known and so far enjoyed as my chosen professional career, or should I take the view that the sooner I get back to the UK the easier it will be to find another before they all get taken up by other Colonial Service officers retiring from other about-to-be independent colonies?

A major instrument in helping retiring members of the Service in their search for a 'second career' was the British government's Overseas Services Resettlement Bureau (OSRB), opened in 1957 to assist retiring officers from Malaya. Later it extended its services to all Colonial Service officers. It is discussed here by its founding director, R.L. Peel. The cumulative total of Colonial Service men and women who registered on the OSRB books shows 6508 names for the founding years of 1957–64, of whom 5911 were placed. Of these, 2381 went into commerce and industry. Of those still awaiting further employment through the services of the OSRB in 1962, *Corona's* final year, the largest number (188) came from the ranks of the provincial administration, followed by police and prisons staff (168) and PWD technical staff (135). Only 22 medical officers, 17 surveyors and 12 legal officers on the OSRB books in 1962 had not yet found further employment.

Corona closed before OSRB attained its peak years, when it cumulatively registered 7981 names in 1965, rising to 9194 in 1968. Otherwise it is likely that its pages would have carried many articles on 'second careers' from those who had been obliged to retire prematurely from their first. Anne Hutchinson's experience offers a neat preview of what was to come. A move to Australia was particularly commended, as W.H. Swaffield's contribution reveals, for ex-colonials in search of an attractive relocation.

Focus on Pensioners

I n an earlier issue of *Corona* we recorded the House of Lords Debate on pensions of former Colonial Service Officers. In the small space available we confined ourselves to remarks by Viscount Boyd of Merton as typical of the feeling displayed during the debate. We have now been asked to give some of the statements made by others who supported the proposal for action by Her Majesty's Government on pensions, and we are glad to do so.

Lord Ogmore:– 'The Government's case is that they deny responsibility and they state that the Colonial Service, or, as it is now called, the Overseas Service, and its officers, were the employees of territorial Governments – that is, Colonial Governments of the various territories – and these Governments are responsible for the payment of basic pensions and of increases to offset rises in the cost of living and inflation. In other words, they say, 'It is nothing to do with us. It is purely a matter of the Colonies in which you were engaged prior to their becoming independent, and you must deal with them.' ... It is a little difficult to know why the Government are taking up this attitude, because throughout the whole history of the Colonial Service the constitutional responsibility of Her Majesty's Government was clear and was admitted for every aspect of selection, appointment and conditions of service of these particular officers. It was clearly reiterated from time to time, and eventually in a Colonial Office Paper in 1954 called *Reorganisation of the Colonial Service*, paragraph 3 of which reads as follows: 'They' – that is, the officers – 'are servants of the Crown and the conditions of their employment are embodied in Colonial Regulations. These regulations constitute the Secretary of State as the ultimate authority for appointment, discipline, promotions and general conditions of employment.'

'In view of that statement, made as recently as 1954, how can anyone say that these unfortunate people are not the responsibility of Her Majesty's Government but must go to countries, which are in most cases independent, to try to make a bargain with them? In fact, these pensioners never had any contractual responsibility or relationship at all with the present independent Governments, but were always servants of the Crown and were paid out of budgets approved by Her Majesty's Government. It is to Her Majesty's Government that they look, and have always looked, for redress; and up to now I regret to say, on this particular issue, in vain. Regretfully, many territories, both dependent and independent, have clearly failed over a period of years to award pension increases to those retired Colonial Service officers at rates which Her Majesty's Government consider necessary for pensioners in this country. Obviously, for political reasons, it would be most difficult in most of these cases, particularly in independent countries, to get them to alter that point of view, and I, for one, should not care to accept the responsibility for so doing.... .

'My Lords, today I am not asking for charity; I am asking for justice ... I am asking for justice for long and faithful service. These are elderly people, living in poverty, in many cases, and, in others, on the borderline of want. I will not reiterate the fact that these people helped to build our Colonial territories, and enabled them to be brought to the position in which we could hand them over as going concerns. Their work set these territories on the road to independence.... .

'These old Colonial servants were devoted to their task. They served on low pre-war salaries which are today made derisory by inflation. They served in times when there were very few amenities. There was a great deal of loneliness, of sickness (modern methods of preventing things like malaria had not been developed then); and there was, what to my mind was one of the worst things of all in those days, the separation for years at a time of a man from his wife and family. These are the people for whom I am asking.... .'

The Earl of Listowel:– '... The principle upheld by the Government – and no doubt it will be repeated by the noble Lord, Lord Hastings, when he replies – is that the overseas Governments themselves have a duty to 'top up' or increase the basic pension of these retired officers, and that this is therefore not a responsibility which falls upon Her Majesty's Government. I have no doubt that the noble Lord will go on to say that, if Her Majesty's Government assumed this responsibility, it would mean that the overseas countries would be encouraged not to make these payments. But there is one question which I should like to ask the noble Lord. If this is the case, why have the Government already paid these post-war increases in the case of civil servants who have retired from service in Burma and Pakistan? ...

'In any event, I feel that there is a moral duty on the part of Her Majesty's Government to see that these pensioners receive, from whatever quarter it may be, what is due to them and what they are not receiving, through no fault of their own – and nobody has for a moment suggested that it is any fault of theirs that these payments are not being made.... .'

Lord Milverton:– 'Over the past few years I have spoken on this question several times in your Lordships' House. My interventions have generally been treated with a very definite *non possumus* from the Front Bench. Indeed, on the last occasion, a year ago, when I asked a number of questions, some of which have been asked again today, I was completely ignored. No reference whatever was made to them. However, hope springs eternal in the human breast, even in the breast of a Colonial servant, and perhaps the cogent speech with which this debate was opened from the noble Lord, Lord Ogmore, to whom I am sure the Service will be deeply grateful, will move the brain of Her Majesty's Government, even if its heart has been petrified beyond resurrection. I am sure that the men and women of the Service will be grateful for this effective and, to my mind, unanswerable advocacy of their cause.

'I do not propose to detain your Lordships with a needless reiteration of the points, but they do follow a definite sequence. First of all, there is the substance of the complaint, or the request, which is made by these pensioners for an improvement of their conditions, which I need not go into now in any detail. Secondly, there is the responsibility of Her Majesty's Government. . . . I appreciate the principle that the territorial Governments are technically responsible for the payment of these pensions. But do not let us forget that none of the Colonial and ex-Colonial Governments has failed to pay the basic pension. The question today does not deal with the basic pension. We are not asking the British Government to undertake that responsibility. We are merely asking them to 'top up' the pensions in order to meet modern conditions and the depression of the value of currency and to bring Colonial servants who were fortunate to serve overseas into the same position as their fellows in the home Civil Service.

'It is not possible, surely, for any Government to adopt this Gallio-like attitude and say that it is the responsibility of the various Colonial and ex-Colonial Governments, because that is manifestly an attitude unworthy of a good employer and the Government are supposed to be a model employer. . . .

'In conclusion, I should like to draw attention to a curious anomaly, as it seems to me. Her Majesty's Government hand out millions annually, by the goodness of their hearts, in grants in aid to other races, but they seem reluctant to give assistance to the pensioned men and women of their own race, about whose past service to this country and to mankind such beautiful speeches are so often made. As I have said before in your Lordships' House, laudatory sentences form a very unsubstantial diet. . . .'

The Earl of Swinton: – '. . . There must be great anxiety among those civil servants who are now serving, and who we are most anxious should stay as long as it is necessary. I think we all realise that we have an obligation to them when their employment in the self-governing State comes to an end. I should like to put this point to the Government. Suppose – and I will not re-argue the case that has been so well argued – that if a little help is given (and it is not very much) other Colonies which are already paying cease to pay. I do not think that is in the least likely to happen; but it is not a very good argument for doing something dishonourable, even if it did. Suppose self-government, independence, is given to a territory tomorrow and a number of civil servants are got rid of: do not the Government accept responsibility for those civil servants? I think they do, and they have clearly said so. Some may be on the verge of getting their pensions. Do not the Government accept the responsibility for their pensions? And would not those pensions be paid at whatever is considered, on the analogy of the pensions increase in this country, the appropriate rate for that territory? . . .'

Lord Saye and Sele: – 'I would suggest to your Lordships that in putting right this disgrace in the Civil Service you should base your ideas not upon so much extra cash as on keeping up the standard of living that a pensioner – or a pensioner's widow, for that matter – is enjoying at the time when he is suddenly cut off, by age or whatever it may be, from the position he has occupied. Pushing up their pension by so many pounds is not a true standard. To my mind, one must consider what their standard of living was originally when they left the Service, and then attempt to keep up that standard within some reasonable distance. That would give a young man entering a Service a much better outlook than he has now. ....'

And finally Lord Ogmore again, after Lord Hastings had spoken on behalf of the Department of Technical Co-operation and given Her Majesty's Government's arguments for placing responsibility for pensions on overseas Governments:–'This is the first occasion on which the new Department of Technical Co-operation has appeared in this House, and I must say that its baptism of fire has left it, so far as I am concerned, in a very unmilitary situation. It has not stood up to the fire; it has dug itself in. It may be said that that is a perfectly good military thing to do, as, indeed, it may be; but at all events we have had little response to the ammunition that came from this side of the House.'

'I will put this matter very shortly, because I think it was a most inadequate reply ... Here we have the Colonial White Paper of 1954, which I will quote, as it has not been quoted before, and in which this very point of new political developments was raised. Paragraph 3 begins: 'The political developments now taking place or likely to take place in many of the territories, in pursuance of the declared policy of Her Majesty's Government in the United Kingdom to further their advance towards self-government, make it necessary to review the situation of the Colonial Service.' In other words, in order to deal with this problem that was obviously facing the Colonial Service at that time, and of which they had some apprehension, this particular Paper was produced.

'It went on to say that Colonial servants are servants of the Crown. We have heard today, from two distinguished former Secretaries of State for the Colonies how the system works. These Colonial servants cannot say where they are going; they are told the territories to which they must go, and the better the man the more likely he is to go to the most difficult territory. I will say this to the noble Lord, Lord Hastings, if I may: that he can take back this impression to his Right Honourable Friend, as be has kindly agreed to do – namely, that every single speaker has spoken in support of the Motion, that it is not a Party Motion, that it has been subscribed to by noble Lords in every part of this House, and that, I think I am right in assessing that the general feeling of your Lordships is also strongly in favour of the Motion.'

Several noble Lords: 'Hear, hear.'

To Stay or not to Stay

T his number of *Corona* went to press as the White Paper on service with overseas Governments was published. By the time the journal reaches readers they will have been able to form their own opinions and to study the reactions of others. *Corona* looks at the proposals from its position as the journal of Her Majesty's Overseas Service. For the Governments which participate in the scheme the advantages are clear and of great benefit. How far will they go to reassure the Service and diminish fears for the future?

Our fear, like that of many others, has been that too little would be done too late. It has sometimes seemed that, with the best will in the world, the wheels of Whitehall could not revolve fast enough to keep pace with the rush to self-government in the Colonies – and not, of course, the wheels of the Colonial Office only: one can guess at the negotiations with the Treasury over the finance involved, and the seemingly endless search for and reconciliation of views from territorial Governments and Civil Service Associations. That stage is now over. The Queen's Speech on the Prorogation of Parliament referred to the proposals as providing greater security for members of the Service and we can expect that by the time this number of *Corona* appears a general welcome from all Parties in the House will have shown that this aspect of the scheme is regarded as no less important than its assistance to overseas territories.

The proposals rest on the principle that the home Government will take on financial responsibilities in part or in full which previously fell, or would have fallen, on the employing Governments. One of the Service's hopes for greater security has been that it could be 'under-pinned' by the home Government, and the principle has now been accepted. (It must, however, be remembered that payments by Her Majesty's Government will be in the form of assistance to overseas Governments to which serving officers will continue to owe their duty. Further measures may be found necessary if the Overseas Service is to retain a strong identity.) While the acceptance by the United Kingdom of full responsibility for 'expatriate' pay (and where that is meant the word is preferable to 'inducement') will undoubtedly relieve overseas Governments of a potential financial embarrassment, it will also relieve them of an actual political embarrassment. At a time of pressure for increased 'localization' of Services the advantage of not having to put the question of 'expatriate' pay to local legislatures is obvious and should be a potent factor in decisions to invite overseas officers to remain. The same consideration applies to the other proposals designed to relieve officers of burdens arising from their overseas service by payment of education expenses and children's allowances at rates payable to members of the Home Civil Service posted overseas, and to make their service generally acceptable by part payment of leave and passage arrangements (including visits by children). The home Government will also bear an equal share with overseas Governments of compensation for loss of career.

The question of compensation has long been a difficult one. It has been said that too much attention was paid in the past to compensation for those who wished to go and not enough consideration was shown to those who wished to stay. The present proposals seek to strike a balance: to incline officers to stay where they are needed but to provide compensation for those who go, without, however, making such compensation an inducement to early withdrawal. The success of the proposals in following a middle course will only be seen as they come into practice and they will be watched with the closest attention. A question that has been asked on several occasions is what will be the position of an officer who accepts an overseas Government's offer to retain him but who finds later that the climate of his work changes to an extent which makes him feel morally bound to retire. This contingency is much in Service minds and it is hoped that the sections of the White Paper dealing with compensation will be sufficiently flexible to cover any such cases.

Given that the proposals do find a middle way and that many officers remain who might otherwise have retired prematurely, it should not be overlooked that there are many others whose keenest wish has always been to stay. Those who are already willing to do so for an unspecified time are doing, without inducement, precisely what the proposals set out to achieve. Is it not possible to advance from this point by estimating the numbers concerned and trying to fit them into the pattern of expected progress in each territory? The difficulties of forecasting and the impossibility of binding independent Governments are very real, but it is also difficult to see how the proposals can be wholly successful without a longer look ahead by the home Government than seems to be envisaged in the White Paper. To whatever extent these officers are 'under-pinned' the phrase 'so long as their services are needed' will be paramount and the vital question in their lives will be 'how long?'

The wish to have some idea of 'how long' is not a request for a guaranteed career. For some time now the Service has realised the difficulties in the way of any such guarantee and the White Paper does well to point out those difficulties unequivocally, while showing the considerable efforts the home Government is making to help those whose careers are interrupted. There is every reason to think that there will be nothing static about those efforts and that they will expand as time goes on.

The proposal that the home Government should bear that part of the cost of the pension or gratuity stemming from the payment of inducement allowance is welcome. In effect it guarantees that pensioners would not lose everything in the event of default by overseas Governments (doubts in this connection may also be voiced over the share of compensation payable by overseas Governments). But there are many other problems concerning pensions which need to be faced and which are indivisible from security for the Service. They will, no doubt, be heard in the growing voice of the newly unified Overseas Service Pensioners Association, now conveniently housed on the Colonial Office doorstep.

Too little too late, or enough in time? We cannot yet tell but our own view is that after a long time in which the Service wondered if words would ever be translated into action, the proposals are a real step forward and deserve a quick response. At last something has been done to help officers to stay for some time longer in their jobs while keeping in close view the needs of those who go. Those who want to prolong their service overseas may well find that their best chance to do so will come from making a success of the crucial years not only preceding but also immediately following independence.

Selling the Service to Employers

by SIR JOHN RANKINE, K.C.M.G., K.C.V.O.

C hanges in staff in the Overseas Services Resettlement Bureau, and its transfer from the Colonial Office to the Department of Technical Co-operation, provide an occasion to pay tribute to the invaluable work the Bureau has done for so many members of the Colonial Service.

Mr. Macmillan's graphic and much publicised reference to the wind of change blowing through Africa was no understatement. There have been many swift and dramatic changes, not only in Africa but in other parts of the Old Colonial Empire. How many of us are there, for instance, who were serving before the war who foresaw that in the short space of less than twenty years from its conclusion Ceylon, Malaya, Ghana, Nigeria, Somaliland, Sierra Leone and Tanganyika would have gained independence and that others, such as Kenya and Uganda would be on the threshold? These changes inevitably have had far reaching effects on the lives and future of many people, not the least of whom are the members of Her Majesty's Overseas Service.

The task of carrying out Britain's policy of bringing the Colonial peoples as rapidly as possible to self government, if at times stimulating and exciting, is also an exacting one. The pace has been tremendous. Officers have seen the fruits of their labours since the war to an extent undreamed of by their predecessors. In Nigeria, for example*, they have seen greater progress in many directions, such as the provision of schools, hospitals, roads, during the last few years than in all the years before the war. This reflects no discredit on past administrations for the simple reason that before the war the money to finance it just was not there. Nevertheless, in fairness to the new African Governments, it must be admitted that their enthusiasm has given the greatest stimulus to development. African Ministers when presented with the opportunities of power have not been slow to seize it and have exercised it with imagination and drive.

During this period British officers serving overseas in territories which have reached or are approaching self-government have born heavy responsibilities and have had to make radical adjustments. As self-government has become a reality, so their role has changed from administrators to advisors and from initiators to executive officers implementing policies laid down by African Ministers. At times these changes, especially when regard is paid to the speed at which they have had to be made, have not been easy. Many have seen fundamental changes suddenly made to policies or to the structures which they had painstakingly built up over the years. Often they must have wondered whether according to the ideas with which they have grown up these changes were for the better or whether the standards they had set were not in danger of being lowered. The field of promotion is continually being reduced as the Colonial Empire contracts. Posts to which they could legitimately have aspired are now closed to British candidates in the interests of 'Africanization'. They have accepted all these in their stride, in good part, as the inevitable concomitants of constitutional advance, and have carried out the instructions and policies of their new masters in accordance with the highest traditions of the British public service. The smoothness with which territories like Nigeria and Tanganyika have come to independence, their desire to remain in the Commonwealth, their continued friendliness towards Britain, and the harmony existing almost without exception between African Ministers and their British staff, are eloquent testimony to the loyalty with which the latter have carried out their duties. It is a tribute no less, of course, to the wisdom and sense of fair play of many of the African leaders, such as Sir Abubakar Tafawa Balewa and Julius Nyerere.

Nor has the work of British officers gone entirely unrecognised and unrewarded. One of the writer's most vivid memories of the best part of thirty years in Africa is the manner in which during Nigeria's independence celebrations the Prime Minister expressed his country's gratitude to the 'British officers we have known first as masters and then as leaders and finally as partners but always as friends.' There were other no less generous and sincere tributes. It was both a moving and a humbling occasion. One felt that anything one had been able to do had been worthwhile. One could not help wondering at the same time whether one could have done more.

On the other hand, at the present time the Service has its bleaker side. Material rewards in the Colonial Service have never been great. Salaries judged by those in some other walks of life have not been high. Duty frequently took one to unhealthy places where many of the amenities and conventional necessities of modern life were lacking. One of the greatest disadvantages was the enforced separation of families and the cost of sending children back to this country for education when they reached school age. But there were compensations to set against these disadvantages. Life in Africa, or the remoter parts of the Empire, might be more exciting than, say, catching the 9·15 from Croydon with bowler hat and umbrella to spend the rest of the day on an office stool. Some could expect a fairly open air life with perhaps the added glamour of safari or big game shooting. There was the chance of substantial responsibility at a comparatively early age. One might be called upon for duties like evacuating the entire population from a volcano threatened island. Work was with people rather than things, and for those with the spirit of service there was the satisfaction of doing something to improve the lot of one's fellow beings. Above all there was security. Even if the material rewards appeared small and the prospects of promotion continually contracted, officers felt secure in the knowledge that if they gave good service they could continue in employment until they were 55–60 and then retire on pension; indeed the conditions under which most officers joined the Service required them to continue until they were 55 in order to qualify for pension.

But this sense of security has been suddenly shattered. Obviously Her Majesty's Overseas Service is now being wound up. For many officers there is no longer the prospect of a career. They find themselves in the invidious position of knowing that they are working themselves out of a job; the better they do it the sooner they will find themselves unemployed. Few people in this country, even those who have themselves faced the spectre of unemployment, can understand the desperate anxiety which this situation causes, especially to those with wives and family commitments. At least they have a base, are in touch with conditions and can begin to search in the fields of employment similar to those in which they have been employed. The officer from overseas has no such advantage. His compensation for loss of career may be more than swallowed up in setting up a new home in this country. He is out of touch and may not know where to begin. Unless he is a professional officer, his training and experience overseas do not appear to qualify him particularly for any occupation in this country. Even if he wishes to transfer to another overseas service, the Commonwealth Relations Office, he must first sit a written examination and then if he is successful compete for selection with many other candidates.

It is a grim prospect, but the Service had a good friend in Mr. Lennox-Boyd, now Lord Boyd, at the time Secretary of State for the Colonies. Thanks to his initiative and help the Overseas Services Resettlement Bureau was opened in 1957 for officers returning from Malaya. Two years later, on the earnest representations of the Nigerian Governors, its services were extended to officers returning from that country. The manner in which the Bureau functions and the way in which it can help officers were described in an article in *Corona*, April, 1959, so no attempt will be made to repeat them here.

The Bureau was faced with an uphill task from the beginning. Within a few weeks of its opening 180 officers had registered for employment. At that time it had not a single vacancy on its books, no recognised status in the employment world and no contacts. It has been estimated that there are more than 500,000 firms in the United Kingdom alone which might offer employment; in addition there are other potential fields in local government, education, health and welfare, trade associations, chambers of commerce and the like. Somehow the Bureau had to penetrate these and sell the Service to employers. The difficulties of doing so appeared immense.

In the first place there was a general lack of knowledge in this country about the potential of the Colonial Service. The other Services are well known. For a long time now men from the Army, for example, have been finding their way into civilian occupations. It is not uncommon to find majors and colonels among the senior executives of a large company and a general on the board; on the contrary it might be difficult to find an important company which does not boast men from the Services among its senior staff. Once the men are known and a connection is established it

naturally leads to more. How often has an employer been heard to say that if
he is looking for more staff preference will be given to men from his old
regiment? By contrast what firms have an ex-District Commissioner as
head of the executive staff or a 'Sanders of the River' in the boardroom?
The explanation is, of course, that up to now the Colonial Service has
provided a full career, and its members have not had occasion, or indeed the
opportunity, to seek a career in commerce or industry. It was not until
comparatively recent times that there was even the option of retirement at
45: the conditions under which the vast majority were recruited required
them to serve to the age of 55 in order to qualify for pension. As a result the
Service was virtually unknown in the employment field. Unlike the other
Services it had no headquarters office in this country, staffed largely by its
own members, which could act as a shop window and give a picture of
its quality. Incidentally the War Office and the Admiralty, through their
supply and contract branches, have what must prove an extremely useful
direct contact with many of the more important industries. Nor had the
Colonial Service anything comparable with the Officers' Association or the
British Legion, which have wide contacts and can provide great assistance
to ex-servicemen seeking employment. Music hall jokes about irascible
gentlemen in topees, swigging gin under the waving palms and waited on
by hosts of servants, were accepted as not too wide of the mark. They might
be good at dealing with a tribal riot but most unlikely to be of much use in
modern industry.

This problem of making the potential of the Colonial Service known to
employers was not made easier because the strong feeling which existed in
certain quarters against unsettling members still in the Service and possibly
encouraging them to leave it led to an official ruling that the Bureau must
employ no publicity either at home or abroad. Its work had to be carried
on by personal contact alone. I am glad to say that this ban has since been
removed but it certainly was a severe handicap at the beginning. Furthermore, by unfortunate coincidence the Bureau was opened just at the time
when the Government decided drastically to cut the size of the armed
Forces. The Bureau was therefore faced with massive competition. Because
its problem was then thought small by comparison it had to take second
priority. For instance, the Forces resettlement problem received maximum
publicity, an eminent businessman was put at the head of the campaign
to interest businessmen in the employment of ex-servicemen, an Air Chief
Marshal was appointed to the Ministry of Labour to take charge of the
resettlement of ex-servicemen and a considerable part of the Ministry was
especially geared to deal with it.

In seeking employment, however, the Service had two assets. The first
was its own quality. The problem of maintaining morale among those
registered in the early stages was almost wholly psychological for there was
little, if any, practical comfort to offer. It speaks volumes for the courage of
its members that they remained cheerful and indomitable at this time in
their search for a new career. Many have now found it and through them
the Service is becoming more widely known. They have borne the brunt of
these difficult times and those who follow will have much for which to

thank them. It is a sad reflection that by the time the reputation of the Service becomes fully established it may be at an end and there may be no more to place!

The second was in the person of the first head of the Bureau, R. L. Peel. Starting absolutely from scratch, with a tiny staff, housed in a dingy little office at the back of Sanctuary Buildings, he has built up a very successful organisation. By hours of talk, touring the country, visiting firms, writing articles in trade journals, and, when the ban on publicity was somewhat relaxed, by interviews with the Press and on the B.B.C., he has gradually broken down prejudice, established many fruitful contacts and begun to sell the Service to British employers. In all this work Sir Humfrey Gale, adviser to the Bureau, has given invaluable help. Of the 2,600 who have registered approximately 1,700 men have been placed. It is perhaps significant that the first 500 took two and a quarter years to place; the second 500 one year and the third 500 only nine months!

Although, as has been seen, many of the initial difficulties have been overcome we should be deluding ourselves if we assumed that all in the garden is now lovely. Much has been done but much remains to be done. The Bureau has made the break through into the employment market, but has not yet landed any top level jobs. Many officers have had to accept posts which are well below their real potential. There are of course reasons for this. First, in fairness it must be admitted that, although excellent material, many are not already qualified for a business career. Some period of adjustment and training may be necessary. By far the most important, however, is that it has been found in practice that if firms are really to be interested it is essential to make a contact at the top. Later, if this contact is successful and the green light is given, profitable discussions can be carried on at the personnel officer level. The writer remembers being told by the head of one of the largest firms of staff consultants that nearly all important appointments are made on the 'old boy' basis. Even where vacancies are advertised there is usually a candidate, already known or who has been brought to notice through this network, who will get the appointment. This is where Peel, starting from scratch and handicapped by a lack of status and the ban on publicity, probably experienced his greatest difficulties, and where in spite of all handicaps he has had some of his outstanding successes. He has made many good contacts. Moreover the Bureau has been assisted by Sir Anthony Abell whose standing and reputation have enabled him to make connections at the right level. But there is an enormous field to cover and it is worth considering whether the work of the Bureau would not be further facilitated if it were supported by a powerful committee drawn from the top level of industry, who know it, are well disposed towards it, and would use their influence in encouraging firms to try men from it.

Meanwhile, Dick Peel who has built the organisation up from nothing is now leaving it for a new post in the Foreign Office. There must be many ex-Colonial servants now in new occupations who owe much to him. They and others still to come who will benefit from the foundations he has laid will pay a well deserved tribute to his invaluable work. All will join in wishing him success in his new post. The Service will be glad that he is to be followed by another member of the Service whose heart will be in his job. (The new Head of the Bureau is Mr. H. A. S. Johnston, C.M.G., O.B.E., D.F.C., formerly Deputy Governor of Northern Nigeria ... *Ed.*)

Note

* *Author's note*: I have cited Nigeria because I happen to be more familiar with recent developments there, but no doubt the same can be said of other parts of Africa.

Selling Yourself to Employers

by RONALD BROWN, O.B.E.

After reading Sir John Rankine's article in *Corona* of April. 1962, on 'Selling the Service to Employers' and his well-deserved tribute to Dick Peel, here are some suggestions to those now leaving the Service on how to set about getting themselves a job.

First and foremost put right out of your heads any idea that your life's work is finished. Remember that in the United Kingdom 65 is still the normal age for retirement and that if you are not more than 43 you are not yet half way through the working life of a university graduate. Aspire therefore to something more exciting than a club secretaryship or other dead-end jobs, for there is a serious lack in Britain of first-class management personnel and with training, experience and determination you have the qualities which can take you to the top. Britain needs you.

If you have been in the Colonial Administration let's face facts and admit that in the Service we tended to regard ourselves as the chosen race. Get that out of your heads right away. British industry certainly needs administrators badly but it is most unlikely to recruit them as such. You must get into industry on other qualities; your administrative ability will have its chance to manifest itself once you are there.

If you have a professional qualification and have been practising your profession as, say, a doctor, dentist, engineer, accountant or teacher you should find yourself a worthwhile job without great difficulty. So, too, will those inclined towards teaching, even if they have not been trained as such.

The world of industry and commerce is an exciting new field into which to venture, but don't try to enter it if you wish your retirement from overseas service to be leisurely. If a firm is worth joining it will be one in which everyone works hard, even if when Friday evening comes round you can retire to your home in the country and concentrate on lawn mowing or more sociable pursuits until you catch the 7.30 to town on Monday morning.

How best to get into industry at plus or minus 40? There are various points of entry. You may in your leisure hours overseas have studied for and subsequently passed the final examination of the Chartered Institute of Secretaries. With an element of luck this may enable you to secure an appointment as Assistant to a Company Secretary from which you may perhaps soon graduate to a position as Secretary of a subsidiary company and so on to bigger and better things. One former colleague of mine, starting this way four or five years ago, is now a member of the main board of a well known public company. Legal qualifications acquired in the same way can lead to good appointments, especially in the larger companies which have their own legal departments as part of the Company Secretary's function.

If you haven't qualifications, don't despair. Unless you have unexpectedly lost those personal qualities which got you into H.M. Overseas Service in the first place, there are opportunities in commerce and industry for you. 'Selling' in our unsophisticated minds used to be associated with ringing front door bells and getting a foot in once the door was unlocked. It is, in fact, a far more skilful and important occupation. As for all jobs worth having, hard work is involved, but skill at selling, whether to manufacturers, wholesalers, distributors, factors, retailers, or direct to the consumer, has its rewards. I have recently met a man of under 40 whose only formal training was for work as a radio officer on a ship, who has just been appointed Sales Director of a well-known company at a commencing salary of £6,000. Although he had been selling for fifteen years he had been earning over £2,000 for the last ten. His case may be exceptional, but it indicates the opportunities which are available for men of drive and ability. Successful selling is, in any case, of first importance to British industry, so why not give it a go? You will almost certainly have to start as a Representative; then it's up to you to earn promotion, in turn, to Sales Manager, General Sales Manager, Sales Director and – why not – to the post of Managing Director itself. Some ex-Colonial Administrators, after being trained at their new employer's expense, have got into industry as Work Study men. A year or two of this and the deserving man will have his chance to tackle something bigger. Personnel work is not everybody's cup of tea, but having got into it there is a professional qualification to be obtained, made easy for the man over 35 who can produce evidence of having done somewhat similar work overseas.

For the younger man intent on an industrial career the best plan may be to seek an appointment as a Management Trainee with one of the larger firms. Such training lasts two or three years and will include spells of service in all the main functions including the shop floor itself (where one probably starts). By the end of the training period it will be evident for which side of the company's business the trainee has the greatest flair and thereafter he can specialise accordingly. There was a time when a man could obtain a job largely on account of his detailed knowledge of some region overseas. It is no longer so, and more important today is a thorough knowledge of the product or service which the overseas traveller is out to sell.

It is as well to realise from the start that job-hunting is a full-time occupation, so having arrived on these shores and settled the family in what is probably temporary accommodation, get down to the business in earnest. Don't depend too much on personal introductions. You may be lucky, but there is normally considerable resistance from those actually responsible for making appointments to taking on an unqualified or inexperienced individual just because some V.I.P. has said that 'he's a jolly good chap'. It is easy enough for the V.I.P. to give introductions, but not nearly so easy for the individual himself to make successful use of them. There will probably be many disappointments before a reasonable job is found. Even then it may not be THE job, but that does not matter. The important thing is to get started. You can always use the first job as a corner of industry in which to establish a new reputation and then after a year or two get something far more worthwhile.

A word on the way in which to apply for a job, and in the course of my post-Colonial Service career I have read thousands of letters of application. The important thing is to catch the eye of the person to whom your application is addressed. Remember that he probably has several scores of applicants for the same job and is not going to be interested in a duplicated or printed *curriculum vitae* which tells in detail about the hundreds of thousands of Africans whom you administered with such skill before you were thirty. Every application should be tailor-made for the particular job and I personally now believe it to be a great mistake to attach a *curriculum vitae* which has obviously been produced in large numbers and which creates the impression that it comes from a desperate man who is anxious to get any job and is not quite clear in his own mind as to what he would really like to do. A tailor-made application is so very much better. If it is for a post which has been advertised, it can indicate how far one possesses the specific qualifications and experience called for and be a personal rather than a mass-produced document.

I read the *Times* but undoubtedly the national daily which contains the greatest number of advertised jobs is the *Daily Telegraph*. Of the weekend papers the *Sunday Times* is probably used just a bit more than the *Observer* but both are worth close study. Don't only read the display and semi-display advertisements. Sometimes a worthwhile job will appear under a classified heading. Finally, don't ignore the personal column of the *Times*.

It is very tempting to apply for a job while you are still overseas but it is really a waste of time. The interview is the most vital part of selection procedure and no employer is likely to want you so badly as to be prepared to wait until your return to England or to offer to finance a special trip home. Once you have arrived in this country you will find the response to your applications much more encouraging.

The better-known executive selection consultants exist to find 'Chaps for jobs' not 'Jobs for chaps' and the two services just don't mix. They therefore derive their fees entirely from employers and although they will always treat you most courteously there is little to be gained by approaching consultants unless you are actually applying for one of their jobs. If you want to teach, you can always make use of the services of such well-known scholastic agencies as Gabbitas-Thring or Truman and Knightley, or contact the Incorporated Association of Preparatory Schools, but the one or two agencies which exist for launching you into industry are less well known.

Starting salaries vary considerably and one should not attach too much importance to them so long as there are good prospects. One feature of industry and commerce is that although increments may not come as regularly as on the long grade in the Colonial Service, when they do come they are well worth having. The progressive employer will always see that his key men are being paid not less than their market value.

Finally, a word on a more domestic matter. On our return to the United Kingdom our wives would not be human if they did not yearn to have a home of their own. Unless you are prepared to live in central London resist the temptation to buy a house until you know where your work is going to be. If, for instance, you live on the wrong side of London, crossing the metropolis by public transport twice a day at rush hours will quickly exhaust you both physically and mentally. It's far, far, better to live on the same side of London as your job. If you can't bear the thought of living in a big town or of being a commuter, then it's perhaps best if you follow the example of two of my former colleagues and establish yourself as a village grocer-cum-subpostmaster. They are, at any rate, still in touch with their fellow men.

Are we Employable?

I. THEORY

by V. E. DAWSON

C*orona* for March, 1956, quoted a *Daily Telegraph* report that 'a scheme for introducing retired senior officers from the Services and the Oversea Civil Service into industry has been launched by the Federation of British Industries. The Federation says that many of them are potentially of 'first class value.''

This news cannot fail to be of interest to many members of Her Majesty's Oversea Service in view of the widespread and rapid political and constitutional developments in their territories.* It is surprising, though, that such a scheme should require 'launching' as if transfer from responsible public service to industrial (or commercial) management were comparable with violent movement from one element to another. It is by no means uncommon for public administrators (and professional officers) to enter industry or commerce on their retirement and sometimes to retire before the normal age in order to do so. Is there, in fact, so much difference between public administration and industrial or commercial management that it cannot be bridged by a moderate adjustment of outlook, by learning a new trick or two, or modifying old ones, and by a zest for mastering relevant detail?

Firstly, how do those who serve the public differ, initially, from those who 'go into business?' For many years, the standard of qualifications and the personal qualities required for acceptance as a public administrator have been high; and in the Oversea Service a spirit of adventure, a sense of mission, and dedication to the principles (as well as the ability to teach the practice) of public service have been essential. Recently, and particularly since the war, it is a fact that industry and commerce have competed strongly with the Civil Services for the best products of our educational and social system, often with attractive financial incentives. For the men of whom I write, financial incentives are subordinate to the stimulation of the task and the satisfaction of ideals but, nowadays, there need he no such conflict between money and motives. Peter F. Drucker says in *The Practice of Management* (first published in 1955):

'... authority ... requires of the manager that he assume responsibility for the public good, that he subordinate his actions to an ethical standard of conduct and that he restrain his self-interest and his authority wherever their exercise would infringe upon the common weal and upon the freedom of the individual.... The public responsibility of management must therefore underlie all its behavior. Basically it furnishes the ethics of management.... Even the most private of private enterprises is an organ of society.'

These words, by one who is regarded as an authority on all aspects of business management, are equally applicable to any public administrator, in Britain or the oversea territories, of any period. The conclusion must be that the emotion, sentiment, ideals, qualifications and qualities now required in a manager are similar to those which have always been, and still are, the prime necessities of a public administrator.

When they have been recruited, what do administrators and managers do? The administrator, who is by derivation a person of service, is one who is required so to arrange the affairs for which he is responsible as to give the widest possible benefit whether (in the writer's opinion) the public stands to him in the relation of taxpayers or consumers. To achieve this aim, he must link his abilities, strongly, to those of his superiors, colleagues, and subordinates. When the Administrative Staff College at Henley was established, Sir Hector Hetherington wrote in an article in *The Times:* 'The administrator's business is to provide the conditions under which the work of a team can come to good effect in the achievement of some co-operative purpose.' This, surely, is equally a definition of 'management.' Drucker has, however, defined management (in *The Practice of Management*) as 'The specifically economic organ of an industrial society for making a productive enterprise out of human and material resources ... and for managing workers and work.'

On the face of it, this specifically economic emphasis of management seems to open a gap between the work, and the aims, of the public administrator and the manager. In bygone days, when managers were less conscious of their public responsibilities, and when spending by the Government and by public authorities did not have such a large effect as it does today on the national economy, there may have been reason for regarding public administrators and managers as comparable with chalk and cheese. But, nowadays, no one could be more conscious than the responsible administrator of the economic effect of his activities. His horizon includes, however (especially in Her Majesty's Oversea Service), political and social, as well as purely economic prospects and his constant challenge is, 'can we afford *not* to do this, or that?'

So far, the scales are fairly evenly balanced between the public administrator and the manager. Similar qualities are required and the manager's slightly weightier economic ingredient is offset by the administrator's heavier public responsibility. The evidence supports the view that administration and management are not divergent paths, nor yet parallel roads, but that they are opposite sides of the same street.

This view, I believe it is true to say, is not generally recognised, or accepted by either administrators or managers, possibly because the words 'administration' and 'management' have been somewhat loosely used in the past. Yet it is by no means new. Henri Fayol, who died over 30 years ago, honoured for his practical success as an administrator (or manager) and for

his teaching of administration (or management), said in his address to the
Second International Congress of Administrative Science:

> 'The meaning which I have given to the word *administration* and which
> I has been generally adopted broadens considerably the field of
> administrative science. It embraces not only the public service but
> enterprises of every size and description, of every form and every
> purpose. All undertakings require planning, organisation, command,
> co-ordination and control, and in order to function properly, all must
> observe the same general principles. We are no longer confronted with
> several administrative sciences, but with one which can be applied
> equally well to public and to private affairs.'**

There are further similarities. The remuneration of public administrators is in the range of £1,000 to £5,000 a year, with the majority in the
£1,500 to £3,000 a year bracket. Managers appear from a study of *The
Times's* vacancies columns to have the same salary range (although there are
some no doubt heavily surtaxed exceptions). Public administrators are
not specialists – except in administration; any other kind of specialisation
would impair their value as administrators. Many other managers are
wanted who 'need not have a detailed knowledge of the company's product,'
Proved experience, initiative, drive, organising ability – those are qualities
required and which take precedence, in a manager, over technical
knowledge. (This supports an attempt by Fayol to evaluate the relative
importance of the abilities required in a 'boss' in which the need for
managerial (or administrative) ability equalled, or exceeded all the other
abilities – technical, commercial, financial, accounting – combined.) The
following quotation, again from Sir Hector Hetherington, explaining
administration, embraces equally management:

> 'At one end of the scale is the simple executive function of applying
> known rules to the given case – sometimes not so simple. At the other
> end, administration shades off into leadership, policy making and
> planning; it may be a sphere of genius.'

In this search for a common denominator between public administration
and management, enough has been said to suggest that they are, basically,
the same and that public administrators and managers, needing similar
qualities and having comparable conceptions of their tasks could, given a
settling in period, successfully transfer from one to the other. The point has
also been made that an administrator or manager does not need to have
technical qualifications but a technologist may well become a manager. This
point was summed up succinctly by N. U. Akpan in *The Scaffold and the
Structure* (*Corona*, September 1955) with:

> 'Good administration springs not from formulas but from a quick
> ability to assess and judge values. It requires great mental skill and

because it deals with human beings, their problems and even their destiny, more delicacy than any normal technical duty.'

There can be no doubt that the 'identical twins' of administration and management are, and will be, increasingly required in this technological age to keep mankind – workers, customers, and 'the public' – in the picture, and in perspective.

II. PRACTICE

by JOHN MORLEY, M.B.E.

S econd only to the problem of how to mitigate the severity of United Kingdom Income Tax, the question what to do to get a job if, or it may be when, one retires is a firm favourite for sundowner or cocktail parties in the now not so dependent overseas territories. Unfortunately, by the nature of things, the person best qualified to lead this discussion is never present. He has already gone to the United Kingdom, where he has either already found a job, in which case he has ceased to think about how he accomplished such a feat, or else he is lying low, writing vague but hopeful letters to his friends which give little indication of how his affairs are progressing. Thus in neither case does he communicate his hard-won experience to his former colleagues who when, or it may be if, their turn arrives to follow him, have only their own native intelligence, and no body of acquired precedent to guide them. This is a sorry state of affairs which surely ought to be remedied.

Here then is a voice from the beyond, the genuine message of one who is still seeking and has not yet obtained. Like most communications from the other side, its contents will be platitudinous rather than startling. It may therefore be judged authentic.

The first and most obvious piece of advice is not to be in too much of a hurry. Be prepared for the long haul. You may be one of the lucky few who land the dream job in a matter of weeks, but it is much more likely to take months. A calm acceptance of this practically inevitable waiting period is partly a matter of cash, or of accumulated leave which comes to the same thing, and partly of temperament or nerve. It is essential to recognise but not to be frightened by the basic facts of the situation, that employers generally while valuing overseas experience are sceptical about its relevance to conditions at home (and who will say them wrong), that even where a post is advertised for public competition there is very often a previously favoured candidate with a prior claim to it, and that the competition is very keen – for example, a recent advertisement for a bursar's post attracted 300 applications. This incidentally means that there is usually a considerable time-lag between the submission of an application and notification of appearing in the short list for an interview. Personal introductions matter

more than anything, but it is wise to assume that only one out of many of
these will actually lead anywhere, not because the others have not tried but
because they just have not heard of any vacancies. It has to be remembered
that in business, as in Government, the greater number of posts are filled on
promotion.

Let us first consider, but very briefly, what sort of institutional help may
be available. There is the Appointments Service of the Ministry of Labour,
with offices in London (Tavistock Square), Manchester and Glasgow. Its
main usefulness perhaps is to bring to the attention of those who register
there notices of any posts for which they appear to be suited. Then there is
the Appointment's Board of one's former University, which will try to be
helpful but is bound to point out at the start that it was set up to help
undergraduates, and not to tackle the quite different and much more
difficult problem of the 'over-30's.' Lastly there is a scheme sponsored
jointly by the Officers Association, the Colonial Office and the Federation of
British Industries, for the introduction of retired senior officials to industry.
A pamphlet on the subject may be obtained from the Federation (21, Tothill
Street, S.W.1) for the price of threepence; the emphasis, it will be noted, is
on introduction to, and not placing in industry.

For that, one can really only rely on one's own efforts, helped out by
whatever influence one can command and with the addition of a strong
element of luck. But it is no use hoping to begin the hunt too early. 'It is
not uncommon,' one agency wrote, 'for Colonial officers whose retirement
or resignation is in sight to ask us to look for vacancies on their behalf.
While they are actually serving overseas, however, we run into the perennial
difficulty that employers will not make appointments without personal
contact with the candidates. I usually suggest that men in your position let
me know two or three weeks before they leave for the United Kingdom so
that we can put them on our active lists.' On the other hand it is commonly
and no doubt truthfully stated that it is easier to get a job when one is in a
job. Bearing this in mind, it is usually better to describe one's status as 'on
leave' rather than 'retired' when making an application, provided of course
one is able to assure the prospective employer that one is at liberty to take
up employment at once. It does happen not infrequently that immediate
availability is a decisive factor, in which respect the Colonial applicant
has an advantage over a rival candidate who may be bound to give several
months' notice.

A typewriter is really indispensable, Even those forceful characters who
have no compunction about storming Chairmen in their private offices,
must be able to leave behind some literature for them, or more likely their
staff, to read. The form of written approach will of course depend on
circumstances but there are three possible elements. First, especially if one's
past has been at all varied, there should be a brief *curriculum vitae* containing
the bare outline of one's past career, with dates and retiring salary (more of
this later). Second, there is the question of testimonials. For many public
posts, the advertisement specifies both referees and testimonials; in one
case *only* testimonials were required. Referees do not usually present any
problem, though it may not be easy to find anyone who is both accessible in

the United Kingdom and can reasonably be claimed to be acquainted with one's work. Testimonials are rather a problem. The Colonial Office cannot give testimonials to officers in the Oversea Service, for the obvious reason that they are not in its employ. Most Colonial Governments have, in their General Orders, some provision for giving them, but the value of these outside the territory may not be very great. It is certainly worth trying to find a way round this difficulty, as a really first class testimonial can be worth a lot in breaking the ice and showing an employer that your application is worth following up. For the same reason, even if he does not ask for one, it may be worth inventing a reason for sending it.

The third element is the letter of application itself, which is where the typewriter comes in. There is no good at all in thinking that a standard form will do. On the contrary each letter of application should be worded very carefully with an eye to what the particular post requires. Thus the appointment of, say, Secretary to the Rock Lobster Authority will require quite a different approach from that of Bursar of St. Botolph's. Reading through the copies of the applications in your file (I forgot to mention the file) you will be amazed to observe how, in the one case, your whole career has been concerned with various aspects of the fishing industry and, in the other, has been devoted with single-minded intensity to the problems of education.

If you have done your job properly with the preliminaries, you may find yourself on the short list for an interview. Having sat on many selection committees yourself you will no doubt have observed that there are a number of different techniques of being interviewed, as of interviewing; I should hesitate to say which is the right one and in any case no one can escape from being himself. One hint may be valuable here, which is to try to find out as much as possible in advance about what the job entails. In the case of a new post, its creation may have been due to a report, so read it if you can. If there is no special situation, read up the general background. In this connection it is worthy of note that up to date reports on a wide variety of subjects can be found in the retail shop of Her Majesty's Stationery Office in Kingsway. Before the interview is over you are most likely to be asked whether you have any questions on your side, and it is not difficult to frame these so that they give a hint (it should not be more than a hint) that you have been to some trouble to get properly briefed. If on the other hand the interview ends without such an opportunity presenting itself, you will at least have acquired additional self-confidence from being armed with this knowledge. Sometimes it is possible to find out indirectly who the members of the interviewing Committee will be, after which it is not so difficult also to find out something about them. Being human, they will certainly not take it amiss if they realise you know who they are, while on your side it will be easier to anticipate questions and answer them adequately.

A word about salaries. After studying the advertisements, it is very difficult to conclude that there is any such thing as 'market value' for administrative work. Some posts have twice the salary of others in which, so far as one can see, the amount of responsibility is just as great. Where the salary is advertised (as in the case of public appointments it nearly always is) there is not much room for argument. In other cases where the prospective employer has a fair measure of discretion, a common first reaction is 'of course we couldn't pay you anything like that figure (the one quoted in the *curriculum vitae*) for a post here.' Bitterly conscious though one may be of next term's school fees already due, it is best not to react too quickly to this one, either by being adamant when one is in fact prepared to give some ground or, rather more likely, by allowing oneself to be beaten down. Nearly always there is a chance to think it over and this should be taken, even though one may feel certain at the time. Many things appear quite different on reflection.

You are now as far as these words of advice can take you, in the ante-room waiting for your turn for an interview. These affairs are often so conducted that one sees one's fellow candidates both before and after. There is a strong silent type in the corner who looks pretty confident; perhaps he is engaged to the Chairman's daughter. Perhaps he is thinking the same about you.

Note

* *It would be a mistake, however, to think that the F.B.I. scheme has yet advanced to the stage where posts in industry are readily obtainable.—Ed.*
** *From Administration Industrielle et Général translated, for some reason, as General and Industrial Management.*

'O.S.R.B.'

by R. L. PEEL

Regular subscribers to *Corona* will have read the entertaining articles by John Morley on the art of job-hunting (November, 1956, and April, 1957). He set out the general lines to be followed in seeking a new career after several years of civil service in the Colonies; the hundreds of applications neatly docketed in files, the few replies, the flame of hope raised by seeing posts advertised at £3,000 a year which seem so absolutely 'up one's street', and the shock of finding that they have been filled by some Admiral coruscant with stars.

The general principles remain much the same, although the degree of competition is probably greater. Where formerly there were 300 applicants for a Bursarship, today there are 400 for the lesser and 1,000 applicants for the better paid vacancies. Personal introductions still help enormously and the best jobs are obtained after the third Martini at a cocktail party or with the nuts at a British Legion dinner.

Since John Morley wrote, however, more official help has been given to men who retire from the Overseas Service. Those who are about to enter upon another winter of discontent in England may be rejoiced to learn that that well-loved Santa Claus of official Britain, the Treasury, whose kindly mouth is so effectually hidden behind the false beard of disapproval, has agreed that the functions of the Bureau, set up in 1957 to assist in the resettlement of officers retiring from Malaya, shall be extended to cover men and women retiring from any Overseas Territory. The office, now known as 'The Overseas Services Resettlement Bureau', is situated in the Sanctuary Buildings block of the Colonial Office.

Before setting out to describe what the Bureau does, it would be as well to say what it does not do. It does not crimp men from the Service and it refuses to register any who have not retired or opted to retire. It is, therefore, no good writing to the Bureau in the hopes of obtaining employment while on leave with a view to exercising the option to retire thereafter. The Bureau has frequently gone further and advised men in certain age groups to return to their posts abroad and not to retire at any rate for the present. It may also be of interest to overseas Governments that, since the life of the Bureau has been extended, a number of officers have decided to remain at their posts for a further period in the knowledge that the Bureau will still be there when they finally do decide to retire. It is food for speculation whether, if the Bureau were made permanent, officers would be even more willing to remain abroad for a longer period.

Secondly, the Bureau does not place people in jobs. It can given them introductions to an ever increasing number of prospective employers and it does give advice on what lines offer the best chance in each particular case, but it is up to the officer concerned to get himself or herself across to the employer or interviewing board. In this connection, interviews are an art in themselves, especially so far as the person being interviewed is concerned. Not only does he have to keep his temper when the interviewer is exercising his privilege of baiting the victim; but he has to gauge to a nicety what limits he can go to in disagreeing with the interviewer on a matter which may be his pet subject or may only be a kite flown for the fun of it. It is always useful, therefore, to seek interviews even for posts which are not of great interest. Strangely enough, it is when one is least interested in a job that one makes the best impression and receives an offer. Over anxiety to obtain a particular post often leads to disappointment.

Having said this, what more does the Bureau do to help officers to start a new career? Well, it provides an answer to one of the problems raised by John Morley: that of finding someone in England capable of giving a testimonial or reference to prospective employers. To some extent it is, of course, dependent on Heads of Departments in the various territories concerned writing a report which will give a really good pen picture of a man, while at the same time bringing out his special qualifications. A statement that an officer is of exemplary conduct but has shown no outstanding characteristics is valueless. Similarly, a report based on the headings contained in the official Annual Confidential Report tends to be too impersonal and staccato. A good report of the type needed calls for imaginative writing and a deal of human sympathy. Some reports have been excellent and give a really live portrait of the man on one page of foolscap.

Then, the number of contacts made by the Bureau is slowly expanding, slowly because of difficulties over publicity, but efforts over the past year have borne fruit and, of course, every man who obtains a post and makes a success of it acts as a good advertisement for the Bureau. Thus, its fame is gradually spreading. One measure of its success is that out of 537 who have registered up to the end of last November, 244 have secured employment.

Nevertheless, do not think that jobs are to be found in England for the asking. There is a general view current that anyone who has served overseas has lived a life of indolent luxury. Few realise that the five-day week of England has still not penetrated the tropics, despite the climate, and that the official hours of work (let alone the many hours of work in districts and on committees out of office) are longer there than here. It is, of course, everyone's privilege to regard his own particular work as possessing some esoteric quality beyond the capacity of anyone else to master, but this seems especially strong in all walks of life in England. Not, mind you, that they deny the grave need for men of intelligence, integrity and ability to take responsibility at the higher levels, but the necessary vacancies most unfortunately always exist in some else's business.

So far as the Service is concerned, there seems to be a feeling that the Bureau cannot help the technical or professional officer. This is quite erroneous. A very large field of vacancies for technical officers and teachers is available in the Bureau and it helps greatly to keep in touch with business and other organisations if it is possible to send names of suitable candidates for such vacancies. It costs nothing to register, nor is any charge made for matching up applicant and employer. At the same time, it is essential, when job-hunting, to keep as many irons in the fire as possible. It is, therefore, strongly recommended that technical and professional officers should register on retirement from the Service.

Finally, a word of advice. Job-hunting is a serious business. Do not take too much leave on retirement before doing the daily search of the newspapers. Up to six months inactivity is acceptable to prospective employers; beyond that time makes the applicant's abilities suspect.

Preparing for Retirement

by A. E. HAARER, F.L.S.

I t is so easy to take up service abroad and feel that the future can take care of itself. With training behind, and the confidence of youth, all that appears necessary is to apply oneself to one's job, to climb up by sheer brilliance and hard work as high as possible in the Service, before retiring gracefully on pension. Given an honest determination to please, and good health, retirement seems a long way off.

The trouble is that the years pass by all too quickly, and retirement comes before most of us are ready for it. With regard to age, a man can still feel young at fifty-five; he may have grown wise and tolerant, and have a brain which is at its zenith, filled with accumulated knowledge that ought never to be wasted, and yet, who wants to employ a man of such an age in England? There are very few openings indeed, and these are very specialised. A man may go to his local council and find them only too willing to fit him into some volunteer organisation – some unpaid job. Better, this, than sitting by the fireside waiting for death! But the times are hard in England, nowadays, and seem likely to get harder. The savings of a lifetime may go in providing and furnishing a home, and it is a struggle for a family to live in Britain now on less than £1,000 a year.

Experience in the Administration and most of the technical services abroad is not enough to fit men for jobs in England or, if it is, then it is hard to find employers who think so. As an ex-planter from Uganda years ago – before I joined the Colonial Agricultural Service – an interviewing clerk at a labour exchange in London told me 'We don't grow coffee and bananas in Clapham Junction you know!' He regretted this statement before I had finished with him, but this did not help to recommend me to whatever central organisation the exchange might have had.

It may be easy to get some clerical or manual work to do at £4 or £6 a week, but by the time income tax and fares and subsistence is withdrawn from these amounts, a soul-killing, life-shortening task has been done for less than half a labourer's pay. The conclusion must be reached, therefore, that if a man has no private means, nor special plan for falling on his feet, he must deliberately prepare himself to earn good money in after life, long before the day for retirement arrives. He must start, in fact, at the very beginning, and not put off the day.

How can folk prepare themselves to earn reasonable incomes during retirement? A few have become successful writers, but this is not easy, unless one has a flair, and drive, or the cheek of the very Devil. A good correspondence course in the beginning is helpful to avoid the usual errors, but success is only obtained after long and painful endeavour, by having

256

extreme patience and the ability to bob up again and again with the will to try again after every disheartening disappointment. It has taken me nearly twenty years hard work to reach an average of £12 a week, and this has only come during the last year or two. I wrote three full-length books before the abridgement of one was at last accepted three years ago, and though I am convinced it will sell moderately well, I must wait at least another year for royalties because it has only just appeared in print.

Five more books are now travelling the same weary road to publication, and a technical one just commissioned will cost money, and take three more years before royalties begin to come in. As for magazine articles and short stories, rejection slips would fill a sack.

There are so many things I wish I had done to prepare myself for retirement during twenty-two years overseas; things that anyone could do by devoting just a little time each week, or month, to something which might be called a hobby. One does not have to be a forestry officer to study timber, for instance.

The world is short of timber at the moment, and firms are importing hard-wood supplies with little more than the foggiest idea of what they are getting. There are many kinds of hard-wood cut in forests overseas, each with its distinctive grain and its special qualities for various purposes. Were a man an expert in hard timber he could easily command a worthwhile post on retirement without knowing how to grow or cut down a tree. It would be just a hobby to collect neat little plaques of wood; to learn to recognise the grain, the smell, the microscopical texture of each piece; adding this knowledge to weights, values, characteristics, durability, and suitability for commercial purposes. Gradually throughout the years the practice of such a hobby would build up expert knowledge to such an extent that one would become an authority, just as one can become an authority on anything else in half a lifetime.

During those years abroad I took hundreds of photographs, but rendered most of them useless for money-making by sticking my family or friends bang in the middle of each picture. As for the others, I snapped at things haphazardly, never thinking they might be of use. Many of these I have used over and over again for illustration at a guinea or half a guinea a time. On occasion I have sold the rights to reproduce one picture for four guineas, and if only I had taken sets – if only I had taken thousands more with deliberate intent, what a gold mine they would have been!

Just ordinary sights and scenes abroad become of value if good clear pictures are taken artistically in sets of say half-a-dozen. Such sets would illustrate customs of living, local industries, scenery, townships, and vegetation, the collecting of which would not only be an interesting hobby, but an investment for the future. There are firms in England who specialise in buying and selling photographs for illustration, and it is surprising how hard it is to get from any one of them just the right material to illustrate an article, a brochure, or to make up a film strip for educational purposes. Many a picture-paper has to write round the illustrations it can obtain – not illustrate what has been written!

During twenty years abroad it should be easy to add to one's collection by contracting with friends, with a view to starting up an agency. Pictures that are collected should not 'date' too easily, unless they might have a historical interest in future, such as 'the building of the Owen Falls dam, and what the Ripon Falls looked like before they disappeared!'

Our schooldays were rendered laborious by having languages such as French and German to learn, and it may be a bore in later life to learn Swahili or some other local vernacular, at least until one realises that proficiency in certain languages may bring good money during retirement. Boredom vanishes as one becomes more proficient, and is replaced by a pride in achievement, so that the learning of a language becomes yet another hobby.

Why not study the whole gamut of local vernaculars if one has an aptitude, remembering that there are schools of oriental languages needing experts, and that translations are required by publishers to supply reading matter for educational purposes, and for illiterate peoples who are only now learning to read? An extra efficiency in the local languages would enhance one's Service life.

Russian may be a difficult language to learn fluently, and why should anyone bother to learn a language of an unfriendly nation? Folk who become fluent and expert in such a language, however, would command good pay and interesting occupations during retirement so long as they could keep out of a bath chair. Among the entourages of committee men and government representatives travelling about the world are vacancies for experts in foreign languages. There are broadcasting staff vacancies, censorship departments, foreign departments of banks and commercial houses all extremely short of reliable people who can speak and read difficult languages. Is it too great an effort to spend a little spare time during twenty years overseas to make retirement a time of comfort and interest and freedom from worry?

The Candidate's Wife

by ANNE CLARK HUTCHISON

T he occupations people take up when they leave the Colonial Service would keep 'What's My Line?' going for weeks – mink farming, the Church, golf club secretary, prep school master.... But whatever it is, wives find themselves at the old game of 'adapting yourself to a new environment.'

I found myself 'adapting' as the wife of a Parliamentary Candidate, for three hectic weeks without much warning in the 1955 General Election, and for another three at a by-election in 1957. Colonial Service life proved to have been a good apprenticeship, for after her daily dealing with the unexpected, both in places and people, it is pretty hard to take a Colonial Service wife unawares.

In fact, *plus ça change* ... In 1955 my husband was contesting a seat in an industrial town, which he was not expected to gain, and thereby he escaped all limelight. It was in many ways like being on an outstation, where you make your initial mistakes away from the eye of authority, learn the hard way, and the officer's wife is willy-nilly much involved in his work. Problems are solved there in ways that would make the hair rise on the Secretariat-minded head, or, in our new context, the Central-Office-minded. The merits of the blind eye became obvious, too. We didn't, officially, know who applied the blob of tar which deleted the 'n't' from the Socialist posters which announced 'Toryism Doesn't Work'; but we knew exactly to whom to have the word passed by bush telegraph that his operations with long-handled broom and bucket of melted tar would please stop short of the point where they might draw reprisal from the other side.

This foray with broom and tar reflected the atmosphere of amateur effort and cheerful improvisation which permeated the shabby hall which was our committee room. It was a bush station working on a pinched budget, all over again. Index cards seemed to home in shoe boxes, like the files in paraffin crates in the old days in the Hadramaut; campaign policy was worked out at odd moments round one end of a trestle table, all in the tradition of informal conference, of talking shop wherever the parties to a problem find themselves, at sundown or on trek or in a village compound. I sidled the portable typewriter into any clear space I saw among the slithering piles of election literature, and banged out last-minute press handouts, much as I had seen a letter to the District Commissioner raced off, while a truck driver fumed to get away before the rains came. And all with endless cups of tea! Substitute squash for tea, and one might have been back in the bustle of a morning spent helping in an Aden hospital outpatient clinic.

Although none of the three local weekly papers which I fed with
handouts could produce the awful joy of 'English as she was writ' in
the earlier numbers of the *Aden Chronicle*, there was enough provincial
journalese to make our children hoot derisively to see parents referred to as
'the couple' and mother described as 'doing her best to secure for her man
that ticket to Westminster.' Press photographs, overseas or at home, rarely
flatter anyone, so there was no surprise in seeing the variations on the theme
of the Candidate's features – boot-button eyes, blank expression, sardonic
smile, evil leer – the lot. If there were such a thing as libel by photograph,
we could by now make a rich haul in damages. It makes one think of
passports.

They say a good officer takes an interest in local custom. This virtue was
forced on us one lovely sunny May evening in a mining village, in which
my husband was billed to address a meeting. Men were arriving at the hall,
not strolling up as usual but with a brisk purposeful air. Was strenuous
heckling being plotted? Our local branch chairman came timidly towards
us as we sat in the waiting car and said, 'I'm afraid no one has come to the
meeting – fine evening and all that, I suppose.' We pointed out that people
had been going in. 'Oh, aye, but they're all round the back at the Doos.' A
wood pigeon is a 'cushie-doo' in Scotland so that gave us our clue. To the
rear of the hall we went and found men and boys busy handling racing
pigeons, taking their ring numbers and packing them into hampers, to go
with others from all over Lanarkshire to Stafford, there to be released to race
home. The Candidate's speech on the Budget stayed in his pocket, and he
soon found himself immersed in the economics of pigeon racing, the price
of feed, and the cost of transport; I heard all about the trips on which the
handlers go to release the birds, as far afield as Rennes and Poitiers, and I
tactlessly asked if the birds always got back safely: sardonic laughter! Next
we strolled down to the miners' welfare club where a game of bowls was just
ending. I was more at home here than with the Doos, for my father was a
keen performer on the local greens at our holiday haunts on the Moray Firth
and I knew the jargon of 'touchers' and 'fine back bools'.

Soon the talk turned from bowls to politics, and I remembered the
advice that officers' wives should never involve themselves in argument,
advice strengthened by the memory of how I transgressed as a greenhorn in
Palestine, by embarking on a fruitless discussion on their way of life in a
Jewish communal settlement. So when an elderly miner, harking back
firmly but without rancour to the bad old days of the early '30's, said to me
with a smile: 'You see then, ma'am, why I aye votes my class,' I resisted the
temptation to name a few public school Front Bench Socialists, and
returned his smile. I met him again on polling day, outside a polling
station, where he told me he had just 'voted his class'.

On polling day the candidate and his wife are, as one worker said, just
'perambulating smiles', and how one hopes that smile will last till after the
count! All day you are both quite superfluous, obliged to be on view, but
with nothing real to do, while others work at top speed. I suspect it might
be like that sometimes for a Governor and his wife at a tribal gathering or

great show put on in their honour. They are necessary to the occasion, but the performers are having all the fun.

The seat in that 1955 Election went to the other side as expected, but there was the same satisfaction an officer feels on coming in from a district, basking a little in the District Commissioner's praise for tackling a job he knew was pretty impossible even when he gave it, and being made to feel that even if his efforts hadn't exactly made the desert blossom as the rose, at least a blade or two of green was visible – and am I wrong in thinking that the attractions and humours of outstation life are more clearly visible in retrospect?

In 1957 the task was to hold a city seat that had not changed for many years. The atmosphere was pure Secretariat or Provincial Headquarters; everything was planned to work according to the book, the registry functioned smoothly out of orthodox cabinets, there was an array of experts on procedure, local history and geography; campaign policy was debated in the office punctually at 10 a.m. each morning (men only). Someone took care of the Press; I had a walking-on part. No racing pigeons, no bowls, but there was still a worthy or two – and those posters. Nothing in Colonial life is comparable to the curious experience of seeing the face you know so well in the opposite arm chair or across the dining table, staring down at you from hoardings, stuck up in windows or flapping on the sides of loudspeaker vans.

I am now the Member's wife (Candidate and Member are always somehow pronounced with capitals). With a husband on safari between Edinburgh and West-minster, I know grasswidowhood again. More I shall not say, lest I invite comparison with that well-known type who comes to your Colony on a three weeks' visit and then goes home to write a book on it.

Back

by PATRICK SMARTT

The tin trunks have been stored away for the last time. Such tattered remnants of tropical kit as were not given to the stewards on the homeward voyage are in them. No more labels bearing the legends 'Cabin Baggage' or 'Not Wanted on the Voyage' will be pasted on those trunks. Home again for good. For better or worse.

Now I can, when not acting as assistant washer-up, do some of the things that I have pictured over the years. Simple things. I can lean on the sill of an upstairs window and watch a cock pheasant perambulating with his marionette strut in the stubble field behind the house. At breakfast I shall be entertained by tits, chaffinches, sparrows, and a robin as they flutter and feed on the bird-table outside the window. When the front door is opened on frosty mornings the black labrador will gambol ecstatically on the white powdery grass of the lawn.

On the walk to the village shop, up the road, over a stile, across a field and down the lane the animals that catch the eye will not be the snake, the white-throated crow, vultures, and emaciated goats. Sparrows will cascade down on to the hedgerows, a blackbird will volley noisily out of a bush. Here on a barb in the wire a fox has left a tuft of his coat marking a foray into a chicken farm. There will be cheerful and genuine greetings from ancients on their way to or from the daily pint.

Coming in from the afternoon walk a ruddy-faced sun is subsiding into a grey-brown veil of haze through which the trees loom in a filigree pattern. There is the hollow sound of a distant shot. A rabbit rustles the leaves as he scampers away.

The red cheeks of my youngsters rival the holly berries. It is true that later in the evening no servant will bring me a whisky and soda. There will be no whisky, no servant.

There will be no mosquitoes. There will be a fire, and a pipe that does not become over-heated in the first few draws; a cat on my knees and a dog twitching in a hunting dream at my feet. There will, of course, be days of teeming rain, days of biting winds, slush, and snuffly colds. There will be no malaria. Not much sun – no sunstroke. The jabber of Swahili, Chinyanja, or Hausa will be stilled: the comfortable, measured, earthy rumble of the countryman's voice will take their place.

I shall see horses and hounds again; thatch and red brick; moss and lichen; crooked chimneys and old gardens – these quiet restful things that are not to be found under the garish light of a tropical sun.

Back – The Other View

by C. D. WILKINSON

Our backs are broken with the hefting of heavy trunks and furniture and we sit exhausted with our efforts of persuading order out of chaos in our new, and final, home. Outside, the rain falls in dreary monotony from a sick grey sky; and here, in the cold and the damp our thoughts wing 3,000 miles and more to the south, and we see Africa, colourful and expansive, under its hot blue sky.

We see no sooty privet or sodden grass, but morning glory trailing down our *stoep*, and great scarlet sprays of bougainvillea. Our inner eye leaps to appraise the gorgeous splash of colour of the Flame of the Forest tree which was the centre piece in our compound, while here, through the streaming window pane looms a black and dripping leafless sycamore. No more darting lizards pulsing in the sun, no gekkos take their evening meal on our sitting room walls. No life, no movement.

In place of graceful coconut palms aslant the warm sea breeze, with white beach and whiter surf beyond, are soot-encrusted canyons of brick and stone, shrouded in thick December fog. Left behind are smiling African faces, their sauntering walk, their bright dress. Instead are the pale strained looks of factory and office worker, hurrying from work. Gone for ever is our boy's cheerful 'Wel-come, master, wel-come, madam', as he comes to meet us from the car. Here is a cold and empty house with fumbling for door-key, a fire to light, a meal to cook.

A dry expensive grape-fruit starts our breakfast now. Where is our lime and paw-paw of lost delight? Where the mangoes and the nutty-flavoured avocado pears? A world away are the sauces round the curry, African curry – roasted, salted groundnuts, shredded fresh coconut, fried banana, bright red peppers. We are back to cabbage and nourishing broth, to dumplings and steamed puddings.

As our warm tan fades, the pale sun barely quickens our thin blood. We gather round the fire. It smokes; not the spicy wood smoke that we knew, but sulphurous fumes. The chimney sweep can come in six weeks' time.

No more the pleasant evening parties with friends and cocktails, and our white-uniformed steward in his element and on top form. Television claims our neighbours nightly. Large bills and small pay. Children coming home from school wet and cold. No time for relaxation. The nights are deathly quiet. Gone is the shrill song of the crickets, booming of frogs and the late night rhythmic drumming from the village.

What have we gained? No daily paludrine routine, only cough linctus. No perspiring noonday, just frozen hands and feet and the insidious onset of creaking rheumatism. No 'Accra tummy' any more, only dyspepsia.

But – it's home.

Four Steps to Separation

by KATHARINE SIM

I wonder how many people, looking back now on twenty-five years of service in Malaya, feel that their work there fell roughly into four periods – the pre-war period of youthful enthusiasm and the search for experience; the immediate post-war one of compromise and diplomacy, followed by the years of consolidation and approach to independence; and lastly the post-independence period, fraught by a certain amount of frustration – the handing-over, the actual separation of oneself from the work, the country and the people one loved.

Looking at our own immediate pre-war period, we must have seemed very young, unconventional and no respecters of persons, falling into all the traps and pitfalls that beset the enthusiasm of youth. I can just imagine how the old hands must have disliked us both; uppish youngsters, over-full of zeal, too critical of the old regime, intolerant and much too outspoken. I can recall a dreadful dinner party at Lumut when, smug-faced as I must have been, I got up and left abruptly because I had taken objection to something belittling said against someone else in whom I believed, by the 'ruling' planter! And I remember the time when my husband (who was in the Customs) ran in 'the King of the Dindings' – a highly irascible, influential and lordly planter – and had him brought to court and convicted over a minor I toddy issue; thereby making himself *not* exactly popular.

But I think I can say we did seek to be honest and in our own ways to be creative – and those were wonderful days: my husband walked down every morning to the white office building by the sunlit estuary, while I sat peacefully up in the little house on the hill and painted and wrote, listening to the sounds of watercraft below, sounds that rose up against the hill above the flowering trees. Beyond, far away were the angled limestone hills of the main range which, east of Ipoh, stood jewel-blue ejaculations, sharp along the horizon, set off by towering white galleon clouds so typical of the Malayan midday scene. But it was a peace that was only too soon shattered by invasion.

The three immediate post-war years in Penang were ones of very hard work for members of the Service. Many changes were already in the air; as far as my husband was concerned, shortage of staff meant that many jobs were thrust upon him. It was a hard but ultimately rewarding period, and perhaps rather a breathless one. In it one had to learn to compromise, to be diplomatic and to cope with jobs for which one had not been trained.

When independence came near, many members of the Service knew that the end of their work was already at hand – although they were still only in their thirties. Those in responsible positions had to look around for local people, the right ones, to take over. But it was difficult to find people willing to break from under the umbrella. Many good ones were capable but unwilling to come forward, fearing to be labelled as stooges of the colonial regime. Others felt that when independence came they would not be able to face the new regime and, like ourselves, would do best to retire.

In Penang, and our own departmental life, for part of this period, normal routine Customs work, Import and Export Control and Foreign Exchange all fell on one pair of shoulders. It was a busy life but those years were intensely happy ones for both of us. We were both working hard, rebuilding, and trying – as people must always do, I suppose, after a war – to catch up on lost years. I was very happy there, working harder than I had ever thought to do before and, although the terrorist emergency started during that time, in June, 1948, we were left more or less in peace by it; for the terrorists, so it was said, were inclined to use Penang Island as a holiday resort and therefore created little or no trouble there. So we were free to walk deep into the hills, to bathe in cool streams, and explore the numerous Chinese temples of the island.

Then followed a long tour of nearly four years in Seremban, the capital of Negri Sembilan, a very Malay State of Mingankabau (Sumatran) influence. Our district covered as well the State of Malacca. It appeared at first to be a quiet station, possibly even boring from the work point of view, and I remember my husband's predecessor saying that there were one or two sleeping dogs whom it was best to let lie. But the sleeping dogs were soon prodded awake and they proved to be of great interest. From them was created the Central Information Office of the Preventive Service, Malaya, which set out to correlate and disseminate all available information about smugglers throughout the entire country. Until then this information had been kept, unshared, to individual stations. It was a wide and enormously interesting job, and it led to several outstanding arrests. The other dog was the Central Assessment Office – the aim of which was to assess the valuation of goods charged on an *ad valorem* basis. The idea had originally been conceived by Don Dawson and my husband in 1937 but, delayed by war and for financial reasons, it had long been shelved at the quiet station of Seremban. Now it was resurrected. Later, at Customs headquarters in Kuala Lumpur, Kenneth Hardacre became responsible for developing the project.

During our time in Seremban the idea was born and developed of a Customs Training School which was eventually founded and built at Malacca. It was the first of its kind in Asia. The whole emphasis of it was that it should be a *Malayan* Service in the full sense of the word – not Malay, Chinese, Indian, Bengali, or so forth, but truly Malayan. The school was built on a barren piece of ground north of Malacca town and, when we last visited it, the angsana and flame trees had grown fast, and the attractive red and white houses – school, museum, living quarters and other buildings – that fill its green compound were well-kept, with an air of usefulness.

No other Customs Service in the Far East, I think, has a fully-fledged residence Customs Training School. Applications were received by headquarters from as far afield as Nepal and Borneo for men to attend courses there. The courses, of about six weeks, included learning the many ways of smuggling, especially of opium, in cars – the false petrol tanks, floors and so on; the tracking down of stills for brewing *samsu*, the illicit rice wine, hidden in the undergrowth, and the thousand and one other ways the law-breaker devises for defeating the rules of the Government. The museum houses a fascinating collection of objects revealing the smuggler's ingenuity – from hollowed wooden clogs and prayer bundles (joss paper) to cricket stumps with false centres.

It was pleasant to feel my husband was identified with the school's beginning and had worked for its development.

Then came our last five years at headquarters in Kuala Lumpur, two before and three after *Merdeka* ('freedom'). This was the final era of 'working oneself out of the job.' There was much writing to be done, putting on record all the experience and knowledge that would be helpful and laying down a reasonable set of standing instructions (during a period as Director of Preventive Service). There was travelling widely all over the country, keeping green the idea of inter-communication in the Central Information Office, and encouraging the local people to take responsibility on themselves – and from all we hear they have done it extremely well and are carrying on in the tradition of the Service.

Although this was a very active and most enjoyable period in many ways for us both, it was also not unnaturally a rather sad one – especially towards the end. It was sometimes frustrating, too, in that there was nothing more creative to be done. It was the end of the road: it was no good looking back, and it was difficult to look forward. Like many others, we had worked ourselves out of the job, and it now remained for others to carry on.

From Colony to Commonwealth

by W. H. SWAFFIELD

I n a previous article I mentioned that Australia offers the Overseas Service man, thinking of early retirement, scope for his ability, a good standard of living, and a bright future for his children – with plenty of sunshine! The following details may be of interest.

Australia's main source of income comes from the export of wool and primary products. However, since the war secondary and heavy industries have expanded enormously and much capital has flowed in from overseas. This great expansion has placed heavy strains on available manpower, including trained personnel – both administrative and technical. But as the high cost structure, chiefly brought about by the 40-hour week (which boils down to about 36 hours), is pricing Australia's manufactured goods out of the world's markets, it is essential that the population should continue to increase and take up the expanding supply of goods. Australia is in fact one of the fastest growing countries in the world. In the last ten years its population has grown from 7.6 million to 9.6 million. In the next ten years it is expected to increase by a further 2.3 million. The 'White Australia' policy precludes immigrants from the East and Far Eastern countries.

Against this background let us suppose, say, that a married officer is retiring from Singapore at the age of 45 years, and that he has a daughter of 8 years and a boy of 12. His pension is £(S)800 per annum. Our ex-Overseas Service officer will want to purchase a three-bedroomed home in a good locality. With the block of land this will cost him from about £A6,000 to buy or build. It will be an attractive detached brick bungalow with a garage. It will cost him another £A1,500 to equip this home, and this sum could be spread over a period. If he is unwilling or unable to put up the whole of this sum he will probably be able to obtain a bank or insurance company loan at 6 per cent, per annum at present.

To give a general idea of living costs, here are some rough figures covering our family of four. They do not include any bank/insurance company repayment and interest on any loan:

Income

Pension £(S)800	£A1,000
Australian salary, about	1,300
	£A2,300

(Pay-as-you-earn local income tax has been deducted from salary)

Major Outgoings per annum

House maintenance and rates	110
Food, clothing, medical and hospital insurance	800
Education – two day children at a good grade grammar school	280
Holidays and entertainments, say	150
	£A1,340

If our man is on the technical side, he should have little trouble in obtaining a suitable post. As elsewhere, the administrator will be on a different wicket, but should be able to fit into this expanding industrial life, as does the local retired officer of the Armed Forces.

Income Tax. As he will pay a small Singapore tax on his pension it is not liable to Australian tax. Local income tax has been deducted from salary at source.

The foregoing will show that our man can balance his budget and put most of his pension away to meet any rainy days.

Under the Commonwealth Child Endowment Scheme he will, on behalf of his two children, receive £9 quarterly. Very useful and reasonable Hospital and Medical Benefits Funds are available to cover his family against the possibility of heavy sickness costs. However, they do not include medicine and dental costs.

Although general public transport is available, a high proportion of people run their own cars – so our man would do likewise. If so, he must allow another £300 per annum. If he travels to country centres, or interstate, he will most likely use the very efficient air services. Children to and from school receive special travel concessions.

Most grammar schools are well endowed with scholarships, and Commonwealth scholarships ensure that many bright students are able to go on to a university.

Our ex-officer and his family will be able to find, at reasonable cost, recreation in almost any sporting activity – from glorious surfing to snow sports in the Australian Alps. In Melbourne and in Sydney with its 1,500,000 people, one expects and finds clubs of all types to suit one's interest and pocket. Our man and his family may, however, prefer to live in a smaller inland country town like Tamworth, Geelong or Rockhampton where business life is less hectic, but where most facilities of the large city are available on a smaller scale. (If, owing to my particular work, I was not tied to life in a big city, I would have another look at Hobart in the lovely island of Tasmania.)

The cultural and entertainment field has greatly widened during the past two decades, partly from the influx of people from the European Continent. World-renowned symphony orchestras and distinguished overseas artists can be enjoyed in the major cities; playgoers are well catered for, and the Elizabethan Trust is doing good work here. The Sydney Opera House, to be built on the wonderful Benelong Point of the harbour, will be among the finest. A world-wide competition for its design was won by Joern Utzon, the Danish architect, and the grace and beauty of the great soaring concrete roof shells, reflected in the waters of the harbour like huge white sails, will create a fantasy of superb grandeur.

I am perhaps one of the few people who believe that in the years to come, when the great problem of insufficient inland water supply has been eased by vast national works on the scale of the present Snowy River scheme and when waters now running to waste into the ocean can be turned back inland, that very large numbers of British people, factories and industries will be transplanted from the old to this new world. I feel that the potentialities of development in this huge continent have not yet been fully realised.

Since the last war there has been an upsurge of large capital investment flowing in, chiefly from the United Kingdom and also from the United States. But much more is needed, and while United Kingdom funds are preferred because profits generally are ploughed back (whereas United States profits are taken out), if sufficient British capital cannot be obtained, then American investments will be encouraged.

Let us face up to two facts. If this vast continent is not fully developed and populated by people covered by the 'White Australia' policy, then it is likely to be done by others. Secondly, there now exists here, and is growing, a political, financial and industrial interest in the United States, with obvious results to the United Kingdom. This applies chiefly to the heavier populated Australian industrial states.

Australia is a young virile country, now forging ahead to a bright future: it will need all the brains and brawn it can attract. The 'Expatriate' settling down to live and work in another country must endeavour to push his former years and memories behind him, to devote his mind and energy fully in order to get the best out of his new life. This is not easy; sometimes an unusual smell or the odd sound of a drum instantly takes him back to other places and to days that are spent – no matter how busy he becomes, the colourful memories of his Colonial life will keep on thrusting through until the end. But the average Australian, kindly fellow though he is and always willing to lend a helping hand, quickly weighs you up for what you are – not for what you may have been.

IV. THE COLONIAL SERVICE
AVE ATQUE VALE

I t was both timely and appropriate that the editor of *Corona* should give centre-stage in his search for copy for the final issue of the journal at the end of 1962 to contributions, looking back as well as forward, from leading Colonial Office and Colonial Service figures of 'the Corona years'. Among them were a retrospective article from one of the doyens of colonial governors, Sir Hilary Blood; a speculative scenario from the long-serving and last Permanent Under-Secretary of the Colonial Office, Sir Hilton Poynton; an overview of the Colonial Service from a senior official long and intimately concerned with the affairs of its Colonial Service Division, Sir Charles Jeffries; and a challenging call for a future role in the newly independent territories from one who had been both a Whitehall mandarin and a colonial governor and was now Permanent Under-Secretary of the new Department of Technical Co-operation, the visionary Sir Andrew Cohen. There was, too, A. Creech Jones' reminiscence of what he, as Secretary State for the Colonies responsible for its founding, had envisaged *Corona* should mean and offer to members of the Colonial Service and of the Colonial Office. The selection concluded, fittingly for a journal that always emphasized the personal as well as the institutional in its articles, the private as well as the official – and was already well ahead of its time in the space it gave to contributions from women, both wives and female officers – with a look back on *merdeka* from the perspective of a Colonial Service wife at the end of a quarter of a century's residence in Malaya, along with a pair of lighter-hearted impressionistic vignettes on what being 'home for ever' might well mean at the end of the day.

Finally, there were two messages from Secretaries of State for the Colonies: one from the current holder of the office, Duncan Sandys, with his toast of 'to the Service, Past and Present'; and one from that Secretary State, who, to so many members of the Colonial Service whose job it had been to oversee the transfer of power, personified 'the best friend' at the Colonial Office that the post-war Colonial Service had ever had in the Cabinet (and later in his devoted service to their Overseas Service Pensioners' Association), Alan Lennox-Boyd.

The End of an Avenue

by SIR HILARY BLOOD, G.B.E., K.C.M.G.

Ever since I retired I have sat on the Overseas Civil Service Appointments Board, the body charged with the duty of selecting candidates for the Colonial Administrative Service – a fascinating occasional occupation for the declining years of an old Eastern Cadet. I am deeply grateful to the Colonial Office for the opportunity, through meetings of the Board, to get and to keep in touch, albeit tenuous, with well-educated, representative young men, about to leave or having just left, their Universities. The thorough way in which the Colonial Office staff screened and sifted candidates, and the full documentation with which we were provided, always excited my admiration. If the members of the Board did their home-work properly beforehand they had a very fair idea of what manner of men would present themselves, at half-hourly intervals throughout a Board meeting day, as candidates for administrative work overseas.

These interesting and intimate encounters helped to keep the 'retired' members of the Board up to date. We were able to learn something of modern fashions. Not fashions in garments – candidates tended to be conventional, and properly so, in their clothing – but fashions in the courses of university discipline followed; in vacation activities; in hobbies and pursuits; in newspaper and other reading; in all the details, in fact, which go to make up undergraduate life. And we were repeatedly struck by two interesting facts: the changing sources from which candidates came – the grammar school and modern university boy applying in increasing numbers; and the remarkable contrast in maturity between those candidates who had, and those who had not, done a period of national service.

As the years have slipped by, the shrinkage in the areas staffed by the Overseas Civil Service has been reflected first in the countries which candidates noted as their preferences – *'Why do you want to go to Tanganyika?' 'Because I think there is the best chance of a career there'*: the question and answer used regularly to feature in interviews not so very long ago – and then in the long intervals at which it is only now necessary to assemble meetings of the Board. Soon, I suppose, its operations will cease altogether and there will be a letter saying that someone is directed to inform us that, in view of so and so and such and such, the Minister has decided that the Board's services are no longer required.

When a piece of apparatus has served its purpose and is no longer required it is better scrapped. But I am concerned here not with the Board, rather with the Service itself: and a Service is more than a piece of apparatus. The inception and growth of the Overseas Service have been described in a number of books by distinguished writers in the Colonial Office – most recently by Sir Ralph Furse who initiated the modern method of recruitment after World War I. The earlier candidates after selection were posted to local services, and unification was largely the work of Sir Charles Jeffries. Appointments to Eastern Cadetships came *via* the United Kingdom Civil Service Commissioners, not through the Colonial Office; but the result in terms of calibre was much the same.

Now I am not all starry-eyed about team work and loyalty and high ideals. We were not, normally, men with vocations; we were men with a job to do, a fascinating job; and we meant to give their money's worth to the Colonial Governments which employed us. But, largely I suppose because we – and by 'we' I mean the invaluable technical services as well as the administrative service – were all facing similar kinds of problems, because we were all trying to do the same sort of thing – to keep the King's peace, to administer justice, to protect the weak, to heal the sick, to encourage trade, to increase the national wealth, and to teach the art of running public affairs – the Service, though scattered over every continent and all the seven seas, became close-knit and integrated, a world-wide, not a local service. A District Officer in Fiji was doing work closely resembling that of a District Officer in the Gambia: an Assistant Secretary wrote the same sort of minutes in Cyprus as in Singapore: there was little difference between the problems of one Medical Officer or another whether he was stationed in Trinidad or in Tanganyika – and the same applied to Education Officers, Agricultural Officers and all the other technically skilled members of the Service. The Service spoke a common language: it developed its own form of pride, its own standards, its own sense of duty. Its success is marked by the speed with which it has trained others to do its own members out of their jobs. And so it is coming to an end. It will linger on for a time, of course, on the 'old boy' basis: the Corona Club tie will have a nostalgic meaning for some years to come. But the days of the Overseas Service are numbered. I hope someone will write it up – as has been done for other Services – that it may not fall altogether into oblivion.

I think a way of life also is perhaps over. The administrative officer certainly very soon found himself differing a little from his brothers and friends who had stayed at home. He ripened, and indeed aged, more quickly. Heavy responsibilities came to him early. Keeping the peace in a vast, thickly populated province was more wearing, and more rewarding, than teaching in a prep. school. Sitting on the bench required more concentration than sitting in an office chair, and so on. With this form of occupation went a more formalized and, in some ways, a higher standard of living. Government servants 'went out to dinner' in overseas territories long after that excellent habit had to be given up by their equivalents in this country: hospitality presented no difficulty nor washing-up any embarrassment. On leave there were, of course, those who spent their days huddled over a gas-fire in a London boarding-house or cheap hotel and longed for the sun: but, for the most part, overseas men and women were eager to recharge the batteries of their minds as well as to refresh their tropics-jaded bodies during the reasonably frequent spells which they could spend at home.

In the result, though it was only too delightful not to be ever on guard lest one missed a face which should be recognised, and would be hurt if it were not, and to pass utterly unknown in a crowd with no official ticket, so to speak, on one's back, the overseas civil servant on leave was in fact always a little bit apart, a conscious spectator of scenes and incidents of which other people were integrated parts.

But there is another, perhaps more important, aspect to be considered. Fifteen years or so ago, when India became independent, one of the great outlets for the young men of this country was closed. The end of the Overseas Service shuts another of the important and rewarding avenues along which the youth of Great Britain could go out adventuring into life. So then what? Youth will in the end not be denied its avenues to adventure: what will be the break through? To what form of activities, perhaps at present unknown, will this youthful head of steam give impetus and power?

We have seen something of an attempt to find a safety valve in the small stream of recruits for Voluntary Service Overseas and for similar organisations. The work of V.S.O. – the only one of these various projects of which I have some personal knowledge – has been remarkably successful. It has been widely praised by competent and unbiased judges. Thrown slightly off-balance by President Kennedy's Peace Corps, it is not at the moment clear just how V.S.O. will develop in the future. But certainly an organisation with its aims and methods can render most valuable service in the Commonwealth countries, or in the remaining dependent territories, at the same time provide an outlet for the youthful adventurous spirit. But a period of service with V.S.O. is short, a year or so – eighteen months at the very most: it is an incident, a short chapter in a life, not a way of life.

Alongside this must be set the opportunities afforded by the new Department of Technical Co-operation for service on contract – particularly in the newly emergent countries. Here the appeal is to older people, men and women who naturally look for a measure of security, not for an opportunity for adventure, and very largely to the technically trained, the professional class rather than to the straight administrator. In the circumstances we cannot expect the contract officer to approach his work overseas in the same spirit of adventure – perhaps of service – as the young cadet, or the probationary member of a technical department. And again, a period of service on contract is a bit only of life, not a way of life.

It has been suggested that the creation of a Commonwealth Service is the solution. Such a service would, it is said, on the one hand produce the staff required to help emergent territories and, on the other, provide an outlet for young people who wish to go adventuring abroad. The idea is very attractive: but the administrative difficulties are obvious. I would like to see the arguments for and against set out very fully before I finally made up my mind that this really is what we are looking for. How far can the idea of service in and to the Commonwealth have the emotional appeal of service in and to the Empire, and can the conception of Her Majesty the Queen as Head and Symbol of the Commonwealth be as evocative as the conception of her as the Sovereign to whom we owe personal loyalty and service? I wonder.

But of one thing I am certain: purely commercial opportunities will not altogether satisfy the youth of Great Britain. However sensible and far-seeing are the banks and the firms and the trading organisations which select with care their young men for service here or overseas, and train them with diligence, and post them with intelligence and understanding, there will still be, I believe, and not only among the choicer spirits, a striving for something less and something more: something less commercial, less self seeking; something more idealistic, more humanitarian, and above all more adventurous. Is the harnessing of space and the planets to human needs perhaps the answer? I don't know.

Speculation in Church House

by SIR HILTON POYNTON, K.C. M.G.

I t is a sad honour to have been asked to contribute to the last issue of *Corona* which was born in 1949 and is now being cut off after a life of fourteen years. Each issue contains a reservation in the following words:

'The Secretary of State does not necessarily endorse any opinions expressed in this Journal nor does any of its contents necessarily represent the official policy either of the Secretary of State or of the Government of any Colonial territory.'

I presume that the Permanent Under-Secretary is as much protected or exposed by this reservation as any other contributor.

When I took over from Sir John Macpherson in August, 1959, the Colonial Office, notwithstanding the independence of Ghana and Malaya in 1957, was still responsible for 43* territories containing an aggregate population of some 80,000,000 people. By the end of this year we shall have seen the successive independence of Somaliland, Cyprus and Nigeria (1960), Sierra Leone, the Southern Cameroons and Tanganyika (1961) and Jamaica. Trinidad and Uganda (1962); the transfer to the Colonial Office of responsibility for Basutoland, Bechuanaland Protectorate and Swaziland: and the transfer away from the Colonial Office of responsibility for Northern Rhodesia and Nyasaland; a net diminution of eight territories. The net effect of this in terms of the number of territories under the Colonial Office and their aggregate population is that by the end of this year, though we shall still be responsible for 35 territories, these comprise an aggregate population of only 20,000,000. This progressive decline in the territorial responsibilities of the Colonial Office obviously involves a progressive reduction in its establishment and there are other factors apart from independence days which also tend in the same direction. I do not for a moment pretend that in terms of the individual officer of the Colonial Office this progressive redundancy has anything like the serious effect that it has on members of the Overseas Service. Indeed, the running down of a Service, like H.M.O.C.S., and the running down of a single Department within a Service, like the Colonial Office, are processes essentially different in kind. Nevertheless, there is, undoubtedly, a personal problem involved in London as well as overseas. When every allowance is made for the argument advanced in some quarters that these changes are no more than a necessary corollary of the progressive fulfilment of Britain's Colonial policy which is, so to speak, part of the terms of reference of all of us whether in the Colonial

Office or in the Colonial Service, it does not alter the fact that the task of a Permanent Secretary who is faced with the necessity of progressively dismantling both the Overseas Service and his own Department (which in one form or another and in various combinations has existed for just over 300 years** and as a Department under its own Secretary of State since 1854), is not exactly congenial. I say this in no spirit of complaint. If the progress had been faster the problem would have faced my predecessor; if we had gone slower it would have been left for my successor. It is a historical accident that the big run-down has come during my period of office.

Readers of *Corona* may be interested to know something of the problems involved in the run-down of the Colonial Office. To understand them it must be borne in mind that the Colonial Office, which in earlier days was organised almost wholly on a geographical basis has, particularly since the Second World War, seen a great expansion of advisory services administered by 'Subject Departments.' When I first joined the Colonial Office in 1929 there were eight geographical departments and a sort of 'rag bag' General Department which dealt with every kind of economic and social problem, defence problems, personnel problems and a whole host of minor matters affecting all territories. By the earlier part of 1961 the Office had grown to ten geographical and twenty subject departments (in both counts the Establishment Branch and the Legal Adviser's staff have been omitted).

The predominantly geographical structure of the Colonial Office in earlier days was necessitated largely by the fact that at that time almost all Colonies were still under the official type of Government, i.e. they had Legislative Councils with an official majority or at least with substantial powers reserved to the Governor and very often wholly official Executive Councils. This in turn meant that the Secretary of State in discharging his responsibilities to Parliament could not shrug off an awkward question of detail by contending that the point at issue was a matter for the local Government, since the local Government was in effect composed of Civil Servants to whom, through the Governor, instructions could be sent by the Secretary of State. It was therefore important that the Secretary of State of the day should be advised by, and that his delegated authority should be exercised by, officers who were specialising on the particular territories. Admittedly, they could never hope to have such a close knowledge of the territories as the members of the Colonial Service who were working in them; but at least there was less chance of decisions being taken in London which bore no relation to the local circumstances than would have been the case if the office had been staffed predominantly by functional specialists to whom, as a critic once put it to me, Trinidad and Tanganyika were just 'two territories both beginning with "T" '.

There have, I think, been three main reasons for the gradual transition to what by 1961 had become a predominantly functional structure. One was the growing attention given to economic and social development, the opportunities for which were greatly increased by the enactment of the

Colonial Development Act and the very much greater revenues available to Colonial Governments immediately after the war as compared with anything that had been known before. It made it both possible and, indeed, necessary to augment the staff of professional advisers at the Colonial Office and to see that they were properly serviced by administrative departments. Secondly, and precisely because the United Kingdom was now contributing development finance to the Colonies on a much larger scale and over a wider field than under the Colonial Development Act. 1929, it became necessary for Colonial development policy to be much more closely integrated into the machinery of Whitehall generally. There were other pressures too, tending in the same direction, particularly in the early post-war years when exchange controls and shortages of materials presented acute problems for the sterling area as a whole. I do not think it would have been possible for the Colonial Office to hold its own on equal terms with other Departments, with which it frequently had to do battle, unless it had been organised in a way which enabled it to talk on level terms with those Departments on their own subjects and command their respect. Thirdly, there has been an increasing amount of international collaboration and interest in matters in which the Colonies are affected. I am not thinking here of the persistent and misguided attempts by the United Nations to meddle in our affairs, but rather of the more fruitful general discussions that go on about economic and social matters in 'G.A.T.T.'; in specialised Agencies such as the World Health Organisation, Food and Agriculture Organisation and other similar bodies; or in commodity Study Groups and Councils. For this purpose again it was necessary to organise the Colonial Office functionally and to make arrangements for associating Colonial Governments themselves over a wide field of international work. There has, too, been a growing practice of associating Colonial representatives with Commonwealth economic or social confer-ences. At the same time the progressive constitutional evolution of the Colonies made it less necessary for the Colonial Office to exercise such detailed control over their local affairs. In short, the role of the Colonial Office has changed from that of a controlling Department to that of being very largely an advisory Department: and in consequence many of the reasons described above which necessitated a predominantly geographical structure in earlier days ceased to be so important.

Having thus traced the gradual change in the structure of the Colonial Office from a predominantly geographical to a predominantly functional organisation I now come back to the main theme of this article, namely, the problem of redundancy created in the Colonial Office by the progressive independence of former Colonial territories. Practical manifestations of this problem are themselves conditioned largely by the internal structure of the Office. At first sight it might seem easy to say that 'X' officers were engaged in dealing with Nigeria and that, therefore, from the 1st October. 1960, 'X' officers became redundant. In practice it does not work like this since, although there was an immediate redundancy in the geographical department that dealt specifically with Nigeria, a great deal of work in connection with Nigeria was carried out by the subject departments and the loss of one territory even so big as Nigeria does not in fact necessarily mean a substantial loss of work in these subject departments. Take for example the section of the Finance Department which deals with the Colonial Development and Welfare Acts. To work out the proper allocations between, say, forty territories involves no less work than for forty-one territories. The same problems of building up the size of a new Act, negotiating with the Treasury, putting the Bill through Parliament and supervising its administration are involved. Similarly with the commodity work of the Economic Division. The independence of Ghana, the biggest cocoa producing country in the world, did not involve any diminution of the work of the Colonial Office on cocoa since Nigeria was also a big cocoa producer and there are a number of other small ones; and the work on international cocoa problems continued unabated until Nigeria, too, became independent. The same papers have to be read; the same interdepartmental meetings attended and the same problem of representation at international conferences arises so long as the Colonial Office is concerned with that commodity at all. Consequently the reduction of work in the subject departments is much slower and spread over a longer period than might apparently seem to be the case.

There are, however, other factors affecting the work of the Colonial Office as well as the loss of responsibility for particular territories. There is plenty of evidence to show that many Colonial territories on attaining independence would like to continue to receive the professional advice and help which they have had from the Colonial Office. But there are two difficulties, one political and one administrative, about this. The political difficulty is the obvious one that a newly independent country, though willing to obtain advice and technical assistance from the British Government, and indeed from the experts whom they know and who know their problems, would not wish to be beholden to the Colonial Office for it. The administrative difficulty is that these services have been financed from monies voted by Parliament to the Secretary of State for the Colonies to enable him to carry out his responsibilities towards the Colonial territories. Except for minor services which do not involve costings it would be impossible for staff on the Colonial Office establishment to be engaged on work for territories for which the Colonial Office was not responsible except on repayment by the Government concerned or perhaps on some other United Kingdom Department's vote. For some years therefore the Colonial Office itself has taken the initiative in trying to divest itself of these services in order that they may be placed under some agency of the British Government which is not exclusively concerned with the Colonies. The first example was the former Colonial Products Laboratory, the value of whose work was certainly not confined to Colonial territories. In that case the problem was solved by transferring it to the Department of Scientific and Industrial Research and renaming it the Tropical Products Institute. In 1961 a much more sweeping change was made by the creation of the Department of Technical Co-operation which, working ultimately under the joint authority of the Colonial Secretary, the Commonwealth Secretary and the Foreign Secretary, is able to provide a service to countries in all three categories. To this new Department the Colonial Office transferred all the professional advisers and their supporting administrative departments (except the Inspector-General of Colonial Police), the Directorate of Overseas (Geodetic and Topographic) Surveys, the Overseas Geological Surveys and the Overseas Personnel Division, in all over 1,000 staff of all grades, i.e. including executive, clerical and subordinate staff. (The Commonwealth Relations Office, the Foreign Office and the Ministry of Labour also transferred to the new Department all their staff dealing with the work which was similarly transferred, but this is not a matter that concerns an article on the future of the Colonial Office.)

As a result of these various changes, territorial and functional, the staff actually on the establishment of the Colonial Office has been reduced from 2,029 in 1958/9 – its zenith – to 874 at the present time. It must be borne in mind, however, that these functional transfers such as the creation of the Department of Technical Co-operation do not involve redundancy since the officers are transferring to a new management, taking their work with them.

I said at the beginning of this article that although the question of redundancy in the Colonial Office had nothing like as serious consequences to the individual officer as redundancy in the Overseas Service, there was nevertheless a personal problem and many officers are worried about their future prospects. I began this article some time before the Cabinet changes were made which resulted in a single Secretary of State, Mr. Duncan Sandys, assuming responsibility for the Colonial Office as well as the Commonwealth Relations Office. This, I must emphasise, is not an amalgamation of the two Departments: Mr. Sandys holds two distinct portfolios and his two Departments maintain their separate identity and establishments. Although, therefore, as Mr. Sandys himself put it in his inaugural message to Governors when he assumed office, 'the combination of the two Departments under a single Minister will greatly facilitate the co-ordination of policy in their closely related spheres,' the change does not immediately affect the staff problem which I have described in this article.

It is true that as members of the Home Civil Service there is in theory no problem about transferring officials of the Colonial Office to other Departments. In practice, however, this only works as long as the numbers involved are small and are matched by vacancies in the other Departments. But if the numbers in any grade were considerable, there would be a problem of a net redundancy in the Civil Service which could only be met by abolition of office (in the Home Civil Service the term 'abolition of office' means no more than that an officer can retire with his pension earned to date, but with no addition). Naturally we hope that this can be avoided but, whether or not it can, there is much-natural sorrow amongst us (whatever our critics at home and overseas may feel!) at the thought that in a few years the Colonial Office may disappear. It has been, and still is for those of us who work there, a fascinating Department to work in, and whether we move to other Departments or retire, we shall sadly miss the variety and the excitement of work here, and the opportunities for meeting so many people of all races and of travelling to so many interesting parts of the world.

Note

* I never care to count my chickens before (or even after) they are hatched. Are the Windward Islands to be reckoned as one or four, for example? The most authentic count yields 43. A.H.P.

** The first separate organisation for the central administration of Colonial affairs was a Committee of the Privy Council for the plantacons which was appointed by an Order-in-Council of the 4th July. 1600. A few months later (1st December, 1660) a separate 'Council of Foreign Plantations' was created and it was on this body that the diarist, John Evelyn, later served with 'a salary of £500 to encourage me', as he records in his Diary. A.H.P.

The Colonial Service in Perspective

by SIR CHARLES JEFFRIES, K.C.M G., O.B.E.

M y official life in the Colonial Office – 1917 to 1956 – covered the official life of the Colonial Service itself. For, although the Service was not formally constituted until 1930, it took shape from 1918 onwards; and it was transformed into the Overseas Civil Service in 1954. During all these years I was personally very much mixed up in the affairs of the Service. From 1918 to 1928 I dealt with personnel matters in relation to Eastern and Central Africa; in 1928 I went into the personnel section of the General Department of the Office; and in 1930 I became head of the Colonial Service Department in the newly created Personnel Division under Mr. (afterwards Sir George) Tomlinson, whom I succeeded in 1939 as Assistant Under-Secretary of State.

I can, therefore, put forward some claim to be able to see the Service in perspective, as one who was outside it, but intimately connected with it. Of one thing I am certain: none of us who had a part in creating and expanding the Colonial Service during the exciting constructive years of the inter-war period had any conception that the Service was to have such a short period of existence. That it did was due to many causes far outside Colonial Office control; but one at least of the major causes was the excellence of the work of the Service itself. From the time that the policy of 'trusteeship' was officially adopted, that work was avowedly devoted to helping the peoples of the Colonial territories to overcome their handicaps and achieve self-government. The work was so well done (with the co-operation of the Colonial peoples themselves) that in a shorter space of time than the boldest prophet would have contemplated, the transfer of power to local authorities became not only possible but inevitable; and, except in a few cases where external influences bedevilled the issue, that transfer was affected without disturbance and in an atmosphere of friendship and goodwill which has persisted after independence.

It may be asked whether, if the Service was to have so short a life, it was worth while to create it at all. I do not hesitate to assert not only that it was worth while but that if it had not been done the Colonial territories could not have developed politically, economically and socially as they have, and that, when world conditions made the continuance of Colonial rule an anachronism, we might well have seen something very different from the peaceful evolution of the territories into sister nations of the Commonwealth.

It is perhaps true to say that the creation of a Colonial Service did not make a great deal of difference to Ceylon or Malaya, which could have carried on as self-contained administrations; it certainly made all the difference to the territories of tropical Africa and the island dependencies of the Crown. In West Africa, something in the nature of a regional Service had been built up before the first world war. The only branch with a formal constitution was the West African Medical Staff; but in the other professional and administrative branches (then necessarily almost entirely staffed by Europeans recruited in England) uniform salary scales and conditions of employment had been applied, and a certain amount of inter-change between the territories went on. After 1918, a similar process went forward in the Eastern and Central African territories which had more recently come under the Colonial Office. (Zanzibar was not taken over until 1913, Tanganyika came in after the war, and Northern Rhodesia as lately as 1923).

For all these territories, as well as for the old-established island Colonies and the new mandated territories, staffs had to be recruited, not only in ever increasing numbers but in an increasing variety of professional and technical skills. The job of recruitment rested, from 1910 onwards, with Major (afterwards Sir Ralph) Furse, who was nominally one of the Private Secretaries to the Secretary of State. In his fascinating memoirs (*Aucuparius*, published this year*) Sir Ralph has explained how it became clear to him that he could expect to recruit staff in the quantity, quality and variety required, only if he could offer the inducement of a career in a world-wide Service. Not even a West African, an East African or indeed a Tropical African Service would do the trick – or if it had, it would have left the rest of the Colonial Empire in an impossibly weak recruiting position. Thus was set in motion the series of developments which led to the constitution of the 'unified' Colonial Service in 1930. The results justified the foresight of Furse and those others who had worked towards this end. The fact that the Service was well established by 1939 enabled the Colonial territories to weather the storms of the second world war and to be ready to face steadily the political problems which followed the cessation of hostilities.

So far so good; but the conferment in 1948 of Dominion status on Ceylon was a pointer to things to come. The probability of other territories claiming and achieving independence within a measurable time became a practical and no longer a theoretical issue. In the immediately post-war years it did indeed look as if the need for some kind of a British Colonial Service would last out the official life-time of most of those then being recruited; but it was seen even before the war ended that there would have to be changes in the pattern.

Those of us in the Colonial Office who were directly concerned in these matters at the official level felt that the right course was to convert the Colonial Service from a body of people employed and paid by the several Colonial Governments to one in which the staffs were employed by the British Government and supplied on secondment or loan to those territories which wished to use them, the conditions of service being fixed by the British Government, and some kind of equalisation fund established to enable the poorer territories to have the staffs they needed but could not afford to employ at the standard rates.

Various schemes on these lines were devised in the office from time to time, but for a number of reasons none of them came to fruition. I hope that some day the full story will be told, but this is not the occasion to go into detail. It must suffice to say that the difficulties were partly political and partly financial, and that they were of such a kind that officials in the Colonial Office had no power to set them aside.

Meanwhile, political developments in the territories made it increasingly undesirable to continue recruiting for the Service on the cheerful assumption that the old security of tenure would hold good and that the ultimate control of appointments, salaries, promotions and discipline would remain indefinitely with the Secretary of State. The interests of serving officers, and the growing unrest of those who saw their future careers in jeopardy made it imperative to take some action.

The first need, as it seemed, was to define precisely the categories of officers for whom the Secretary of State accepted responsibility, and to set forth in clear terms what that responsibility implied. This was the purpose of the White Paper of 1954 (Colonial No. 306) in which – both in order to mark the break and to get rid of the word 'Colonial' – the officers to be brought under the new arrangement were constituted 'Her Majesty's Overseas* Civil Service' – H.M.O.C.S.

The important point of this paper was the definition of those who would be members of the new Service. The term 'Colonial Service' had been loosely used to cover both members of the unified Services and the general mass of officials in the employment of the Colonial Governments, most of whom were locally recruited under conditions fixed by the several Governments at their own discretion. The Secretary of State had special responsibilities for those whom he had recruited or who had been recruited under his authority. Most of these, but by no means all, were included in the unified branches, while the latter included several officers of local domicile who might not wish to be merged in a general Service. The creation of H.M.O.C.S. was to make it possible for the first time to distinguish those officers for whom the Secretary of State had a responsibility from those who were purely employees of local Governments.

As regards the guarantees included in the 1954 White Paper, it must be admitted that on examination they did not amount to very much. The British Government did not in fact promise more than that when any territory became independent, it would make an agreement with the Government of that particular territory to secure the rights of serving officers of H.M.O.C.S. These were the best terms that could be obtained at the time after exhaustive inter-departmental discussion and negotiation; but from the point of view of officers in the Service, they were not very satisfactory. Officers were not so much interested in the agreements which would be made as in the prospect of those agreements being carried out. They would have liked some specific undertaking by the British Government that it would in all circumstances ensure that officers and their dependents should receive the salaries, pensions and other conditions to which they were entitled; but it was clearly difficult for the British

Government to tie themselves down in advance as to the way in which they would deal with the hypothetical situation which would arise if an overseas Government defaulted on the agreement. To do so, it was argued, might indeed have the effect of making such a situation more likely to occur.

From 1954 onwards it was this aspect of the matter which became increasingly a live issue, with the prospect of Malaya, the Gold Coast, Nigeria and other territories becoming independent in the near future. It was not now merely a question of providing adequate guarantees but of preventing, if possible, the general and immediate exodus of the British staffs on which those countries largely depended for the efficient working of the administration and the successful progress of their development plans. The 1956 White Paper (Cmd. 9768) was the result of many months of intensive and often frustrating argument. Here, again, the terms were the best that could be secured, but they fell far short of what the Colonial Office would have liked to see done. In the result, the British Government did indeed accept in principle direct responsibility for the employment of some officers, but this acceptance was hedged about with so many limitations and came so late in the day as to impair very seriously any favourable effect it might have had on the morale of the Service; and, as is well known, the British Government subsequently was obliged to incur far wider obligations and very considerable expense in the endeavour to secure some continuity of administration and technical assistance in the territories as they emerged into independence.

I still firmly believe that better results could have been obtained at a fraction of the cost if the Government had been willing at an earlier stage to listen to the advice of the Colonial Office and to take imaginative and positive action which would have ensured the enthusiastic co-operation of the Service as a whole.

It was certainly my own hope that the transformation of the old Colonial Service into H.M.O.C.S. and the acceptance by the British Government of direct responsibility for officers serving oversea Governments would lead to the transformation of H.M.O.C.S. into a Corps of British officers qualified in various professions and skills who would be employed and paid by the United Kingdom and made available as required on loan or secondment to the oversea Governments needing their services. We managed, not without difficulty, to secure inclusion in the 1956 White Paper of a statement foreshadowing such a development, but nothing came of it in the end. The difficulties have been held to be too great. That there are substantial difficulties no one can deny. I obstinately remain, however, of the opinion that the difficulties need not have been considered insuperable and that the great work of technical assistance, to which the British Government is now committed, would have been tremendously helped if steps had been taken, while there was yet time, to constitute such a Corps as I have described.

However, this is straying beyond my subject, which is the Colonial Service in perspective. Nothing that might have been done could in any case have materially altered the fact that a large proportion of the members of the former Colonial Service were bound to find themselves out of a job as one territory after another became independent. I believe that, so far as monetary compensation goes, the officers concerned have been treated with reasonable generosity. Some have no doubt welcomed the opportunity to make a fresh start. Some, I hope, have been able to turn the change of fortune to their advantage. Many, however, not only regret the premature termination of what they had looked forward to as a career of public service, but have found difficulty (especially if they have no professional or technical qualifications) in establishing themselves in new and satisfying work.

On the face of it, it is absurdly wasteful that men who have been handpicked for one of the finest Services in the world and who are still in full vigour should be put on the shelf at a time when their experience and qualities could be of the greatest value to the community. The difficulty is to find the right channel for making use of their services. The Overseas Services Resettlement Bureau is, I know, doing a splendid job in finding outlets for individuals, and it provides the retiring officer with first-class and detailed information and advice. All I would venture to do here is to offer a very tentative general observation. There are, as it seems to me, two callings which are not overcrowded, are of immense social and public importance, and demand the very qualities which the good Colonial civil servant possessed. I refer to the Ministry of the Church and to the teaching profession. The first, of course, can appeal only to those who are convinced Christians, and of those only such as are conscious of a call to service in this particular way. Quite a number of former Colonial civil servants are already members of the ordained Ministry of the Anglican and other Churches; one of them, a former Governor, wrote movingly of his own experience in the March, 1954, number of *Corona*.** Another, who had also been a soldier, told his story in two later issues.† The Churches certainly have room for many more.

Teaching has a wider appeal. Some people are clearly not gifted that way, but there are surely many more who, though they may never have considered themselves as possible teachers, would in fact be most valuable acquisitions to the profession if they would consent to undergo the necessary training. The layman is apt to think of teaching only in class-room terms, but it means far more than that and can offer a wonderful opportunity for the most useful kind of social service.

The passing of *Corona*, the journal which was one of the few outward expressions of the unity of the British Colonial Service, marks the ending of a brief but glorious chapter of British history. Under the able guidance of its editors, the successive volumes of *Corona* have become a library in themselves of the work, the problems and the personalities of a Service of which it can truly be said, in the words of Winston Churchill, as Secretary of State, at the Corona Club Dinner in 1921, 'There has never been such a varied charge confided to so few men.'

And in many a tropical land where freedom flourishes, the rule of law prevails and the handicaps of poverty, ignorance and disease are slowly but surely being overcome, the epitaph of Sir Christopher Wren may serve for those who have lived – and died – to make these things possible:

SI MONUMENTUM REQUIRIS, CIRCUMSPICE

Note

* *At first it was 'Oversea', but a later Office ruling added the final 's'.*
** The Rev. Sir Reginald Champion, K.C.M.G., O.B.E.: *From Government House to Country Vicarage.*
† The Rev. G. W. P. Thorne, O.B.E.: *Interview with a Bishop*
(November, 1957)
A New Line of Country
(December, 1958)

Good-Bye

And so *Corona* comes to its end after fourteen years of vigorous life. For a long time it has been a constant factor in changing conditions, not only for members of the Colonial and Overseas Services but for others. If the copies which have gone behind the Iron Curtain have caused there no visible change of heart towards British Colonialism, the journal, we believe, has made some impression on American thought and it was also used regularly at an Australian University as a practical expression for the teaching of administrative theory. Ghanaians have continued to take *Corona* through all the effects of their independence and there were no signs that an independent Uganda would have given it up. Soon after *uhuru* Tanganyika's University College at Dar Es Salaam asked for and was sent, a complete set of the journal. There will, therefore, be many people of different nationalities, colours and outlook, in addition to members of the Services, who will be sorry to see *Corona* disappear. We thank everyone who has written kindly to tell us so.

If the journal's end is a matter for some sadness, its lifetime certainly was not, and least of all for the editor who now has his chance to say a personal 'thank you' to all those who have made it so pleasant a part of thirty-three years connection with the Colonial and Overseas Services. Taking over the editorship originally for two months only from the first editor who had done all the hard work of organisation and reputation-building, the present editor stayed until the end, ten years later – clear proof that the work was attractive to someone whose previous life had been with the Service overseas and who knew little of Colonial Office ways.

Dependent on the Colonial Office for its existence and the roof over its head, *Corona's* affinities were nevertheless properly closest with the Service whose name it bore on its cover. Having a foot in two places can be uncomfortable; but that it never has been so in the *Corona* office has been due to the help and encouragement which have come in many ways from many people in Church House and Sanctuary Buildings. The friendship of 'The Office' has been an indispensable and much valued part of the journal's life from its first day to its last and has underlined the close ties between Great Smith Street and the Service. It is good that this last number contains an article by a former Deputy Under-Secretary of State which shows where sympathies have lain.

None of the members of the Colonial Office included in these collective thanks would wish to lose anonymity, but mention must be made of one person who was largely responsible for the smooth running of the editorial machine. *Corona* was fortunate in having a Personal Assistant (Diane Morris) who was with it for the whole of its fourteen years. Many of her varied duties were known to the people with whom her work brought her into contact, but they probably did not know that in addition to much else she typed every word that appeared in *Corona's* text. On one task alone – that of preparing articles for the printer – some 10,000,000 words came off her fingers.

Those words came from the people who made the journal: our contributors. Although we believe they enjoyed writing and drawing for *Corona*, a special word of thanks is due to them. How understanding were those whose pet pieces were returned with a letter of regret; how long suffering when their published work showed a scandalous amount of editorial interference; how civilly did even those react to a blue pencil who, during their Service days, slashed red ink onto other people's compositions. And if sometimes a few of those who had promised contributions became deaf and dumb as deadlines approached, how gallantly did others respond when asked to fill a gap at short notice.

We had many visitors from all over the Commonwealth. A great many of them sent us personal letters, and correspondence with others we never saw opened up new friendships and diminished our considerable ignorance. For visits and letters *Corona* has always been grateful; through them the journal could justifiably feel that it was in touch with and a part of the Service overseas.

A verse in *Corona*, speaking of the Colonial Office, once said:
'Sometimes these calm, judicious rooms
'Knew the bright invasion of Africa and the Caribbean.
'Far Eastern casuarinas sang for an instant in the wind of words
'Captured within a file ...'

The *Corona* office at times may have been neither as calm nor as judicious as the other offices which surrounded it, and its somewhat unorthodox files were cautious in what they captured from those who on occasions expressed themselves carthartically; but no office could have enjoyed more the bright invasions, whether in person, by letter, by article or verse, by drawing or photograph, which were the breath of its existence. To our invaders and to our readers of all nationalities we wish good fortune and say good-bye.

EDITOR.

Index of Contributors

The contributions without a name were mostly written by *Corona*'s Editor (K. G. Bradley, 1949–52, and J. J. Tawney, 1952–62), often redacted from Hansard, or White Papers and official reports, or as a personal contribution.

Akpan, N. U.	219	Maudling, Reginald	177
Bates, J. Darrell	19	Miller, Ronald	41
Blood, Sir Hilary	273	Morley, John	249
Boyd, Viscount of Merton	181	Nkrumah, Kwame	215
Breckenridge, J. B. W.	95	Norris, Raymond	16
Brown, Ronald	242	Peel, R. L.	253
Carstairs, C. Y.	64	Poynton, Sir Hilton	277
Chandos, Viscount	117	Purvis, John T.	56
Cohen, Sir Andrew	28	Rankine, Sir John	236
Creech Jones, Arthur	157, 160, 161	Rogers, Philip	25
Dawson, V. E.	246	Sandys, Duncan	180
Franklin, Harry	72	Sayers, Gerald	22
Gitau, Jeremiah	92	Sim, Katharine	265
Haarer, A. E.	256	Smartt, Patrick	262
Hamilton, John	217	Swaffield, W. H.	268
Hutchison, Anne Clark	259	Sweaney, W. D.	185
Jeffries, Sir Charles	283	Thimba, Wilfred	92
Kirk-Greene, A. H. M.	224	Thomas, A. R.	3
Lennox-Boyd, Alan	168, 170, 209	Wangendo, Benjamin	92
Lyttleton, Oliver	163, 164, 171	Whitley, O. J.	68
Macleod, Iain	174	Wilkinson, C. D.	263